Social Movements, Law and the Politics of Land Reform

Social Movements, Law and the Politics of Land Reform investigates how rural social movements are struggling for land reform against the background of ambitious but unfulfilled constitutional promises evident in much of the developing world. Taking Brazil as an example, *Social Movements, Law and the Politics of Land Reform* unpicks the complex reasons behind the remarkably consistent failures of its constitution and law enforcement mechanisms to deliver social justice. Using detailed empirical evidence and focusing upon the relationship between rural social struggles and the state, the book develops a threefold argument: first, the inescapable presence of power relations in all aspects of the production and reproduction of law; secondly their dominant impact on socio-legal outcomes; and finally the essential and positive role played by social movements in redressing those power imbalances and realising law's progressive potentialities.

George Mészáros is an Associate Professor at the School of Law, University of Warwick

Law, Development and Globalization
Series editor Julio Faundez
University of Warwick

During the past decades, a substantial transformation of law and legal institutions in developing countries has taken place. Whether prompted by market-based policies or the international human rights movement, by the relentless advance of the process of globalization or the successive waves of democratization, no area of law has been left untouched. The aim of this series is to promote cross-disciplinary dialogue and cooperation among scholars and development practitioners interested in understanding the theoretical and practical implications of the momentous legal changes taking place in developing countries.

Titles in the series:

State Violence and Human Rights
State Officials in the South
Andrew M. Jefferson and Steffen Jensen (eds)

The Political Economy of Government Auditing
Financial Governance and the Rule of Law in Latin America and Beyond
Carlos Santiso

Global Perspectives on the Rule of Law
James J. Heckman, Robert L. Nelson and Lee Cabatingan (eds)

Marginalized Communities and Access to Justice
Yash Ghai and Jill Cottrell (eds)

Law in the Pursuit of Development
Principles into Practice?
Amanda Perry-Kessaris (ed.)

Governance Through Development
Poverty Reduction Strategies and the Disciplining of Third World States
Celine Tan

Lawyers and the Rule of Law in an Era of Globalization
Yves Dezalay and Bryant Garth (eds)

Policing and Human Rights
The Meaning of Violence and Justice in the Everyday Policing of Johannesburg
Julia Hornberger

Lawyers and the Construction of Transnational Justice
Yves Dezalay and Bryant Garth (eds)

Social Movements, Law and the Politics of Land Reform
Lessons from Brazil
George Mészáros

Forthcoming titles in the series:

From the Global to the Local, How International Rights Reach Bangladesh's Children
Andrea Schapper

Gender, Justice and Legal Pluralities
Latin American and African Perspectives
Rachel Sieder and John McNeish

Justice and Security Reform
Development Agencies and Informal Institutions in Sierra Leone
Lisa Denney

Multinational Integration, Cultural Identity and Regional Self-Government, Comparative Experiences for Tibet
Roberto Toniatti and Jens Woelk

Social Movements, Law and the Politics of Land Reform

Lessons from Brazil

George Mészáros

Routledge
Taylor & Francis Group
a GlassHouse Book

First published 2013
by Routledge
2 Park Square, Milton Park, Abingdon, Oxon OX14 4RN

A GlassHouse Book

Simultaneously published in the USA and Canada
by Routledge
711 Third Avenue, New York, NY 10017

Routledge is an imprint of the Taylor & Francis Group, an informa business

British Library Cataloguing in Publication Data
A catalogue record for this book is available from the British Library

Library of Congress Cataloging in Publication Data
A catalog record for this book has been requested

ISBN - 978-0-415-47771-0 (hbk)
ISBN - 978-0-203-55211-7 (ebk)

Typeset in Garamond
by Cenveo Publisher Services

Printed and bound in the United States of America by Publishers Graphics,
LLC on sustainably sourced paper.

In memory of Creuza

Contents

Preface   xi
Abbreviations   xiii
Interviewees   xv

Introduction   1

1   Shocking the System: Social Movement Pressure as the
    Catalyst of Political and Legal Change   27

2   To Criminalise or Not to Criminalise? Conflicting
    Legal Responses to Social Movement Pressure   57

3   Why Law Fails: The Administration of Land Law in the
    Context of Power Relations   90

4   The Limits of Progressive State Action   127

5   Pushing and Redefining Legal Boundaries through
    Social Movement Pressure   151

    Conclusion   179

    Index   189

Preface

The origins of this book can be traced back to two chance meetings. The first was in 1992 with Brazil's attorney general, Aristides Junqueira Alvarenga, who was then proposing to impeach President Fernando Collor over corruption charges. At the time I thought his task unlikely to succeed (to say nothing of personally risky) given the powerful network surrounding the president. In the event, though, Collor was forced from office, and Alvarenga's standing – along with that of the attorney general's office – was greatly enhanced.

I thought no more of these matters until some years later his deputy, Álvaro Augusto Ribeiro Costa (who later became the solicitor general in President Lula's government), addressed a small meeting in London on the subject of Brazil's human rights record and its legal institutions. I was struck not only by how critical he was of that record and the role of legal institutions, but also by his suggestion that things could be different, and that newly empowered legal institutions, following the constitutional settlement of 1988, could and should help to bring about social change.

That tantalising possibility set me to thinking about one area in which constitutional law has traditionally said much but failed so consistently, redistributive land reforms. Could Brazil finally offer a way forward?

I was also keen to marry these concerns with my longstanding interest in worker struggles in general and the Movimento dos Trabalhadores Rurais (MST), or Landless Rural Workers' Movement in particular. Despite its size and direct action techniques, which included land occupations, relatively little was known about the MST in the English-speaking world. As a Socio-Legal Researcher working at Warwick University I wanted to see how the MST experienced and engaged with law and the sort of impacts it had on the progress of land reform. I wanted to explore the interaction between this globally significant social movement and the legal and political processes governing the progress of land reform. I leave it to readers to judge whether I have succeeded in that task.

In the process of researching this book I have relied upon the cooperation of many individuals and organisations. Among the latter are the Nuffield Foundation, which offered me pilot funding, and the Economic and Social

Research Council (ESRC), which granted me full funding. Without their support this research would not have been possible. Likewise I owe a debt of gratitude to numerous individuals (too many to mention here) who gave me their advice and input generously. They include Jacques Tavora Alfonsin, Tânia Andrade, Ricardo Antunes, Maria Oliveira de Andrade, Alvaro Augusto Costa Ribeiro, Miguel Carter, Guilherme Costa Delgado, José Graziano da Silva, Horacio Martins de Carvalho, Antonio Carlos Peres Gediel, Miguel Pressburger, Marcelo Pedroso Goulart, Plínio de Arruda Sampaio, Sergio Sauer, Bernardo Mançano Fernandes, Ariovaldo Umbelino de Oliveira, Raul Jungmann, Belisário dos Santos Júnior, João Pedro Stédile, Carlos Frederico Marés, Oliver Marshall, Julio Faundez, Colin Perrin and many others. I should stress that I alone take responsibility for the conclusions reached.

Above all, I want to thank Maggie and Katherine for their love and support.

George Mészáros
Leamington Spa

Abbreviations

ABRA	Associação Brasileira de Reforma Agrária (Brazilian Land Reform Association)
AMP	Associação do Ministério Público (Association of the Public Ministry)
ANAP	Associação Nacional de Advogados Populares (National Association of Popular Lawyers)
CNA	Confederação Nacional da Agricultura (National Confederation of Agriculture)
COHAB	Companhia de Habitação do Estado do Rio Grande do Sul (State Housing Corporation of Rio Grande do Sul)
CONTAG	Confederação Nacional dos Trabalhadores na Agricultura (National Confederation of Agricultural Workers)
CPT	Comissão Pastoral da Terra (Pastoral Land Commission)
CRP	Carta de Ribeirão Preto (Open Letter of Ribeirão Preto)
FARSUL	Federação da Agricultura do Rio Grande do Sul (Agricultural Federation of Rio Grande do Sul)
FUNAI	Fundação Nacional do Índio (National Indian Foundation)
GETAF	Grupo Especial de Trabalho sobre Assuntos Fundiários do Oeste Paulista (Special Working Group on Land Issues in Western São Paulo)
IAJUP	Instituto de Apoio Jurídico Popular (Institute of Popular Legal Support)
IF	Instituto Florestal (State of São Paulo Forestry Institute)
INCRA	Instituto Nacional de Colonização e Reforma Agrária (National Institute for Colonisation and Agrarian Reform)
INSS	Instituto Nacional de Segurança Social (National Institute of Social Security)
ITCF	Instituto de Terras, Cartografia e Florestas (Land, Forest and Cartography Institute)
ITESP	Instituto de Terras do Estado de São Paulo (State of São Paulo Land Institute)

MASTER	Movimento dos Sem-Terra do Oeste do Estado de São Paulo (Landless Workers' Movement of the West of the State of São Paulo)
MMPD	Movimento do Ministério Público Democrático (Movement of the Democratic Public Ministry)
MST	Movimento dos Trabalhadores Rurais Sem-Terra (Landless Workers' Movement)
OAB	Ordem de Advogados Brasileiros (Order of Brazilian Lawyers)
PDT	Partido Trabalhista Democrático (Democratic Labour Party)
PFL	Partido da Frente Liberal (Party of the Liberal Front)
PMDB	Partido do Movimento Democrático Brasileiro (Party of the Brazilian Democratic Movement)
PNRA	Plano Nacional de Reforma Agrária (National Plan of Agrarian Reform)
PPB	Partido Popular Brasileiro (Brazilian Popular Party)
PSDB	Partido da Social Democracia Brasileira (Brazilian Social Democratic Party)
PT	Partido dos Trabalhadores (Workers' Party)
RECAD	Recadastramento (INCRA's re-registration department)
RENAP	Rede Nacional de Advogados e Advogadas Populares (National Network of Popular Lawyers)
SESP	Secretaria de Estado da Segurança Pública (Secretary of State for Public Security)
STJ	Superior Tribunal de Justiça (High Court of Justice)
TFP	Tradição, Família e Propriedade (Tradition, Family and Property)
TRF	Tribunal Regional Federal (Federal Regional Tribunal)
UDR	União Democrática Ruralista (Rural Democratic Union)

Interviewees

The following interviews were conducted by the author.

Tânia Andrade (former head of the State of São Paulo Land Institute, ITESP), 3 December 1999.

Paulo Emílio Barbosa (head of INCRA, Rio Grande do Sul), 1 February 2000.

Marcelo Beckhuasen (federal prosecutor), 21 January 2000.

Rose Beltrão (head of INCRA's land acquisition department in São Paulo), 8 February 2000.

Juvenal Boller (lawyer representing Governor Montoro's Agricultural Secretariat and a former head of ITESP), 19 April 2000.

Ministro Luiz Vicente Cernicchiaro (judge in the Brazilian High Court of Justice, also presided over the commission which revised the Brazilian penal code), 22 October 1999.

Valdemir Rodrigues Chaves (a leading MST militant in the Pontal do Paranapanema), 1 January 1999 and 1 September 1999.

Judge Gersino José da Silva Filho (Agrarian Ombudsman), 25 October 1999.

Dra Ines do Amaral Buschel (a member of the Movement of the Democratic Public Ministry), 6 June 1997.

André Felício, Marcos Vizusaki and Mário Coimbra (prosecutors), 6 September 1999.

Paulo Afonso Garrido de Paula (the prosecutor appointed by Sao Paulo Attorney General Marrey to liaise on his behalf with GETAF), 17 April 2000.

Alcides Gomes dos Santos (MST militant), 21 March 2000.

Luiz Eduardo Greenhalgh (MST's leading lawyer), 3 September 1999.

Rolf Hackbart (President of INCRA), 6 July 2007.

Raul Jungmann (Minister in charge of INCRA during the presidency of Fernando Henrique Cardoso, 1995–98, 1999–2002), 5 April 2000.

Six lawyers from the Pontal do Paranapanema, 8 September 1999.

Zelitro Luz da Silva (a leading MST militant in the Pontal do Paranapanema), 20 March 2000.

Zelitro Luz da Silva (a leading militant in the MST in the Pontal do Paranapanema), in conjunction with Jan Rocha and Sue Branford, 20 March 2000.

Benedito Macielo (a senior lawyer responsible for drafting Decree Law 42.041/97 of São Paulo state), 3 December 1999.

Kelly Maford (a São Paulo state MST leader and leader of the Matão occupation), 3 February 2000.

Bernardo Mançano Fernandes (a leading academic analyst of the MST), 7 September 1999.

Carlos Frederico Marés (Formerly Chief Attorney of Paraná state, Chief Attorney of INCRA and head of FUNAI), 17 December 2000.

Luiz Antonio Marrey (head of São Paulo's Public Ministry and Attorney General), 17 March 2000.

Gilmar Mauro (a member of the MST's national executive), 10 August 2000.

Marcelo Pedroso Goulart (prosecutor in the São Paulo state Public Ministry), 10 September 1999.

Miguel Pressburger (CPT's legal advisor and former head of IAJUP), 31 March 2000.

José Rainha (MST's leading spokesperson in the Pontal do Paranapanema), 20 March 2000.

Paulo Sérgio Ribeiro da Silva (the prosecutor who sought the imprisonment of MST militants in October 1995), 9 September 1999.

Neuri Rosetto (a member of the MST's national executive), 6 June 1997.

Urbano Ruiz (senior judge, São Paulo's Audit Tribunal), 2 September 1999.

Judge Catarina Ruybal da Silva Estimo (judge in the judicial district of Mirante do Paranapanema), 17 March 2000.

Belisário Santos Júnior (Secretary of State for Justice, state of São Paulo), 6 December 1999.

João Pedro Stédile (leading spokesperson for the MST), 18 March 2000.

Jacques Tavora Alfonsin (human rights lawyer, Rio Grande do Sul), 17 June 1997, and Sueli Belato (human rights lawyer), 12 June 1997.

Ela Wolkmer de Castilo (senior prosecutor in the Federal Public Ministry), 13 June 1997.

Maria Oliveira de Andrade, the former head of INCRA in Paraná, 20 October 1999.

Introduction

This book offers a socio-legal account of Brazil's Movimento dos Trabalhadores Rurais Sem Terra, the Landless Workers' Movement (MST), a group once described by Noam Chomsky as the most important and exciting popular movement in the world. For well over a quarter of a century now, the MST has openly challenged Brazil's highly inequitable pattern of rural land distribution. The movement's use of controversial direct action tactics, especially mass occupations of rural land by hundreds of poor families at a time, has seized the public imagination and propelled redistributive land reforms from relative obscurity towards the top of the political agenda. By 2009 (the 25th anniversary of the MST's foundation) a total of some 370,000 families had been settled on land acquired as a result of MST struggles and a further 130,000 families were in tented encampments struggling for land.[1]

In some respects the emergence of this movement is just as significant as the election of a former shoeshine boy, Luis Inácio Lula da Silva (more widely known as Lula), to the country's presidency in 2003. His was without doubt an extraordinary personal journey and achievement, one that defied the odds and even became the subject of a feature film. However, the MST's journey also occurred in the face of huge odds, most notably the organised violence and intransigence of powerful landed interests. Its journey entailed the formidable task of transforming literally hundreds of thousands of the poorest and most repressed rural workers and their families into effective agents of political change. That is no mean feat. There are important differences too. Over a number of years Lula's power would increasingly derive from the occupation of high office, the careful packaging of his personality, and the construction of broad electoral coalitions. The MST's power, on the other hand, was not about coalition building, electoral success, or about personalities. Instead its power derived from the mass mobilisation of its grassroots members. Of course other factors came into the equation, but the continuing willingness and ability of workers to organise themselves as a social and political force is what made – and still makes – the MST one of the most formidable extra-parliamentary organisations of our time. During the National Day of Struggles for Agrarian Reform in April 2011, for instance, the MST simultaneously mobilised 30,000 families (120,000 individuals) across 19 of Brazil's 26 states in 70 land occupations.[2] It is hard to think of any rural social movement in the world that possesses this level of organisation. As if to underlie the point, the MST has also succeeded in projecting its power globally. It was central to the foundation in 1993 of La Via Campesina, an organisation which describes itself as 'the peasants voice' and 'an international movement which brings together [200] millions of peasants, small and medium-size farmers, landless people, women farmers, indigenous people, migrants and agricultural workers from around the world'.[3]

Why a Socio-Legal Study?

Much has already been written about the MST.[4] Studies have covered issues as diverse as the educational facilities it provides members (including primary schools and even a university), the prominent role of women in all aspects of its organisation,[5] and the economic viability of permanent MST land settlements. Surprisingly, though, by the end of the 1990s (almost 15 years into its existence) there was a marked absence of accounts dealing with the movement's engagement with legal issues and institutions, yet they were vitally important to the movement's fortunes.[6]

This absence of systematic accounts may have arisen because of the widespread perception across the political spectrum that the relationship was so obviously antagonistic that it required little by way of more detailed explanation. On the one hand, right-wing opponents saw the movement's land occupations as fundamentally subversive, meriting condemnation rather than further research. On the other hand, left-wing supporters prioritised the politics of social justice and direct action over legal forms. This broad consensus about the antagonistic relationship between this movement and law meant that the interface between the two could be explained in relatively straightforward terms rather than constituting an important subject for study.

During the course of the research for this book, however, it quickly became apparent that even if accounts of left and right contained important grains of truth (there were, for instance, major tensions between the MST and the legal system, and legal issues were not of foremost concern to the movement), those accounts nonetheless lacked real depth or perspective. In fact their mixture of uncritical deference to, or exaggeration of, a separation of social movement politics from law did a profound disservice. It engendered a climate in which the MST could be tarred with the brush of illegality and therefore illegitimacy. This book partly offers a corrective to those stereotypes.

The gap in understanding the MST's relationships with law is symptomatic of a broader tendency to portray law and politics as specialised realms that are not just analytically distinct, but largely separate. The separation of powers doctrine is a political and legal theory that lends apparent credence to such divisions by asserting the importance of a functional and institutional separation of state power as a means of precluding its unchecked concentration and abuse. Most constitutions of the world seem to give substance to these functional and institutional divisions by routinely tasking executives with proposing legislation, legislatures with debating and enacting it, and judiciaries with interpreting and enforcing it. But while the simplicity of these demarcations may help outside observers to grasp certain aspects of state power, and offer judges and politicians a straightforward narrative or justification of their actions, that simplicity is beguiling and as an explanatory framework extremely problematic. It relegates other crucial, often quite complex constituents of power, such as social, political and economic structures, as well as cultural and ideological factors, to the margins of consideration if not off the agenda altogether.

Socio-legal studies, the approach adopted in this work, typically seek to overcome these limitations by stressing the contextual nature of legal institutions, practices and outcomes. Using a variety of methods, such studies try to clarify interconnections considered essential to a more accurate understanding of these institutions, practices and processes. Some studies, for instance, focus attention upon the historically produced nature of law and institutions, others examine the role played by class forces in the administration of justice (and injustice), while others have looked at the significance of gender relations in the production – and reproduction – of legal structures and outcomes. Tripartite typologies of state power, on the other hand, reduce complex issues to static components, suggest the possibility of an apolitical division of labour (especially within the judicial branch), and obscure the presence of powerful structural dynamics and behavioural patterns that either defy straightforward compartmentalisation or transcend it altogether.

The title of one work from the late 1970s, Griffith's *The Politics of the Judiciary* typifies one possible socio-legal approach. It cuts across a simplistic separation of powers, rejects the actuality of value-neutral 'technical' decision-making characteristic of legal positivism, and asserts the centrality of politics as a category within judicial decision-making. According to Griffith,

> *judges in the United Kingdom cannot be politically neutral because they are placed in positions where they are required to make political choices which are sometimes presented to them, and often presented by them, as determinations of where the public interest lies.*[7]

What is especially significant about Griffith's work is his suggestion that what he termed 'political cases' (defined as those 'which arise out of controversial legislation or controversial action initiated by public authorities, or which touch upon important moral or social issues'[8]) were not simply decided on their individual merits, as theories suggested, but conformed to certain patterns. These patterns, he argued, were rooted in '*judicial attitudes such as tenderness*

towards private property and dislike of trade unions, strong adherence to the mainte-
nance of order, distaste for minority opinions, demonstrations and protests, support of
governmental secrecy, concern for the preservation of the moral and social behaviour to
which it is accustomed, and the rest.'[9] In other words, there were sociological and
ideological dimensions present in judicial decision-making.

This book on Brazil's Landless Workers' Movement and its relationship to
law similarly looks at socio-legal patterns. It could be argued that a socio-
legal, or contextual approach as a means of both gathering evidence and generating insights is especially applicable to the Brazilian situation because the
mismatch between the substantive application of law and its formal claims,
most notably that of social justice, is so glaring and so consistent. The suffering induced by the failure of land reform to materialise surely constitutes a
case in point that demands some form of explanation.

Land reform has been on the Brazilian statute books for decades, whether
in the form of constitutional provisions, government legislation or administrative guidance. There were hopes that with the end of military rule and
return to democracy (1985), and the advent of a civilian constitution (1988),
the autonomy and efficacy of legal institutions would increase, and with them
the prospects of land reform. But as in so many other parts of the globe where
land reform is a major issue, these expectations did not materialise, certainly
not to the desired extent. It is a remarkably consistent pattern. A major
assumption of this book is that much of the explanation for this lies in the
processes and linkages between politics, law and society rather than in the
operation of any one 'sphere'.

The main research subjects of this book are politicians, judges, prosecutors,
lawyers, administrators, social movement sympathisers and activists. This is
not an anthropological study of how individual grassroots members see their
relationship to law, processes of land occupation, direct action and so forth.
There is no doubt in my mind that there are numerous interesting questions
to be explored in this regard. What, for instance, transforms a group of individuals, who are frequently seen as politically 'conservative', 'passive' and 'law
abiding', into one of the most radical, active and legally challenging of political forces of recent times? Do individuals undergo a personal transformation?
Are notions of law and justice an important part of individuals' worldview or
not? Is the decision to take part in mobilisations influenced by that relationship? Is there a 'disconnect' between their worldview and that of militant
activists?[10] Important though these questions are, this book focuses instead
upon discourses of MST activists and the organisation's sense of itself and its
socio-legal struggles.

Although subsequent chapters touch upon the myth of judicial neutrality,
the focus of attention is in fact much broader than this. Judicial conservatism
constitutes a key variable retarding the progress of land reform, and evidence
is provided to this effect, but it is seen as only one part of the story. Examples
of that conservatism include the reification of old-fashioned absolutist liberal

conceptions of private property relations to the virtual exclusion of modern constitutional dispositions that qualify property rights. This has a number of discernable impacts. Procedurally speaking it slows down government attempts at legalised expropriation of land; and in financial terms it significantly multiplies the cost of compensation to landowners. Likewise, conservatism is evident in repressive judicial attitudes to social protest. The MST's direct action tactics are regarded by many (although by no means all) Brazilian judges, as an assault upon private property relations and even as a challenge to the rule of law itself. The dominant attitude is one of containment or repression of social demand through the eviction and imprisonment of landless workers.

It is important to add, however, that no matter how dominant such attitudes are, or problematic their consequences, they have been challenged from within the judiciary itself as well as from without. Several chapters in this book discuss these parallel developments, suggesting a degree of interrelatedness between exogenous and endogenous factors. Juridical alternatives occur in the context of social pressure rather than springing from the head of radically minded judges. It is precisely because social movements like the MST repeatedly and tenaciously challenge the status quo that these issues find their way onto the courts' agenda and compel a response.[11]

Unfortunately, for the most part that response is negative or wanting. Just how much of that is the stuff of autopoietic theory or judicial 'independence', rather than ideological and class linkages with landed interests, is debatable. Occasionally, though, the response is positive. As well as documenting the obstacles to change, therefore, this book examines a number of instances where legal progress under social pressure did occur. Cases include an instance where the High Court of Justice (Superior Tribunal de Justiça – STJ) responded favourably to the question of whether the MST had the right to take direct action. They also include an instance where a lower court accepted the legality of a land occupation of productive property on the grounds that that property was not fulfilling environmental and labour-related constitutional obligations.

This is an important point, discussed in considerable detail in the last chapter, but which merits brief clarification here. According to Article 188 of the 1988 Brazilian constitution:

> It is within the power of the Union [federal state] to expropriate on account of social interest, for purposes of agrarian reform, the rural property that is not performing its social function....

Article 186 notes that:

> The social function is met when the rural property complies simultaneously with, according to the criteria and standards prescribed by law, the following requirements:
> I - rational and adequate use;

II - adequate use of available natural resources and preservation of the environment;

III - compliance with the provisions that regulate labour relations;

IV - exploitation that favours the well-being of the owners and labourers.[12]

Inevitably there is controversy about how these clauses should be interpreted in the light of Article 185, that firstly puts forward the notion of 'productive property' and then asserts that it 'shall not be subject to expropriation for agrarian reform purposes'.[13] A crucial question is whether that article is a free-standing principle, which many judges take it to be, or whether it must be read in conjunction with other articles that qualify its meaning. Can, for instance, land that is deemed economically productive but which achieves these results on the back of anti-environmental practices and labour exploita-tion, etc., be deemed worthy of legal protection, or does Article 188 take precedence? It is a very old philosophical, legal and social question. According to Catholic social teaching for instance, as expressed by Pope John VI in 1965, 'it is the right of public authority to prevent anyone from abusing his private property to the detriment of the common good. By its very nature private property has a social quality which is based on the law of the common destina-tion of earthly goods.' He also noted that 'insufficiently cultivated estates should be distributed to those who can make these lands fruitful'.[14]

And finally, there is a more indirect case, where the party to the action was not the MST, but a state government seeking to reassert control over illegally appropriated state lands (known as devolved lands, see below) by private land-lords. Although the MST was not a direct party to this legal action, interviews with both government officials and the judge involved make it abundantly clear that its social pressure was fundamental to the presentation, judgment and positive outcome of this case.

Federalism and Case Selection

The foregoing case, which occurred in the state of São Paulo under the gover-norship of Mário Covas (1995–2001), is illustrative of this book's methodo-logical approach. The legal dynamics of land reform are examined in conjunction with political developments and institutional structures located at both federal and state levels. In order to understand this some explanation of Brazil's federal political structure and its implications for land reform is necessary. For reasons of brevity and clarity, this discussion simultaneously includes consideration of how and why the cases that form the empirical core of this work, were chosen. They are drawn from three states of the federation: São Paulo, Rio Grande do Sul, and Paraná, highlighted in Figure 1. It will also include discussion of two other institutions not mentioned so far, the Ministério Público, or Public Prosecution Service, and the Instituto Nacional de Colonização e Reforma Agrária (National Institute for Colonisation and

Figure I Map of the Federal Republic of Brazil

Agrarian Reform – INCRA). Both of these institutions operate at federal and state levels and to varying degrees have significant implications for the MST as well as the progress of land reform.

No book that deals with issues as complex as land reform, and the relations between Brazil's legal system and a movement as large as the MST, can ever hope to do full justice to their diversity or complexity. As the fifth largest country in the world, Brazil assumes continental proportions (more than eight and a half million square kilometers). It borders ten other Latin American nations. Its economy now ranks as the sixth largest in the world. Behind these figures lie populations and cultures of remarkable diversity. Over a period of five hundred years waves of colonisation, European migration, and in the case of African slaves forced migration, have left a rich racial and cultural legacy. Following waves of migration at the beginning of the twentieth century, Brazil even became home to the largest Japanese population outside Japan. Not even the genocide of Brazil's indigenous peoples over the course of several centuries could eradicate their linguistic heritage. Several states have indigenous names (Pernambuco, Piauí, Ceará, Pará and Paraná).

Detailed discussion of the historical origins of federalism lies beyond the scope of this book. For present purposes it can be summarised as the attempt to forge a degree of national unity through constitutional mechanisms that both assert a degree of social, cultural, political and economic unity through the central state and a degree of autonomy within local states. This division of state power between the federal and local, with the latter formally accorded many of the functional divisions of their federal counterpart (a tripartite division of power between executive, legislature and judiciary) can cause confusion to readers who are expected to shift their attention between the two. The shorthand name given to both federal and state prosecution services – the Ministério Público – is a case in point. As will become evident in the course of this book, the two are functionally and territorially quite distinct. That is especially relevant when it comes to an issue like land reform, which is constitutionally defined as an exclusively federal matter. An awareness of these distinctions is important because in theory it means that only the Federal Ministério Público has formal jurisdiction over issues related to land reform. At the same time, however, the reality transcends these formal distinctions. It seeps into other areas, for instance the criminal law, where the Ministério Público within each of the states of the federation carries a great deal of influence, for example in the prosecution of landless workers. Where possible, then, this book draws a distinction by referring to the Federal Public Ministry as opposed to the state Public Ministry, or federal as opposed to state judiciary.

With regard to INCRA, the agency charged with the implementation of land reform, this is a quintessentially federal body, as one might expect given the aforementioned exclusivity rule. Again, though, appearances can be rather deceptive. It was none other than Raul Jungmann, the Minister in charge of INCRA during the Presidency of Fernando Henrique Cardoso (1995–98, 1999–2002) who in an interview with the author acknowledged that: 'No superintendent [from INCRA] can survive in a state, and oversee the agrarian conflict, who does not, in some measure, receive support from within the states. It simply does not happen any other way. You always have to operate within these paramenters.'[15] His comment, made in the context of his own removal of the head of INCRA in the state of Paraná, draws attention to the distinction between formal demarcations of state power and its substantive or operational dynamics. In effect Jungmann was saying 'I have full formal authority, but the reality is that it is contingent – often highly so'. Part of this book's argument is that these externalities of power make themselves felt not simply within the realm of politics, in this instance at the level of the executive, or in an administrative instance like INCRA, but also in the judicial and prosecutorial fields, albeit in more subtle ways given their greater degree of formal autonomy. Judges and prosecutors, for instance, enjoy a much greater degree of employment protection than their political or administrative colleagues. Nonetheless, they are not immune from external pressure or other often politically motivated pressures, such as job promotion.

As regards the sorts of operational parameters Jungmann had in mind, these certainly included the power of landed interests at federal and state levels (interests that partly propped up the Cardoso government, as, ironically, they would do in differing ways with the two subsequent Lula administrations). Crucially, though, those parameters will also have included consideration of the political weight of the MST in the different states. The latter is difficult to quantify. The MST's power will have varied considerably from one state to the next. Rather than being seen as an independent variable, therefore, it should be seen as part of a complex correlation of forces. Such correlations underly the importance of a contextual reading of the issues.

This brief excursion into the federal nature of Brazil's political system and complex power dynamics brings us back to the matter of case selection and composition amidst such diversity. As indicated at the beginning of the Introduction, this book offers a socio-legal account of Brazil's Movimento dos Trabalhadores Rurais Sem Terra. It does so, however, not solely in terms of the MST's encounters with law, critical though they are, but also from the perspective of institutional encounters with the MST. It should come as no surprise to readers that the fate of land reform does not lie in the hands of the MST. More surprising, perhaps, is the view that it does not lie in the hands of INCRA either, or the judges, or even the government. Rather, its fate lies in the interactions of all these elements combined, including, the negative power of landed classes. This book therefore examines the dynamics of land reform law in relation to the interplay of all these instances at federal level and within particular state conjunctures.

Quite a broad range of institutions is therefore considered, foremost of which are the federal and state governments, the federal land agency (INCRA). the federal and state judiciaries, and the federal and state prosecutors' offices. A much narrower study could legitimately have been undertaken, but it was felt that concentrating upon a wider range of institutions did greater justice and more faithfully corresponded to the reality of land reform in Brazil, thereby contributing to a better understanding.

Brief reference to one of the subsequent case studies, which deals with the state of São Paulo, may help to explain this point. Although INCRA had federal competence over land reform, to be effective it had to work through partnerships on the ground with what was the far more powerful (i.e., better resourced and staffed) state agency known as ITESP, the Instituto de Terras do

Estado de São Paulo (the State of São Paulo Land Institute). Legal means were found to do this. In effect law became an expression of this reality. Only through the emergence of a joined-up approach between ITESP, the state government, and INCRA did it become possible to make progress on land reform in the courts and beyond, i.e., in terms of actual land settlements. Similarly in another of the case studies, which deals with the state of Paraná, its state land institute (the Instituto de Terras, Cartografia e Florestas – ITCF, Land, Forest and Cartography Institute) was closely involved in the mediation of land conflicts and thereby regulated significant aspects of the legal proceedings. Rather than being seen as sources of confusion, the blurring of institutional lines of demarcation, and the marked distinctions between formal legality and its operation, should be understood as expressions of the broadly constituted nature of the land problem which demands a multi-agency approach.

Regarding the selection of cases themselves, the overall aim has been to carefully tease out and present some core dynamics at work through detailed empirical accounts. Given the aforementioned diversity of Brazil, this has inevitably necessitated making some strategic choices. Arguably the most important of these was geographic. The study could quite legitimately have focused on Brazil's Northeast, a region of major land conflict, where the MST is active, where land reform is a major issue, and where the justice system plays a critical (and highly problematic) role. Much, for instance, has been made of the precarious nature of the justice system in the North of Brazil in contrast to the South, which is widely seen as possessing much greater institutional capacity. One senior judge, from São Paulo's Audit Tribunal (Tribunal de Contas), puts it bluntly:

> the South and Southeastern region is incredibly different from the North and Northeast, and that partly explains why the Brazilian judiciary is so precarious. While you have a judiciary that works reasonably well from São Paulo southwards, it is very precarious as you move northwards. I believe, without exaggeration, that in terms of institutions and organisation, the North and Northeast are still at a medieval stage.[16]

Even Gercino José da Silva Filho, with experience in the North as former president of Acre state's High Court (Tribunal de Justiça), and later with national experience as the National Agrarian Ombudsman, raises issues about contrasting judicial cultures: 'in Rio Grande do Sul, the judges are always at the forefront of judicial movements that seek to render justice more dynamic and less formal', as opposed to 'those [northern] states, for example Pernambuco, where the judges are still very traditional'.[17]

Doubtless investigations in the North would have raised valuable issues. What was more crucial for this study, however, was the possibility of exploring states and legal systems widely regarded as among the most robust that the country has to offer. For this reason the book is structured around five 'best case' scenarios drawn from three states: two from Brazil's South, Rio Grande do Sul and Paraná, and one from its Southeast, São Paulo. These states account for a substantial proportion of Brazil's industrial and agricultural output, as well as constituting its major centres of population. In 2008, São Paulo, Rio Grande do Sul and Paraná ranked first (33.1 per cent), fourth (6.6 per cent) and fifth (5.9 per cent) respectively in terms of Brazil's gross domestic product (GDP).[18] That makes them politically and economically significant, but legal considerations were important too.

São Paulo's Public Ministry is one instance of legal sufficiency. It is comparatively very well funded and staffed (by far and away the best in the country), and has been at the intellectual forefront of a radically reformed and more autonomous Federal Public Ministry (as enshrined in the 1988 constitutional settlement). One question, therefore, was how effectively that greater autonomy and vision would translate into practice, especially in an area as contentious as land reform. Likewise Rio Grande do Sul was nationally renowned for the progressive stance of its judiciary. As for Paraná state, it also possessed a comparatively well organised legal infrastructure, in addition to which it was home to the most active network of pro-land reform lawyers anywhere in the country. To what extent would these combinations of factors have a discernable impact?

The presence of these different characteristics was especially significant when taken in conjunction with others exhibited by the MST, which had originated in Rio Grande do Sul, had achieved national notoriety on the back of occupations conducted in the state of São Paulo in the early 1990s, and was – and remains – active in Paraná. According to statistics compiled by DATALUTA, between 1988 and 2009 São Paulo, Paraná and Rio Grande do Sul accounted for well over a quarter (16.14 per cent, 8.29 per cent and 2.63 per cent respectively) of the total number of occupations (8,128) in Brazil and of the total number of families (1,156,408) involved (16.73 per cent, 7.50 per cent and 5.20 per cent respectively).[19]

Given the desire to explore the relationship between the MST on the one hand, and legal institutions *at their most functional* on the other, these seemed ideal locations. By implication, if land reform activists encountered substantial difficulties here, or if the legal system was found wanting, then the likelihood was that these difficulties would be magnified elsewhere.

Another key variable to consider was the policy and impact of individual states. To what extent, for example, would they enforce judicially mandated eviction orders of landless workers as, prima facie, law required? The presence of reforming governments in all three states represented an opportunity to explore a series of more positive political conjunctures (often not present in many other states), albeit against the background of sometimes favourable and at other times difficult legal situations. Ironically, the most positive political situation and acutest legal conflict arose not where one might expect it, in Rio Grande do Sul, under the more radical governorship of Olívio Dutra, a leading member of Lula's left-leaning Workers' Party (Partido dos Trabalhadores – PT), nor even in São Paulo, under the leadership of Mário Covas, a member of Fernando Henrique Cardoso's Brazilian Social Democratic Party (Partido da Social Democracia Brasileira – PSDB), but in Paraná, under the governorship of Roberto Requião. Nominally speaking he was to the right of both governors, because of his affiliation to the centre-right Party of the Brazilian Democratic Movement (Partido do Movimento Democrático Brasileiro – PMDB), yet as a trained lawyer he was reluctant to rubber stamp what he understood as socially irresponsible eviction orders. A constitutional crisis thus ensued. His was without doubt a unique, i.e., personalist brand of politics, but the presence of marked regional variations is not. On the contrary, variations constitute the vital backdrop against which the broader theme of land reform is played out and through which it can and must be understood.

A Brief Overview of Land Reform

With the possibility of such variations in mind, some brief comments regarding the generality of Brazilian land reform can now be made. For the sake of simplicity, this book follows the practise of many authors who use the terms 'land reform' and 'agrarian reform' interchangeably.[20] Cox *et al.* have suggested that: 'Agrarian reform constitutes a major change in the ownership structure of agricultural land'.[21] Factors they cite as having justified reforms historically include the 'presence of highly unequal distribution of land assets; large tracts of land with low farming intensity; exploitative labour relations on large estates; extensive landlessness and/or very small uneconomic units; extensive land conflicts (squatting, land invasions, etc.)'.[22]

There is little doubt that Brazil has conformed very closely to this pattern until comparatively recently, and in certain key respects still does. The distribution of land remains highly unequal, exploitative labour relations persist, indices of poverty are more closely correlated with rural livelihoods than their urban counterpart, there is extensive landlessness and the presence of very small uneconomic units, land conflicts and occupations are widespread. With regard to inequality and poverty, for instance, between 1970 and 1980, the number of rural poor rose from an estimated 27.6 to 28.8 million, while the Gini coefficient for land concentration (a key measurement of the equality of land distribution[23]) went from 0.85 in 1960 to 0.86 in 1980.[24] Brazilian government statistics also showed that properties of more than 1,000 hectares increased their share of cultivated land from 47 per cent in 1967 to 58 per cent in 1984, while small properties of less than 100 hectares saw their share of land decrease from 19 per cent to 14 per cent over the same period.[25] Far more troubling, though, is the fact that by 2005/6, some 20 years into the redemocratisation process, the Gini index for land had barely changed from its 1985 level of 0.857. By 1995/96 it was 0.856 and in 2006 (when the last reported census was carried out) it was 0.854.[26] As the table from Sauer and Pereira Leite below shows,[27] 2006 census data revealed that farms of less than 10 hectares still accounted for almost 48 per cent of all rural establishments but only occupy a tiny fraction, 2.36 per cent (7,798,607 hectares) by area. This contrasts with properties over 1,000 hectares which account for a fraction, 0.91 per cent, of all rural establishments but which occupy more than 44 per cent of land (146,553,218 hectares) by area.

Table I Number and area of agricultural and livestock estates by groups of total area: Brazil, 2006

Groups of total area	Number of estates (units)	%	Area of the estates (ha)	%
Less than 10 hectares (ha)	2,477,071	47.86	7,798,607	2.36
10 to less than 100 ha	1,971,577	38.09	62,893,091	19.06
100 to less than 1000 ha	424,906	8.21	112,696,478	34.16
1000 ha and beyond	46,911	0.91	146,553,218	44.42
Total	5,175,489	100.00	329,941,393	100.00

Even the government statistical service itself observes that comparing data from the censuses of 1985, 1995 and 2006 reveals 'continuation of unevenness in the distribution of land'.[28]

Although the deconcentration of land has been extremely limited, in no way does this imply that nothing has changed over the decades, or that Brazil can be characterised in terms of large unproductive landed estates – *latifudios* – that historically dominated the country and much of Latin America since colonial times. To be sure, such formations still exist, but anyone familiar with the term BRICS (a problematic term commonly referring to the large-scale and rapid expansion of so-called emerging economies of Brazil, Russia, India, China and South Africa) will also be aware that over the last few years Brazil has achieved agricultural superpower status. Its model has delivered spectacular results, with agricultural exports reaching US$80 billion in 2010–11 alone.[29] Several factors have contributed to this, not least of which are the so-called green revolution of the 1960s, intensive mechanisation, the pro agro-industrial policies of successive governments (including large subsidies and tax breaks), and the seemingly inexhaustible supply of land permitting the absolute expansion of agricultural frontiers into new regions of the country. That may mean the destruction of biodiversity in regions such as the Amazon, the Pantanal and the Cerrado, but it also means that Brazil is now the world leader in coffee, orange and sugar production, the second largest grower of soya beans, and third largest exporter of maize. The accelerating investment in, and expansion of, highly intensive agro-industrial complexes has led the MST to describe these forms of production and control as 'the new face of landlordism'.[30] As will become evident in Chapter 5, that gives rise to new sources of conflict, and raises important political and legal questions in the process, most notably over the issue of whether these 'productive' lands can be legally occupied or expropriated.

According to the 1988 constitution, no such doubts should exist in relation to so called 'unproductive' or 'underutilised' land, estimated by INCRA at 120.4 million hectares (out of 436.6 million hectares) registered with the organisation.[31] Although this source should provide a vast pool from which the state can legally expropriate land for the purposes of redistribution this does not happen – certainly not on the requisite scale or speed. This leads to the paradoxical situation of land scarcity amidst plenty, and hence landless workers camped on roadsides. Sauer and Pereira Leite note that the second National Plan of Agrarian Reform (Plano Nacional de Reforma Agrária – PNRA) 'estimated that in 2005 there was "a total of 3.1 million families", so-called "landless people", who are "rural workers without access to land, including small-scale agricultural producers – proprietors, partners or leaseholders".'[32]

This paradox is all the more remarkable when one takes into account another highly significant legal category, that of public or vacant land, known as 'terras devolutas', or devolved land, which cannot be privately appropriated except under the strictest of legal conditions. These conditions were originally established under the 1850 Lei de Terras, or Land Law, which asserted that devolved lands – tracts of land that did not as yet belong to private parties, of which there were literally hundreds of millions of hectares – could no longer be appropriated except through means of purchases made directly from the government. Article 1 asserts: '[t]he acquisition of devolved lands by title other than purchase is hereby prohibited.' The sociologist José de Souza Martins notes this would have profound social consequences for it 'would transform devolved lands into a monopoly of the state and a state controlled by a strong class of large landowners. The non-propertied peasants, those that arrived after the Lei de Terras or those that had not had their occupations legalised in 1850, were therefore compelled ... to work for the large estates.'[33] Yet again we find a situation of shortage amidst plenty. In this instance the law was designed to manage the transition from a slave economy to a capitalist one by deliberately locking millions of people (including freed slaves, smallholders and future immigrants) out of landownership and into waged employment on large estates.

Theoretically, as Pressburger explains, from a technical perspective

> The Lei de Terras [Land Law] of 1850 and its regulations determined how, under what conditions, and for how much devolved lands could be sold to private individuals. ... [I]f the privatisation of the public asset was not realised in accordance with the legislation then in legal terms the asset remained inalienable and, as established in the Civil Code, beyond commercialisation.[34]

But that is not what happened. Not for the first time would the law bite off far more than it could possibly chew, in this instance by asserting an untenable monopoly. Dominion over devolved lands was divided between the federal state (especially in areas of strategic concern, like international frontiers and military installations) and local states, which were legally entitled to those areas not destined to federal control. Due to corrupt networks of influence, however, many local states, were either uninterested in enforcing the law, or enforced it in a highly selective fashion that benefited their friends. This was a recipe for social conflict, as small holders sought to eke out an existence, and as putative landowners staked their claim to vast areas through corrupt notaries and officials who produced chains of false documents 'proving' their ownership prior to 1850. It was also a recipe for seemingly interminable legal conflicts, as lawyers waded through mountains of documentation (much of it false) trying to establish the real provenance of land. Market forces further compounded these difficulties, since one of the best ways of realising a gain from land was not by owning or working it, but by selling it to unsuspecting buyers, or to buyers who knew perfectly well its provenance but were nonetheless prepared to take the relatively low risks of potential state enforcement. That process persists to this day.

Although this is the legal background to the first two chapters in this book, which deal with struggles over devolved land in the state of São Paulo, it is also the background to vast tracts of devolved land throughout Brazil. The eminent agrarian geographer, Ariovaldo Umbelino de Oliveira, notes that 'according to data available in INCRA, in 2003 the area occupied by public devolved lands was greater than 400 million hectares, in other words, almost half the national territory.'[35] The key point is not so much the precise figures ('the state does not know who has appropriated the land – whether legally or illegally'[36]), as their broad magnitude. The significance of these devolved lands is underlined by the constitution's assertion, in Article 188, that they must be made compatible with national agrarian reform plans, in other words they should be actively considered for purposes of agrarian reform. When added to the 120 million hectares of unproductive land referred to earlier, the extent of pent-up social demand seems hard to explain. Chapters 1 and 2 go some way towards providing that explanation.

The Trajectory of Land Reform

Numerous studies have made clear the depth of rural poverty and the significant contribution which unequal access to land and income make. According to the demographic census of 2000, five million rural families lived on less than two minimum salaries (a total of $166) per month. Rural areas are where the highest rates of infant mortality, disease and illiteracy occur.

There seems to be little doubt that the two Lula administrations (2003–06, 2007–10) made some headway through a variety of social assistance programmes, most notably Fome Zero (Zero Hunger, a programme designed to eradicate hunger), and Bolsa Família (Family Grant, a conditional cash transfer programme to extremely poor families linked to indicators like school attendance and health visits). Even the minimum wage increased substantially in both nominal and real terms over the period (the latter by more than 60 per cent once inflation is taken into account). But significant though these gains are, especially to the beneficiaries themselves, they do not address structural problems associated with land ownership and use. For that one must look to land redistribution.

The statistical record of successive governments on this question has been hotly debated. Table 2 gives some sense of the progress made in permanently settling families over the last 25 years. The picture is one of progress but with substantial variations. Structural reform of the kind regarded by many as essential to qualify as a genuine land reform, i.e., one that delivers change on a massive scale and in a relatively short timeframe, thereby providing an irreversible political and social shock to the system, has not occurred. To the extent that land reform is a function of the political process rather than more predictable legal or administrative ones, this absence of consistency is to be expected. Thus, for instance, the repressive and anti-land reform government of President Fernando Collor (1990–92) heavily influenced the low settlement rates of the early 1990s (see Table 2). His repressive policies also saw the successful containment of land occupations, as Table 3 indicates. But the same cannot be said for the second Lula administration (2007–10), which rhetorically speaking remained pro-reform, but enjoyed limited success even by historical standards.

The Lula government has attributed these differences in part to the increased priority given to the quality of settlements rather than their numbers. It has argued, not entirely without reason, that the amount of land taken is one variable and that attention must also be paid to qualitative factors, such as the economic viability of settlements, the availability of capital, the educational training of workers, the proximity of settlements to infrastructure and markets, etc. But while there is an important grain of truth in these assertions, and funds related to land reform projects have increased substantially, many observers, including this author, would question whether the diminution in numbers in fact reflects a policy line of least resistance. In other words, the political costs of improving existing settlements are much lower than those associated with the acquisition of new land. For an administration that finds itself presiding over an agro-industrial export boom, the political costs of alienating allies may be too high to contemplate.

President Lula's failure to update land productivity indices – despite repeated promises made prior to his 2006 election victory – exemplifies the problem. These indices (unchanged since the 1970s) are a key variable in assessing whether land is productive or not, and therefore whether it is legally subject to expropriation for the purposes of land reform. The 120 million

Table 2 Number of families settled in land settlements in Brazil: 1985–2011[37]

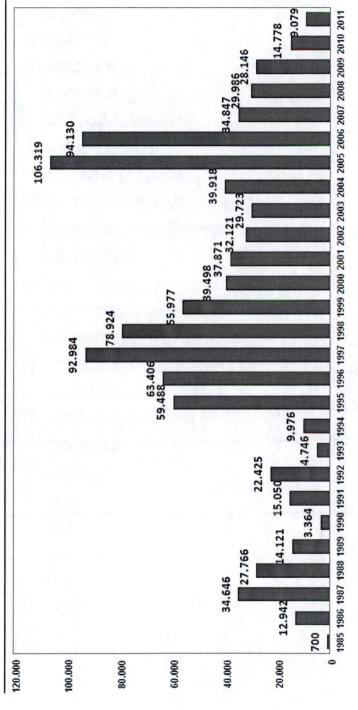

Table 3 Number of families in occupation in Brazil 1988–2011[38]

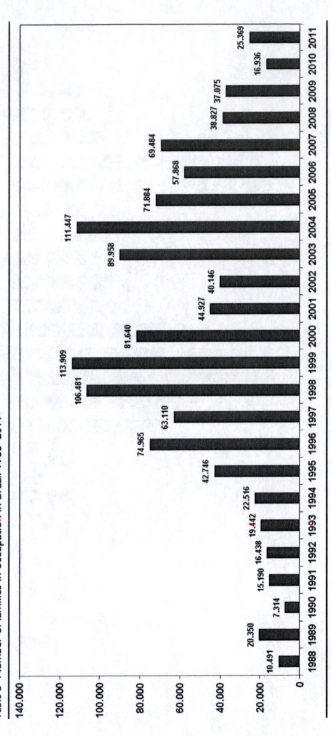

hectares of unproductive land referred to earlier is, if anything, a massive underestimate since it is based upon a test where the bar has been set artificially low, i.e., back in the 1970s. A recalibration of the test to reflect twenty-first century productivity levels would surely lead to an increase in the amount of land currently defined as unproductive and therefore landowners do not want the uncertainty this engenders. Thus despite the compelling technical and political case for revision, or the support of INCRA and the Ministry for Agrarian Development, or the electoral promises made by Lula, powerful interests within the Ministry of Agriculture continue to exercise a veto over this aspect of policy. Chapter 3 sheds valuable light on this problem in the context of Fernando Henrique Cardoso's government. Ultimately one finds that the favourable legal and administrative climate that developed was subordinated to a series of insurmountable social and political obstacles.

The MST's Place in the Wider Spectrum of Rural Struggle

Part of the contention of this book is that the MST administered a much needed external shock to the system, calling the status quo into question and forcing the issue of land reform to the top of the political agenda. Opponents of the movement contend that in so doing it would act in an anti-democratic and illegal fashion (not a view shared by this author). Others have sought to classify the MST as a counter-hegemonic movement, i.e., one that challenges the dominant model and campaigns to change the status quo.[39] Houtzager notes that:

> The MST's strategy is the kind of counter-hegemonic use of law and rights that Santos [40] ... argues is most likely to succeed: it integrates juridical action into broader political mobilisation, politicising struggles before they become juridified, and mobilising sophisticated legal skills from diverse actors. This strategy enabled the MST to engage in the type of sustained and broad litigation – both geographically and across issues – that ... is central to redefining legal terrain.[41]

There is considerable truth in this assertion, but in making it one should not lose sight of the wider historical picture. That includes a vibrant and large rural trade union movement which numerically speaking dwarfs the MST. The National Confederation of Agricultural Workers (Confederação Nacional dos Trabalhadores na Agricultura – CONTAG) is Brazil's largest rural union organisation, congregates 27 federations and 4,000 unions with a total membership of approximately 20 million rural workers.[42] Trade unions also have a much longer pedigree too. CONTAG was founded more than 20 years before the MST in 1963. As for the key policy with which the MST has come to be most closely associated – agrarian reform – this was a cause espoused by rural trade union activists even during the most turbulent days of the military dictatorship, an activity for which some paid with their lives.

The novelty or distinctiveness of the MST surely lies in its coupling of political radicalism, including a trenchant critique of more reformist union strategies, with a high degree of organisational (and therefore political) success. The rural sociologist, Leonilde Sérvolo de Medeiros, notes that for CONTAG 'the struggle for "rights", within legal parameters, came to constitute the basic directive to action'.[43] Similarly Rudá Ricci, notes CONTAG's 'struggle for agrarian reform was confined ... within the limits that could guarantee dialogue with the state, avoiding any kind of mass movement that could signal a possible rupture.'[44] For the MST, which it must be acknowledged emerged under different historical conditions, most notably the gradual return to democracy, the exact opposite was the case: some form of rupture was essential because to all intents and purposes the process of land reform was seen as dead.

Occupations were part of peasant struggles long before the advent of the MST. The novelty of the MST was to reassert this tactic through a process of mass mobilisation. That would enable hitherto geographically isolated struggles and individuals to turn the tables on landowners locally, as well as develop regional and national struggles. Combined with the movement's ability to sustain occupations over long periods it would prove a powerful combination. In this way the MST became a pace setter, spawning other occupation movements (including some dissident groups). Although members of CONTAG would also engage in occupations (it was the second largest such force), their number was dwarfed by those undertaken by the MST. Throughout, the MST remained the principal point of reference. By no means could the MST claim a monopoly on occupations, but there is little doubt that mass occupation became a basic part of the grammar of rural contestation in Brazil primarily because of its actions.

Any appreciation of the undoubted successes and importance of the MST must be tempered by the acknowledgement of the major and potentially increasing difficulties it faces. More than 25 years on and the movement has been unable achieve its primary objective, land reform. That two Workers' Party administrations were unable to deliver that prize indicates the scale of the challenge it faces and extent to which the movement finds itself politically constrained. The diminution in militancy, partly as a result of economic growth and government policies aimed at poverty alleviation, in other words the emergence of some economic alternatives, no matter how fragile or temporary, also constitutes a significant constraint. The adoption of a more conservative stance on land expropriation by President Dilma Rouseff's government (which assumed office in 2011) also leaves the MST with more limited room for manoeuvre. These are sobering trends, but like the MST's past successes, they are not secular. Many observers have come to regard Brazil's economic boom, with its increasing reliance upon commodities, exports to China, and its process of accelerated deindustrialisation, as extremely problematic.

The main concern of this book, however, is the narrower but nonetheless vital area of the MST's relationship with legal institutions and processes. Here too there are many sobering trends, but there is also scope for real progress.

Turning to the organisation of this volume, Chapter 1 ('Shocking the System: Social Movement Pressure as the Catalyst of Political and Legal Change') opens with a brief account of the highly precarious nature of land tenure arrangements in the Pontal do Paranapanema, in São Paulo state. Quite simply land here had been illegally privatised – literally stolen from the state. This status quo was underpinned by a seemingly impregnable political structure. Our interest in the matter initially derives from two factors: first, in the manifest inability – and unwillingness – of the legal system to deal with the problem; and second, in the decision of the MST during the early 1990s to challenge the legal system, landowners and the state through a series of mass land occupations. This shock to the system would provoke a range of responses – many hostile, but it also forced that system to begin to address the problem. As well as discussing these issues, the chapter explores the role of the state as an instigator of change. There is no doubt that it would play a pivotal role in some of the progressive transformations, legal as well as social and political, that subsequently took place. These include providing the judiciary with an opportunity to make a positive contribution to change. That sense of dialectic of law, politics and social mobilisation is one of the clear findings to emerge from this research.

Chapter 2 ('To Criminalise or Not to Criminalise? Conflicting Legal Responses to Social Movement Pressure') also discusses events in the Pontal do Paranapanema, but in terms of the dynamics of occupation itself, and the legal challenges which this threw up for the MST. Put simply, some sections within the legal establishment (police, prosecutors and judges) attempted to criminalise movement members for their actions. A complex game of cat and mouse ensued. The chapter not only gives an insight into the highly problematic and ideologically driven nature of the Brazilian justice system, but also its deeply divided nature. This is significant, for as well as pursuing the MST relentlessly, that system, through a ruling of the High Court of Justice (STJ), was able to provide the movement with one of its most notable political and legal victories. A closer look at São Paulo's Public Ministry also reveals how its most senior members refused to buckle under explicit pressure by the federal government of Fernando Henrique Cardoso to take a tougher line on the MST. As São Paulo's Attorney General explained, 'a straightforward and formal application of the law will not resolve the extra-legal situation. It is a social problem that will not be resolved by repression.'[45] Once again, this case study underlines the importance of looking at social, political and legal institutions in terms of their dynamic interaction, whether that is between federal government and local prosecutors or local prosecutors and the MST. Whether the legal establishment chose to admit it or not, it was deeply rooted in the ideological conflicts of the day, conflicts that persist to this day.

Chapter 3 ('Why Law Fails: the Administration of Land Law in the Context of Power Relations') arguably offers some of the most worrying evidence in this book concerning the obstacles to land reform. Although based on events that occurred in the state of Rio Grande do Sul in the late 1990s, the issue discussed – namely the fate of rural productivity indices – is of strategic significance and goes to the very heart of the land reform issue in both the Fernando Henrique Cardoso and Lula da Silva administrations. Given the poor track record of the legal system on other aspects of the land question, it is perhaps surprising that its actions on this occasion were not found wanting. Nor, indeed, were those of the land agency INCRA. Both were keen to enforce the law on land audits designed to measure productivity. Both, however, would be met with sustained and, ultimately, successful resistance from landed interests. Unusually, that resistance took the form of civil disobedience by landowners, as well as more traditional political pressure exerted upon (and from within) the federal government of Fernando Henrique Cardoso himself. The case is significant not so much because it deals with the failure of the justice system, but rather because it points to some of its fundamental limitations, and underlines the enormous magnitude of the obstacles facing those sectors within the state who want to give practical effect to constitutional injunctions on land reform.

Chapter 4 ('The Limits of Progressive State Action') is primarily centred on the diametrically opposed policies of successive governments in the state of Paraná on criminalisation of land occupations. One governor, Roberto Requião, sought the creation of spaces of mediation with the MST. On one occasion this led to the MST's leading spokesman, João Pedro Stédile, to give an invited lecture on land evictions to the military police. Requião's policy, which included exploring crucial issues such as whether the land actually legally belonged to landowners, ultimately culminated in a constitutional crisis between himself and a judiciary keen that he should enforce what he regarded as socially irresponsible eviction orders. The chapter explores some of the contradictions in the policy itself, notably the difficulty of 'managing' landless worker expectations. In sharp contrast to Requião's approach, Governor Jaime Lerner was happy to evict and, as part of an electoral deal, effectively handed over his security apparatus to paramilitary interests keen to crush the movement. What is interesting about the case of Requião in particular, is just how difficult it was for the state – even with the active support of some of the most brilliant and progressive legal minds in the country – to establish a policy in the face of landed interests and judicial hostility. The case of Judge Elizabeth Khater, also discussed in this chapter, is symptomatic of that hostility. The chapter also looks at the case of the head of INCRA in Paraná, Maria de Oliveira, who failed to settle 1,500 landless families, despite her best efforts and the support of the Minister of Agrarian Reform. Her failure, together with that of Governor Requião, are presented as symptomatic of the huge challenges facing land reform.

Finally, Chapter 5 ('Pushing and Redefining Legal Boundaries through Social Movement Pressure') deals with the aforementioned issue of how the constitution deals with the social function of property but in the context of an occupation by the MST of productive land near the town of Matão, in São Paulo state. As João Pedro Stédile explains: 'In the case of some specific regions there aren't large unproductive ranches. ... So the workers are obliged to choose areas which, although they are productive, can lead on to the debate over their social function.'[46] Like the events discussed in other chapters, the issues are as current as ever. The fact that they remain so, even after the passage of a decade and two Workers' Party governments points to their deeply engrained nature and underlies the value of exploring them in an historical context. With regard to the issue of productive property and the case of Matão, I suggest that actions by the MST represent a form of offensive legality – in other words, the movement has extended its legal discourse. This is partly, it must be acknowledged, because in regions like the Southeast it cannot so easily opt for unproductive properties and therefore has less choice. Nonetheless, the willingness of the MST to do so in these specific terms illustrates just how sophisticated the movement has become and, as the chapter makes clear, just how willing a surprisingly wide legal constituency is to take on board, develop and support its arguments. That is simultaneously an exciting and a daunting prospect. In the Conclusion I set out some of the implications of all these developments.

Notes

1 Cited in '"Ocupação de terra é a única forma de questionar o latifúndio"', diz integrante do MST', *Folha de São Paulo,* 19 January 2009, www1.folha.uol.com. br/folha/videocasts/ult10038u490004.shtml
2 'MST mobiliza 19 estados e faz 70 ocupações de latifúndios', 28 April 2011, www. mst.org.br/MST-mobiliza-19-estados-e-faz-70-ocupacoes-de-terras This number includes other actions such as the occupation of 14 INCRA state headquarters and the closure of some major highways.
3 'What is La Via Campesina?', 9 February 2011, http://viacampesina.org/en/index. php/organisation-mainmenu-44/what-is-la-via-campesina-mainmenu-45
4 There is now a substantial and rapidly growing body of literature on the MST. For an informative collection, see Miguel Carter, ed., *Combatendo a desigualdade social – o MST e a reforma agrária no Brasil,* São Paulo: Editora Unesp, 2010. For discussion of the MST in the context of neoliberal transformations, see James Petras and Henry Veltmeyer, *Social Movements in Latin America: Neoliberalism and Popular Resistance,* New York: Palgrave Macmillan, 2011.
5 See, for example, Caroline Lamar Pihl, 'A caldron of militancy: construction of feminine consciousness in the Movimento Sem-Terra', School for International Training, Harvard University, 2007; and Renata Cristiane Valenciano and Antonio Thomaz Júnior, 'O papel da mulher na luta pela terra: uma questão de gênero e/ou classe?', *Scripta Nova, Revista Electrónica de Geografía y Ciencias Sociales,*

Universidad de Barcelona, vol. VI, no. 119 (26), 1 August 2002, www.ub.edu/geocrit/sn/sn119-26.htm

6 A notable exception in this regard was John L. Hammond's 'Law and disorder: the Brazilian Landless Farmworkers' Movement', *Bulletin of Latin American Research*, vol. 18, no. 4, 1999, pp. 469–89. See also George Mészáros, 'Taking the land into their hands: the Landless Workers' Movement and the Brazilian state', *Journal of Law and Society*, vol. 27, no. 4, December 2000, pp. 517–41.

7 John A.G. Griffith, *The Politics of the Judiciary*, 5th edition, London: Fontana Press, 1997, p. 336.

8 Ibid., p. 7.

9 Ibid., p. 336 (Griffith's italics).

10 For an ethnographic study of the MST, see Wendy Wolford, *This Land is Ours Now: Social Mobilization and the Meanings of Land in Brazil*, Durham, NC: Duke University Press, 2010. Wolford examines the processes behind the continuous reconstruction of an identity of struggle. In passing (p. 122) she notes the views of Fransisco Julião, the leader of the Brazil's Peasant Leagues, who 'believed that peasants were generally afraid to contravene the law, he situated the struggle for land within the legal system of rights, and argued that it was the plantation owners who were acting illegally, not the workers.' See also James C. Scott, *Weapons of the Weak: Everyday Forms of Peasant Resistance*, New Haven: Yale University Press, 1985. Scott makes a powerful case for exploring non-confrontational aspects of politics. Although he is right in suggesting that covert, informal and individual practises constitute an underrated aspect of politics, in contrast to high profile forms of resistance (including, one might add, from social movements like the MST), his analysis leaves groups like peasants with little room for struggle except in essentially adaptive and defensive forms.

11 This is an issue taken up by authors associated with '*direito achado na rua*', law found in the streets. Originally coined by Roberto Lyra Filho, de Sousa Júnior notes the expression partly reflected 'upon the juridical actions of new collective subjects of law and upon the experiences developed by the creation of law and citizenship in our country.' José Geraldo de Sousa Júnior, 'O Direito Achado na Rua: terra, trabalho, justiça e paze paz' in Mônica Castagna Molina, José Geraldo de Sousa Júnior, Fernando da Costa Tourinho Neto, eds, *O Direito Achado Na Rua Vol. 3: Introdução Crítica ao Direito Agrário*, São Paulo: Editora UnB, 2002, p. 17. This volume provides a useful introduction to more critical conceptions of agrarian law and the role of social movments in its development.

12 Constitution of the Federative Republic of Brazil, 2nd edition, translated and revised by Istvan Vajda, Patrícia de Queiroz Carvalho Zimbres and Vanira Tavares de Souza, Brasília, 2009, Articles 184 and 186 respectively. Available at: www2.camara.gov.br/english/brazilian-constitution-2

13 Ibid.

14 Second Vatican Council, *Pastoral Constitution on the Church in the Modern World: Gaudium et Spes*, Promulgated by Pope Paul VI, 7 December 1965, Rome, section 71, available at: www.vatican.va/archive/hist_councils/ii_vatican_council/documents/vat-ii_cons_19651207_gaudium-et-spes_en.html

15 Author interview with Raul Jungmann, 5 April 2000.

16 Author interview with Urbano Ruiz, 2 September 1999.

17 Author interview with Judge Gersino José da Silva Filho, 25 October 1999.

18 Source: Instituto Brasileiro de Geografia e Estatística (IBGE), Contas Regionais do Brasil 2004–08, *Contas Nacionais*, no. 32, Rio de Janeiro, 2010.

19 Banco de Dados da Luta Pela Terra (DATALUTA) supplied to the author by Bernardo Mançano Fernandes. Only Pernambuco came close to São Paulo with a figure of 14.76 per cent and 13.57 per cent for the number of occupations and families involved (all other states were in single figures). Its state and legal infrastructure were extremely precarious by comparison.

20 As Henry Bernstein and others point out, however, the relationship between the agrarian question (as constituted in different countries over different historical periods) and land reform is complex. See Henry Bernstein, 'Land Reform: Taking a Long(er) View', *Journal of Agrarian Change*, vol. 2, no. 4, 2002, pp. 433–63. See also, Henry Bernstein, '"Changing before our very eyes": agrarian questions and the politics of land in capitalism today', *Journal of Agrarian Change*, vol. 4, nos 1–2, January–April 2004, pp. 190–225.

21 Maximilliano Cox, Paul Munro-Faure, Paul Mathieu, Adriana Herrera, David Palmer and Paulo Groppo, 'FAO in agrarian reform', in *Land Reform: Land Settlement and Cooperatives*, Rome: Food and Agricultural Organisation, vol. 2, 2003, pp. 12–30.

22 Ibid., p. 13.

23 The Gini coefficient is a widely used and accepted method for calculating general inequality. In the case of land a zero reading represents perfect distribution while a reading of one would represent absolute concentration in the hands of a single individual.

24 This is according to the United Nations Food and Agricultural Organisation cited in Anthony W. Pereira, 'Agrarian reform and the rural workers' unions of the Pernambuco sugar zone, Brazil 1985–1988', *The Journal of Developing Areas*, vol. 26, January 1992, p. 189.

25 Anthony W. Pereira, 'Agrarian reform and the rural workers' unions of the Pernambuco sugar zone, Brazil 1985–1988', *The Journal of Developing Areas*, vol. 26, January 1992, p. 189.

26 Source: Instituto Brasileiro de Geografia e Estatística (IBGE), 5 November 2009, available at www.ibge.gov.br/home/presidencia/noticias/indice_de_gini.shtm

27 Sérgio Sauer and Sérgio Pereira Leite, 'Agrarian structure, foreign investment in land, and land prices in Brazil', *Journal of Peasant Studies*, vol. 39, nos 3–4, July – October 2012, pp. 873–98, 877.

28 Source: *Census of Agriculture 1995–1996: IBGE: Census of Agriculture 2006 makes a portrait of Brazil*, available at www.ibge.gov.br/english/presidencia/noticias/noticia_impressao.php?id_noticia=1464

29 Figures for March 2010 to February 2011. Brazilian Ministry of Agriculture, *País alcança valor recorde de exportações do agronegócio*, 21 March 2011, www.agricultura.gov.br/portal/page/portal/Internet-MAPA/pagina-inicial/internacional/noticias/noticia-aberta?noticiaId=31601

30 Comments made by the MST's National Secretariat March 2011. Source: 'Women in the Fight Against Agrochemicals', *MST Informa No. 189*, www.mstbrazil.org/news/mst-informa-no-189-women-fight-against-agrochemicals-3-4-11

31 Sérgio Sauer and Sérgio Pereira Leite, 'Agrarian structure, foreign investment in land, and land prices in Brazil', *Journal of Peasant Studies*, vol. 39, nos 3–4, July – October 2012, pp. 873–98, 877.

32 Ibid.

33 José de Souza Martins, *Os camponeses e a política no Brasil*, Petrópolis: Vozes, 1995, p. 42.

34 Miguel Pressburger, 'Terras devolutas. O que fazer com elas?', *Coleção Socializando Conhecimentos*, no. 7, July 1990, Rio de Janeiro: Instituto Apoio Jurídico Popular & Federação de Órgãos para Assistência Social e Educacional (FASE), p. 12.

35 Ariovaldo Umbelino de Oliveria, 'Grilagem de terras públicas na Amazônia', 28 July 2008, available at www.ecodebate.com.br/2008/07/28/a-grilagem-de-terras-publicas-na-amazonia-artigo-de-ariovaldo-umbelino-de-oliveira/

36 Ibid.

37 Source: Banco de Dados da Luta pela Terra: Relatório Dataluta Brasil 2011, Presidente Prudente, São Paulo: NERA (Núcleo de Estudos, Pesquisas e Projetos de Reforma Agrária), FCT-UNESP, October 2012, p. 18.

38 Ibid., p. 11.

39 See for example Abdurazack Karriem, 'The rise and transformation of the Brazilian landless movement into a counter-hegemonic political actor: a Gramscian analysis', *Geoforum*, vol. 40, no. 3, May 2009, pp. 316–25.

40 See Boaventura de Sousa Santos, *Toward a New Legal Common Sense: Law, Globalization, and Emancipation*, 2nd edition, London: Butterworths, 2002; and Boaventura de Sousa Santos, *Toward a New Common Sense: Law, Science and Politics in the Paradigmatic Transition*, New York: Routledge, 1995.

41 Peter Houtzager, 'The Movement of the Landless (MST) and the juridical field in Brazil', *IDS Working Paper 248*, August 2005, p. 2.

42 Source: 'Contag representa 20 milhões de trabalhadores e trabalhadoras rurais', available at www.contag.org.br/indexdet.php?modulo=portal&acao=interna&codpag=1

43 Leonilde Sérvolo de Medeiros, *História dos Movimentos Sociais no Campo*, FASE, Rio de Janeiro, 1989, p. 92, my emphasis.

44 Rudá Ricci, 'A Contag no governo de transição: um ator à procura de um texto', *Caderno CEDEC No. 15*, São Paulo, 1990, p. 10.

45 Luiz Antônio Marrey, cited in 'Promotores criam comissão', *Oeste Notícias*, 5 February 1997.

46 Author interview with João Pedro Stédile, 18 March 2000.

Chapter 1

Shocking the System

Social Movement Pressure as the Catalyst of Political and Legal Change

> When we took office there were high court sentences which said that parts of the land occupied by private individuals or groups belonged to the state. This was a big problem for us because it was in precisely these areas that there were invasions [occupations by the MST]. And the invasions in the state of São Paulo, at least at the time, were not merely an issue for the police or the agrarian question; it was a question of justice. They drew attention towards lands that belonged to the state and the state did not take measures. This was the great drama.
>
> Belisário dos Santos Júnior, Secretary of State for Justice, São Paulo[1]

While land conflicts across the globe vary in nature, reflecting local social structures and unique histories, a theme that is common to all is a belief that embedded injustices should be righted. Brazil is no exception. In the Pontal do Paranapanema, a region in the west of the state of São Paulo, for most of the nineteenth and twentieth centuries the authorities turned a blind eye to – or colluded in – the theft by powerful private interests of hundreds of thousands of hectares of state-owned land. During the 1990s, however, the forces underpinning these entrenched grievances were overcome to a sufficient extent to lead one of Brazil's foremost land reform exponents to describe events as 'the closest thing to agrarian reform' he had seen.[2] Significant though these events were on a regional level, they also raise a wider question of why here and not elsewhere? Of note too is how consistently impotent law had proved throughout the decades. A case in point is a 1958 court ruling that declared these lands the state's. This chapter examines law's wider failure, but also traces how, why and to what extent that changed in the 1990s. Undoubtedly the crucial variable was the development of the Landless Workers' Movement (MST) as an effective social and political force. The contingency of law is examined here in the context of the MST's rise to prominence. The chapter also touches upon the extent and limits of the movement's own power. In so doing fundamental questions are raised about role of the state, law and social movements in perpetuating and addressing situations of historic injustice.

Property Is Theft: A Brief History of the Pontal do Paranapanema

Long regarded as an economic backwater, the Pontal do Paranapanema is a vast semi-arid region of almost 1.2 million hectares on the most westerly fringe of the state of São Paulo, bordering the states of Mato Grosso do Sul and Paraná (see Figures 2 and 3). Appearances can be deceptive, however, for the region has undergone immense environmental and social changes. In a matter of a few decades a pristine sea-green landscape, the Mata Atlântica, or Atlantic rainforest, has given way to a desert of sandy browns. Commencing in the nineteenth century, the process of destruction persisted with accelerated intensity during the course of the twentieth. According to the São Paulo State Forestry Institute (Instituto Florestal – IF) for instance, in 1971–73 the region still possessed 203,650 hectares of natural vegetation, but by 1990–92 this had dropped to 94,448 hectares, a decline of 54 per cent.[3]

Alongside the incipient forestry clearance of the 1850s went the slaughter and complete liquidation of the indigenous inhabitants, including the Kaiuás and Kaingang.[4] One graphic account of the time noted that

> On meeting female Indians some were imprisoned and others killed. The same, it is said, happened to the men who were raised from their beds or from the floor, thrown in the air and impaled on the tips of knives; on other occasions they were held by their feet and their heads smashed apart

Figure 2 Map of São Paulo State showing location of Pontal do Paranapanema

Figure 3 Map of Pontal do Paranapanema

on wood. The wombs of pregnant women were sliced open and, after the carnage, the bodies were piled high and set alight.[5]

Cotton, coffee and subsequently cattle would take their place. Out of these destructive processes there emerged a new regional social order of large landed estates whose self-proclaimed owners would retain a tenacious grip on political and economic power well into the 1990s. Predatory speculation played a decisive role in the region's development. Although early phases of the colonisation exhibited semi-spontaneous characteristics associated with a land grab, as thousands of small settlers and squatters were enticed into the region with promises of land in exchange for labour, the venture was in fact hierarchically structured and ruthlessly controlled. Little did these settlers realise that they were merely the foot soldiers for grander, utterly fraudulent claims. Once they became surplus to requirements, they were simply evicted at gunpoint or executed by hired gunmen. Conversely, for the tiny handful of individuals at the top of this system, the genocide of Indians, the destruction of forests and subsequent wholesale clearance of squatters and sharecroppers offered massive rewards, leading one powerful landowner to declare that 'land soaked in blood is good land'.[6]

The 1850 Land Law and its Legacy

What did the law have to say about these seemingly chaotic developments? In theory, with the passage on 18 September 1850 of the *Lei de Terras* (Law 601, basic legislation governing the use and appropriation of land throughout Brazil), the answer is a great deal. This law had asserted that devolved lands — tracts of land that did not as yet belong to private parties — could no longer be appropriated except through means of purchases made directly from the government.[7] Article 1 asserted that '[t]he acquisition of devolved lands by title other than purchase is hereby prohibited.' As noted in the Introduction:

> [it] would transform devolved lands into a monopoly of the state and a state controlled by a strong class of large landowners. The non-propertied peasants, those that arrived after the *Lei de Terras* or those that had not had their occupations legalised in 1850, were therefore compelled ... to work for the large estates.[8]

Thus the law attempted to manage the transition from a slave economy to a capitalist one, deliberately locking millions – whether freed slaves, smallholders or immigrants – out of landownership and into waged employment on large estates.

As in many other parts of Brazil, the development of property relations in the Pontal do Paranapanema highlights the state's consistent failure, despite the *Lei de Terras*, to exercise any meaningful sort of control over devolved lands facing predatory interests. This has not changed even with the superimposition of legislation after 1850. Although the concept of devolved land was incorporated (with some variations) in Brazil's first republican constitution of 1891 and reasserted in the constitution of 1988, the *Lei de Terras* remains a fundamental reference point.

The connections between past and present, and their practical implications, are summarised by Pressburger as follows:

> The *Lei de Terras* of 1850 and its regulations determined how, under what conditions, and for how much devolved lands could be sold to private individuals. Later, other laws regulated the alienation of public lands and, more recently, (Decree-Law 900 of 29/6/1969) established a whole framework of authorisation by legislative power, public competition, etc. Thus, in every analysis of title to private property an investigation is essential so as to determine its origins, that is to say, to check if it is not in fact devolved land (public) 'transformed' into private property and, if the latter proves to be the case, what the legislation was that authorised this 'transformation', and whether all the requisites of that legislation were correctly and fully attended to. That is because if the privatisation of the public asset was not realised in accordance with the legislation then in legal terms the asset remained inalienable and, as established in the Civil Code, beyond commercialisation.[9]

Manifestly the legal requisites to which Pressburger refers were not attended to in the Pontal do Paranapanema (a fact that would later be used by the MST to legitimise its own claims). Instead, landownership in the Pontal was predicated upon an industry of deception.

There are numerous accounts of the illegal transfer of devolved land into private property. A glaring example of this occurred in 1856 when Antônio José de Gouvêa falsely laid claim to 300,000 hectares in the Pontal. His documentation asserting knowledge and ownership included an entirely fictitious river, the Pirapó. He claimed to have been living and farming near there before 1848. Fearing imminent legal action, in 1890, Manoel Pereira Goulart, another owner, took the extraordinary step of simply exchanging his own land with that of the successors to the estate of Gouvêa. Theirs was a blatant attempt to create false trails. Goulart's estate lay outside, but bordered, the Pontal. It shared a number of characteristics in common with Gouvêa's estate. It too could be measured in the hundreds of thousands of hectares, was said to have been subject to occupation and cultivation prior to 1850. Both claims to legalisation were based upon fictitious parish records that proved so full of legal and technical inaccuracies that the governors of São Paulo at the time came to reject them. One governor, Visconde de Parnaiba, even sought to prosecute Goulart.

The legal profession, cartographers and corrupt local priests (acting in their capacity as public notaries) were central to the deception. Along with paperwork of varying degrees of sophistication, these pillars of the local establishment generated powerful cultural expectations. Their work possessed a ring of authority and authenticity. A favoured method of falsification was *grilagem*. The term (which became synonymous with all forms of land acquisition through false title deeds) derived from the word *grilo*, or cricket, and referred to the practise of locking title deeds in a drawer with crickets. Once they died they secreted liquids which discoloured or aged the documents prematurely. Corrupt notaries then authenticated them.

The factors that led to the development of a fully functioning land market in the Pontal do Paranapanema were complex. Paradoxically the *Lei de Terras* was partly responsible. It had deliberately engineered wider conditions for the commodification of land and labour. Men like Gouvêa and others were opportunists who saw the loopholes and played them for all they were worth. Crucially, though, their aggressive confidence was combined with an ambiguous response by the state. The latter could never accept his actions since these were a deliberate attempt to circumvent the legislation, hence periodic legal actions, but there was a sense in which Gouvêa and others were doing the state's job for it, i.e., transforming land into a commodity and developing capitalist relations.

It may seem odd that anyone should have bought into a juridically worthless asset like devolved land. Sale and purchase from generation to generation could not purge these lands of their original sin. And yet, by the 1990s these vast land holdings had been transformed into a fait accomplis of such potency that the ideology of private property was invoked against supposedly lawless land occupations.

How did this transformation of nominally worthless assets occur? Much of the answer relates to perceptions of risk. While fooling purchasers and the justice system were essential to market formation, many market entrants, smallholders, large landowners and commercial organisations alike, were 'knowing' buyers. Their motives varied considerably. For some, like small-holders, it was a matter of survival; for large players there was the potential for vast profits. Crucially, it did not matter that the state had not legally recog-nised these land acquisitions or that, in some instances, it had declared the illegality of occupation and fraudulent nature of the claims. The key issue was – *and remains* – what the state would do about it, especially in such remote regions. Eviction was a possibility as was legalisation. Speculative risks were worth taking. In any case, while the state made up its mind, a process that commonly took years, land could enter commercial production and circulation.

These artifices would not of themselves constitute the sufficient material basis for a self-sustaining economic dynamic. For that one has to look to other developments. Some were speculative. The construction of the Sorocabana Railway, a line reaching the Pontal do Paranapanema in the early twentieth century, sucked capital into the heart of the region. It was a self-fulfilling prophecy of sorts. Partly on the back of this transport network, demography came to play a more significant role. Explosive rates of population growth meant that the demand for land far outstripped supply and gradually helped to bury past crimes, as a self-interested collective amnesia took hold. Although the state government occasionally reminded people of the risks of buying devolved land, the *grilagem* industry's counter claims and offers to help to acquire land proved more credible. Lastly, in what is by no means an exhaus-tive list, cyclical waves of cultivation made the risks sustainable. While the state issued edicts, registered landowners planted crops and reaped the rewards: initially highly profitable coffee (until the crisis of 1929), followed by cotton in the 1940s, and later still, cattle rearing.

Finally, one should consider the role of the state and local governments in the valorisation and commodification of worthless assets. The fate that befell the region's nature reserves illustrates how practices publicly condemned and legislated against were supported from within sectors of the state. Between 1941 and 1942, under the governorship of the former agronomist-engineer Fernando Costa, the state created three reserves[10] totaling an area of almost 300,000 hectares. Collectively these became known as the Grande Reserva do Pontal. Under the governorship of Jânio Quadros (1955–59) the state erected prominent notices within and at the edge of the reserves, declaring them to be 'property of the state of São Paulo'. It was under the governorship of Adhemar de Barros, in 1949, that the technical legality of the reserves was first ques-tioned, and these were reduced to just under 110,000 hectares. Aside from local potentates, like the mayor of Presidente Venceslau, one of the key figures to move into the Morro do Diabo reserve was none other than Antônio Emídio de Barros Filho, the governor's brother. Nepotism of this kind was common. Subsequent attempts to protect the remaining 36,000 hectares, to which the reserves had been reduced, were defeated in the state legislative assembly with the aid, among others, of state deputy Cassio Ciampolini, a purported title holder in the Pontal do Paranapanema. These formidable alliances chipped away at the reserves.

Controlling the machinery of state power was important if only for the potential scope it offered to retard the rapacious appetite of private power. The fortunes to be made when state controls were relaxed made it a highly prized and contested sphere. This explains why one governor who was willing to oppose the designs of the *grileiros*, Franco Montoro, bemoaned the 'wave of criticism'[11] he faced from large registered landowners in 1983. This was a war of attrition in which the historical tendency was one of cumulative defeats. Registered landowners traditionally were technically and financially well prepared, especially in the legal sphere. As the São Paulo State Land Institute (Instituto de Terras do Estado de São Paulo – ITESP) itself noted in 1998:

> 'The state ... failed to equip itself in the sense of monitoring and effectively combating the invasions of these areas. Legally, these reserves still exist, given that the decrees that created them were never revoked. In de facto terms, however, presently only the Reserva do Morro do Diabo exists and even then not in its entirety.'[12]

To summarise, then, the juridical quagmire in which the Pontal do Paranapanema found itself by the early 1990s arose not so much from the arrogance and cunning of a few powerful and corrupt individuals, as from the successful incorporation of their designs within the wider capitalist economy and society. On those occasions when the state did attempt to draw a juridical line in the sand, its efforts were simply eroded by the force of events. The net result was that the fate of devolved lands came to symbolise the incompetence and corruption of the state, the immense power of private interests and the total paralysis of law enforcement. That dynamic would change in the early 1990s as the MST invested major efforts in the region.

The Emergence of the MST as the Leading Contender in the Pontal do Paranapanema

The MST's methods of direct action – mass land occupations – would challenge head-on the corruption and paralysis that the Pontal do Paranapanema had come to symbolise. The region represented a strategic and symbolic target, being located in the richest and most developed of the Brazilian states, São Paulo, a fact that simultaneously highlighted how the land question was not simply a matter for the less developed states, but a national question. As the movement's leading spokesperson, João Pedro Stédile explains:

> Obviously for us it was very important from an ideological point of view because in the Pontal there were, and are, 700,000 hectares of

public land. The property's [status] was clear and decided in the courts as belonging to the state and it had been stolen by large landowners and leading figures of the São Paulo aristocracy.[13]

There was nothing new about the desire for change. In fact, as far back as the late 1950s and early 1960s another organisation, the Movement of the Landless of the West of the State of São Paulo (Movimento dos Sem-Terra do Oeste do Estado de São Paulo – MASTER) was active in the region,[14] and with the decline of the dictatorship, in the early 1980s, other struggles had emerged, 'carried out by homesteaders [*posseiros*], people affected by dams, former sharecroppers, day-labourers [*boia-frio*], unemployed rural and urban workers, etc.'[15] Ultimately, what would make the MST stand out was the political and organisational force it learned to develop with the *sem terra*. When José Rainha, who became the MST's leading spokesperson in the Pontal, arrived in the region in 1990, he had been struck by the movement's limitations. Speaking of one occupation, he noted how:

> The method was wrong for the reality. They had a method of resistance towards the police and they had already suffered the eviction of 700 families who had then been reduced to 100. I asked myself what could be done? The police were surrounding the occupation ... I saw that it was a situation in which a massacre could occur and I was less than happy with the method that was leading to confrontation. I suggested another method – to withdraw the families, negotiate with the police, and encamp by the roadside and analyse the situation. Meanwhile the government was there and committed to supplying water and infrastructure to the people pending the expropriation of land.[16]

Zelitro Luz da Silva, a leading militant in the MST, also acknowledges the difficulties of those early days:

> On 12 July 1990 the MST occupied the Fazenda Nova do Pontal. ... There were a little over 600 families involved. An extremely truculent eviction followed and those families who didn't know the MST well eventually gave up. Those that remained, between approximately 150 and 200 families, went on to occupy the Fazenda São Bento.[17]

Rates of attrition like this were unsustainable. Notwithstanding the pent-up demand of landless workers in the region, the movement was effectively exhausting itself. However, this pattern reversed as the movement changed tactics.

> The MST adopted a method of non-confrontation. It negotiated and stayed there a little bit more time, but at the moment when the police

was just about to go in there, we left. There was no other way. We got out of there and went to a rail siding. We already had somewhere to go, we had worked that out before hand. Two or three days later the injunction, the eviction order – in other words the legal instrument, no longer had validity and we went back into the area, this happened 23 times.[18]

For a movement that had shown signs of exhaustion, the change in tactics opened the way towards a remarkable reversal of fortunes:

You see it was a process; it was a method, of winning through the exhaustion [of one's opponents] without causing attrition, because that spread fear amongst the families and weakened the MST. With these tactics of non-confrontation the movement became a mass movement. On 28 February, for example, we carried out an occupation of the Fazenda São Bento with 1,700 families.[19]

As noted in the Introduction, the movement's relationship with law was difficult to say the least. Those difficulties ran far more deeply than the obvious legal consequences (eviction and imprisonment) arising from direct action (see Chapter 2). They were also present in the movement's DNA. One feature that had marked out the MST since the early 1980s was its trenchant criticism of the historical failures of other rural movements, especially the National Confederation of Agricultural Workers (CONTAG), still by far the largest rural workers' organisation in Brazil.[20] In her work on rural social movements, the sociologist Leonilde Sérvolo de Medeiros notes that with the emergence of the military dictatorship in the 1960s, and the generalised climate of fear and demobilisation of rural workers that resulted, 'the struggle for "rights", *within legal parameters*, came to constitute the *basic* directive to action of CONTAG.'[21] Under dictatorial conditions, it became a question of 'transforming the law, in its diverse forms, into an arena of contestation and, thereby, expanding spaces of organisation.'[22] Medeiros concludes that: 'The point of departure that comes to guide the practise of CONTAG is that rights existed but were not respected. ... In this way the recourse to legal justice became the framework of action.'[23] Ricci adds that for an organisation such as CONTAG, 'the struggle for agrarian reform was confined ... within the limits that could guarantee dialogue with the state, avoiding any kind of mass movement that could signal a possible rupture'.[24] For the MST, however, the opposite was the case: exhibiting elements of rupture was essential to the construction of an active mass base. Far from eschewing conflict, the MST would use the latter as a basis of negotiation.

Although according to Medeiros, 'the struggle for "rights", within legal parameters, came to constitute the *basic* directive to action'[25] of CONTAG, it is nevertheless clear that the MST's own forceful dialogue with legality, including a struggle for rights, became a critical reference point. The MST was itself in no position to eschew legality. The state held most of the cards, including the monopoly of force, and the movement came to understand that notions of legality exercised a profound impact upon its own – and would-be – members. Speaking of his time in Brazil's Northeast, before his arrival in the Pontal to organise its major occupation campaign, José Rainha noted that people there were very 'legalistic': 'We had enormous difficulties. [Our members thought] "gosh, I'm going to enter this man's land". These first moments were extremely difficult because they knew the owners of the sugar plantations. Culturally the owner is like a father.'[26]

Conflicts with the police had also shown the costs of ignoring legal dynamics (including a potential loss of members), and, as subsequent sections will show, the benefits of a proactive approach. Thus, while ideologically speaking CONTAG and the MST were poles apart, in practise there were parallels. The idea that 'transforming the law, in its diverse forms, into an arena of contestation and, thereby, expanding spaces of organisation'[27] is not just applicable to CONTAG, it neatly encapsulates certain aspects of the MST's own struggles.

Whatever the movement's perceptions of the injustices of the legal system, the fact is that references to the legality of the MST's actions came to form a critical part of its ideological discourse – galvanising both internal support and external legitimacy. To be sure, other factors, like the publicity from being in the heart of São Paulo and low rates of land productivity, were at work, but according to Rainha: 'the *biggest* aggravating factor was that the land didn't belong to them. The land belonged to the state, to the government of São Paulo. So they were the people's land. For this reason [we said], we were going to occupy these land holdings to give back to the people their right to a piece of land.'[28] This was the language of popular mobilisation rather than of the law courts. Simultaneously, though, it was the language of rights and legitimacy inextricably linked to a legal category – devolved land – of the state's own design. This made it all the harder to refute. In fact, the idea that it was incumbent upon the state both to assert control over devolved lands and to place these land holdings within the effective reach of an agrarian reform programme has received substantial jurisprudential support.[29]

Rainha underlines the ideological value of legality within the MST's struggle, suggesting that occupations within the Pontal became 'a great deal easier':

> Because one questions the law. Because it is the landowners who bang on about us being the invaders. No, we said, it isn't us. You are the illegal ones, we aren't the illegal ones! You are the illegal ones because the law says that the land belongs to the state! Well the impact of this is extremely powerful. It has an impact upon society. We isolated the landowners.[30]

The movement was more than happy to draw attention to land's devolved status and choose its site of struggle accordingly. As Valdemir Rodrigues Chaves, a leading militant in the Pontal, attests:

We found out that since 1958 the government had already won a case in the highest courts and that the lands were devolved. Once we came across this information ... we decided that we are going to throw our energies behind this, we are going to turn our cannon in that direction. And we went in hard.[31]

The movement could have opted merely to address the social inequalities of land concentration. Its decision to highlight the Pontal's legal dimensions and link these to the state's wider constitutional duty of land reform demonstrates the increasing significance that law was assuming as a source of leverage within its own struggles.

The Dialectic of State and Social Movement Action

Undoubtedly one of the MST's great merits would be to give a new voice to the struggle for land in the Pontal do Paranapanema. To fully appreciate the magnitude of these achievements, including their limits, they should be seen in a broader perspective which includes attempts by the state to address land issues. This chapter contends that the continuous interplay between social struggle and state action had a major impact upon both parties and consequently the prospects of reform.

Arguably the most significant attempt at addressing the Pontal's situation came from the government of Franco Montoro (1983–87) which for all its limitations, was one of the first administrations in the state of São Paulo to pursue agrarian reform with any seriousness or degree of success. As with all such attempts, however, it was met with fierce resistance, a fact, as noted earlier, bemoaned by the governor himself. In 1983 Juvenal Boller, a lawyer representing Montoro's agricultural secretariat, made a visit to the Pontal 'with a view towards negotiating with the landowners', but his proposals were 'consistently rejected'.[32] Faced with this apparently immovable obstacle, Boller proposed a remarkable amendment to an ongoing legislative project that eventually became Law 4.925 of 19 December 1985. 'An article[33] was inserted', explains Boller, 'that authorised the state, in areas of conflict, to negotiate lands and relinquish its right to a Discriminatory Action [see below] provided that it could remain with a portion of the land ... approximately 30–35 per cent.'[34] His comment is extremely telling and goes to the heart of the matter. It highlights both the juridical difficulties as well as political tensions between a reforming state and landowning interests.

The juridical problems facing the state were formidable. According to Boller, who was a highly experienced legal practitioner,[35] 'it was better to obtain this land quickly at zero cost, than to fight in the courts – where we might even fail'.[36] His suggestion, to which there was more than a grain of truth, was that the situation was fraught with legal risk and complexity. The underlying legal principle behind devolved land was relatively easy to grasp, i.e. the notion that at no stage was such land incorporated into the private domain, but establishing this was far from simple. To this day nobody can be sure, for example, where many of these land holdings exist. For the state to establish provenance with precision requires the instigation of a procedure known as an *ação discriminatória* – a discriminatory action, which, as the term suggests, attempts to discriminate between those lands that are public and those that are not. Technically it is a legal procedure (instigated by *procuradores do estado*, prosecutors employed by the state government, rather than public prosecutors from the Public Ministry) whose culmination lies with the binding sentence of the court. It is predicated upon an intensive series of administrative-investigative actions. Evidence shedding light on the status quo, i.e., who was occupying a particular property, the extent of that property (size, precise boundaries, etc.), who had an interest in it, or should be notified of any legal action, was comparatively simple to gather since it could be cross-checked with contemporary archives and even satellite photographs. But obtaining historical evidence was far from simple. As one group of lawyers from the Pontal explains:

> This [evidence] comes from land registers, court records, departments and documents of state – in other words different branches of the state. It depends on the case at hand. Here, in this region, you find it in the land registers. You have to go to the register in the town of Assis, and then you have to look in the town of Botucato – in all registers. Then there comes a certain moment, from 1890 and earlier, when you have to look in the national archive. Sometimes the information is there, and sometimes it isn't, but you still have to go after it. ... Sometimes the property's certificate is there but it doesn't mention the previous registration. If that is the case you have to carry on researching and investigating until you find something [like inventories]. Individual cases may involve eight or ten volumes. It's a lot of paperwork.[37]

It is hardly surprising that the process of discrimination frequently took between 15 and 20 years to complete.

Thus the legal procedure for reasserting control over devolved land had evolved into a practise that was so slow and complex, and subject to the vagaries of judicial conservatism, that to all intents and purposes it became unworkable. According to a 1997 survey carried out by ITESP, some 41 per cent of the region's 1.183 million hectares (i.e., 480,000 hectares) fell into this category. This compared to 231,000 hectares (20 per cent) that was classified as devolved land, and 384,000 hectares (32 per cent) that was classified as private. More worrying still, no legal action had begun in the vast majority (some 336,000 hectares) of these un-discriminated lands.[38] The transaction costs were so high that the state, under Governor Montoro, was willing to relinquish its rights in relation to the overwhelming majority of devolved land – 60–75 per cent.

Were Boller and Governor Montoro wrong to make this sort of a bargain? Certainly the São Paulo Catholic Church's Pastoral Land Commission (Comissão Pastoral da Terra – CPT) thought so. The CPT could not accept the argument (even if made by lawyers sympathetic to land reform) that existing procedures were too complex, risky and time consuming to permit a viable alternative to Law 4.925. Furthermore, in the light of his own experience as a lawyer in Rio de Janeiro under the governorship of Leonel Brizola, the CPT's legal advisor, Miguel Pressburger, argued that:

> One didn't need to initiate any legal action. After all, it was the state that organised Brazil's legal structure, indeed it organised it in an extremely authoritarian manner. The state didn't need to go along this route. All that it had to do was to gather its land. Look, I worked for the state of Rio at the time of [Governor Leonel] Brizola, and I used to gather the state's land. I would give 60 days notice for the person to leave or be evicted. I gathered a lot of land this way. Afterwards we could discuss the finer points, but first we gathered it.[39]

In other words, somewhat as registered landowners had done before, the state would reassert de facto control, if necessary by the use of force, and then leave the courts to work out the problem, thereby leaving registered landowners on the defensive. This was politics followed by proceduralism, rather than the other way around. It is an interesting argument, but what is more significant for present purposes is the fact that, just over a decade later, São Paulo's Governor Mário Covas would introduce legislation (Decree-Law 42.041 of 1 August 1997) that almost exactly reversed the proportions of Law 4.925. Henceforth, the state would retain 70 per cent of disputed lands while registered landowners could keep the remaining 30 per cent. Clearly this too was a political argument, one that raises the intriguing question of what had happened to shift the balance so markedly in the intervening period.

To be sure, shifts within the state itself had played a part. The military dictatorship was no longer in power and Mário Covas, who was at the height of his electoral power, had more room for manoeuvre and was determined to use his mandate. One factor that is also likely to have strengthened Covas' hand was the changed legislative climate. Governor Montoro had been sympathetic to land reform, but his electoral mandate had come to an end in 1987, before the passage of the new Brazilian constitution and Law 8.629 (of 25 February 1993) that sought to regulate land reform in detail. Although this legislative change was not directly relevant to the issue of devolved land, dealing with the social function of property instead, it did, nevertheless, form part of the background – a legislative and political paradigm shift – against which Covas could now operate. However, as the remaining sections of this chapter will make clear, it was the advent of the MST and the eruption of mass occupations onto the political scene that would make a decisive contribution to this shift.

The comments of Belisário dos Santos Júnior, Covas' secretary of state for justice, the man who had to deal with many of the juridical, social and political aspects of the conflict in the Pontal do Paranapanema, gives a sense of the changes underway:

> When we took office there were high court sentences that said that parts of the land occupied by private individuals or groups belonged to the state. This was a big problem for us because it was in precisely these areas that there were invasions [occupations by the MST]. And the invasions in the state of São Paulo, at least at the time, were not merely an issue for the police or the agrarian question; it was a question of justice. They drew attention towards lands that belonged to the state and the state did not take measures. This was the great drama.[40]

This was the background against which the state would forge its political and legal strategy, and against which the judiciary would forge its decisions.

As with any complex historical situation involving multiple variables and agents, the notion of isolating one of these, in this case the MST, is inherently problematic. Although, for instance, the full significance of the MST's role in the Pontal has been debated by experts, there is little point engaging it on the terms cast by two leading academic analysts of the MST, Zander Navarro and Bernardo Mançano Fernandes: 'Zander Navarro often says that it was the Pontal that highlighted the Landless Workers' Movement, while I say the reverse, that it was the Landless Workers' Movement that highlighted Pontal.'[41] Rather like the debate about which came first, the chicken or the egg, this is a fruitless exercise since the lines of causality cannot be established in the unilateral/exclusive terms presupposed by the 'debate'. The fact is that the Pontal gave leverage to the MST, and that the MST was capable of exposing and exploiting it. These reciprocal determinations also hold for relations between the state and the MST. While the MST undoubtedly presented the government of Mário Covas with a 'great drama', his government rose to that challenge by embracing elements of the conflict, i.e., addressing some of its root causes, rather than merely repressing them. Mançano himself notes that 'to a certain degree with this appointment [of Belisário dos Santos Júnior as secretary of state for justice and the defense of citizenship] the historic alliance between *grileiros* and the state was undermined.'[42] As will become evident, this offered opportunities to the MST, but equally the MST's presence on the scene would offer the government an historic opportunity to move forward.

The State's Response

Chapter 2 details the dramatic nature of the crisis presented to the Covas government. Its proximate causes lay in the MST's decision to confront historic injustices through mass land occupations (hundreds of families descending on a *fazenda* at any one time). This provoked various responses. From registered landowners, there were legally sanctioned evictions and illegal armed evictions that they arranged independently. The state's response, however, was more complex as ideological divisions cut across the judiciary, prosecutors and to a lesser extent the government of Covas himself. He wanted to respond to the social demands of MST, but simultaneously assert law and order imperatives in a region where the law had never prevailed. From a broader perspective, i.e., including federal, state and municipal levels, as well as the judiciary and Public Ministry, the response of the state largely took the form of crisis management. Extensive media coverage of workers' imprisonment and set-piece confrontations merely intensified this sense of crisis and denied the state its usual breathing space. A procession of senior delegations made their way from the federal capital, Brasília, to comparatively obscure towns like Teodoro Sampaio and Presidente Prudente in the Pontal do Paranapanema. Members of the External Commission of the Chamber of Deputies (Comissão Externa de Representação da Câmara dos Deputados) made their way to the Pontal in January 1996. In addition to a number of federal deputies and the Workers' Party (PT), senator from São Paulo, Eduardo Suplicy, members of the Commission were accompanied by the Federal Public Ministry's specialist prosecutor in citizens' rights (Procurador Federal dos Direitos do Cidadão), Wagner Gonçalves. In February 1997 São Paulo's Public Ministry convened its Special Working Group on Land Issues in Western São Paulo (Grupo Especial de Trabalho sobre Assuntos Fundiário do Oeste Paulista – GETAF), a belated attempt at pooling local expertise on the land question and at trying to organise a more coherent response. And finally, the Minister for Agrarian Reform himself began to make a regular series of trips to the region and state capital, São Paulo, in an attempt to resolve the problem.

Having focused minds upon the Pontal, the MST could now make its case. At a meeting with GETAF prosecutors, it demanded 'greater agility on the part of authorities in gathering land and turning it over for permanent land settlements', and 'an end to the exaggeratedly bureaucratic nature of Discriminatory Actions'. The MST also reiterated the 'need to accelerate *vistorias* [on site land audits] by INCRA [the federal government's land reform agency] with a view to assessing the productivity of large properties'.[43] After all, the federal government still retained constitutional responsibilities in relation to private land, much of which, in the Pontal's case, was unproductive and therefore potentially subject to expropriation. Backed up by mass mobilisations, these demands formed the backdrop against which the Covas government both legislated and adopted innovatory legal strategies using existing, but as yet untested, legal instruments. The latter included *tutela antecipada*, or interim control, one of a number of changes made in late 1994 to the Civil Legal Code (Código do Processo Civil) which offered at least the theoretical possibility of dramatically accelerated land acquisition.[44]

To some extent the Covas administration was taken by surprise. According to a former head of the ITESP, Tânia Andrade, 'if you take the first programme of the Covas government, there isn't a single word on the agrarian question, there isn't an agrarian policy'.[45] In fact, Belisário, who ended up in charge of this area, had no track record on land issues (although he was a human rights lawyer with known sympathies towards social movements). Mário Covas was different. He had a personal history of active support for land reform, dating back to his work as a representative in the National Constituent Assembly when it was framing new constitutional provisions.[46] That said, his election was very much the product of urban electoral interests.

Several factors would lead to the transformation of state policy. One of these was the actions of ITESP itself. ITESP is significant because over time it would become the pre-eminent organisation responsible for planning and executing São Paulo state's policies in the areas of land tenure and reform. Although formal jurisdiction on matters of land reform were (and remain) largely confined to the federal level, in many respects ITESP eclipsed the activities of federal organisations (INCRA) by virtue of the substantial invest-ment – financial, technical and political – made by the state of São Paulo, and the intellectual and personal commitment of those working within ITESP itself. Thus, upon the election of Covas in late 1994, employees from ITESP went on to the offensive. Rather than waiting for a policy to emerge, they organised a meeting with the Secretary elect, at which they presented a sub-stantial document dealing with the work of ITESP and 'putting forward an agrarian policy to the Covas government'.[47] The whole process was carefully orchestrated by sectors within and beyond ITESP. Even the selection of ITESP's new head, which formally lay within the exclusive gift of the govern-ment, is symptomatic of this reactivation of networks. As Tânia Andrade, explained:

> The employees put him forward and we organised a political campaign throughout the state. More than 500 faxes of support arrived from all over, including trade unions, mayors and deputies – from all over the state, asking that Jonas should be nominated. And he was.[48]

In short, there was a noticeable shift as the work of ITESP moved centre stage and the state government belatedly acquired an agrarian reform policy.

On a purely practical level, though, this still left the government in des-perate need of an effective means of responding to rapidly unfolding events. ITESP, which had more cordial links with rural social movements[49] and extensive experience in the field, offered itself as part of the solution, but the fact was the government's room for manouevre was diminishing. It had a priori excluded a repressive approach to land occupations. Simultaneously, it had accepted registered landowners as respected and legitimate interlocutors to be accorded certain legal protections rather than as *grileiros* who should be expelled along the lines suggested earlier by Pressburger. Finally, the MST, which owed the government no political favours sensed that now was the moment to raise the stakes and press home the attack. As its leader said at the time: 'The region is all made up of devolved and unproductive lands. We are going to occupy it and demand that the government divides up the lots.'[50] The issue now facing Covas and Belisário was how to create a viable margin of action.

In truth the government had more room for manoeuvre than zero-sum scenarios between registered landowners, landless and the state would suggest. For a start it had vital financial and legal levers at its disposal, to say nothing of political ones, for example the traditionally ascribed power to mediate such conflicts. In the Pontal's case there was an added source of power: the state's direct material interest in devolved land. So although the administration faced formidable constraints, with imagination it could exercise considerable power. Nowhere was this more obvious than in the related fields of law and politics, to which we now turn.

Underwriting the Efficacy of Land Law through the Political Process

Mário Covas' administration was a centre-left coalition that did not depend heavily upon the support of the far right. Rather than being imprisoned by a faction, Covas enjoyed a considerable degree of room for manoeuvre in relation to his political bases, and greater latitude when legislating. To this extent law corresponded more closely to the will of the state, and ultimately proved an effective instrument of it. Nonetheless, state policy had to come to terms with the peculiarities and profound limitations of that instrument.

These limitations were essentially two-fold: specialised/technical, and political. Regarding the former, this chapter has already discussed the slowness and complexity of legal processes. It took over a hundred years for the judiciary to decide the status of devolved lands in the Pontal do Paranapanema, and having decided in the state's favour in 1958, it took another 40 years for the state to begin – and even then only tentatively – to assert effective control over devolved land. As an instrument of policy, law proved remarkably ineffective.

While speaking of the debt owed to the Montoro government, Belisário also acknowledged its legal shortcomings:

> Montoro spoke of agrarian reform, he spoke of the use of public land, he created the first laws on the use of public land, and he tried, by legally flawed means, to introduce the first practical examples. He used expropriation that, in legal terms, created some problems for us.[51]

The implication is clear: there was a failure to come to grips with legal discourse within its own terms as a consequence of which the full potential of law as an instrument of state action was never fully realised.

But law cannot be divorced from the second limiting aspect: politics. This is evident from additional comments by Belisário. He suggested that the Montoro administration 'tried to resolve the status of public lands but perhaps there hadn't been a great deal of discussion and, on account of this, he was subject to a number of popular legal actions that continue right up to today. With this experience in mind, we moved forward on the one hand with legal moves to reacquire public land and, on the other hand, with moves to exchange public land for public land.'[52] The basic principle underlying the policy of 'terra por terra' public land for land, was simple. Instead of compensating registered landowners in the Pontal with cash payments, the state offered them the possibility of retaining a portion of their land in lieu of those payments. According to Belisário, 'we created an extremely scientific, in fact extremely complex, set of criteria. In each plot there would be a quotient according to the extent of its use, etc. But more than the criteria being better, we discussed the issue.'[53] Note Belisário's acknowledgement that for all the technical and legal sophistication of his own approach, or attempts to iron out legal flaws beforehand, the essential precondition to implementation was in fact political.

Notwithstanding their obvious differences, law and politics were inextricably linked fields of action. The choice of 30 per cent reacquisition by the Montoro government as against Covas's 70 per cent reacquisition was not just a policy choice; it also represented a commentary upon the legal system's ability to withstand pressures that would inevitably arise. Constructing legislation only to see it immediately entombed by its own shortcomings, for example through widespread and interminable litigation, would have been a pointless exercise for two genuinely reformist governments. Certain presumptions about the operation of the legal system underlay the approaches adopted by the Montoro and Covas administrations. Boller's comment that 'it was better to obtain this land quickly at zero cost than to fight in the courts – where we might even fail'[54] said as much about judicial conservatism as it did about the law itself. Although never written into the legislation, this fear of failure was one of its invisible cornerstones of government action.

Returning to a question posed earlier: what made Covas think he could get away with 70 per cent, when Montoro had faced so many difficulties? It is doubtful, given the active presence of the MST, that Covas could have got away with anything less even if he had wanted to. Legislation constituted just one in a series of political signals the government was sending the movement at the time. To have offered a lower figure, while making claims to reform, would have been unworkable. In any case, the government had to address the substantive issue: the shortage of government land. By contrast, the situation facing the Montoro administration in the early 1980s was far less conducive to sustained radical action.

We will never know whether Pressburger's alternative would have worked, but it is clear that the socio-political demand pressuring Montoro from below was more limited at that stage and that partly as a result the leverage he was able to exercise in relation to conservative social interests was more limited. Far from being on the defensive there is a sense in which registered landowners were very much in the driving seat. By contrast, when Covas assumed office, registered landowners of the region were in the midst of a major political and economic crisis. The speculative value of land had already been declining and the presence of the MST merely exacerbated this situation. Although registered landowners might not admit it publicly, some of them wanted out. This gave Covas an historic opportunity to change the terms of engagement, an opportunity he grasped with both hands.

Ironically, Covas was able to seize the opportunities available to him partly because his government lay to the right of reforming parties like the Workers' Party (Partido dos Trabalhadores – PT). In contrast to the left, whose political capital lay with extra-parliamentary groups like the MST, Covas was better placed to neutralise opposition from *within* the class of registered landowners itself. Through a degree of trust and empathy he could mollify them. Nowhere is this more evident than in the production of legislation. According to Belisário, '[o]ur fear was of acting in such a way as to accentuate the conflict in that region until it reached unmanageable proportions.'[55] Simultaneously, there was a real risk that any legislation introduced, no matter how technically superior to previous attempts, would simply crumble under these colossal forces. An attempt was made to integrate them, to go with the grain instead of cutting across it. In practical terms that meant literally bringing registered landowners in on the Act. As Benedito Macielo, a senior lawyer responsible for drafting the legislation (Decree Law 42.041/97) explains:

> This executive decree wasn't enacted overnight. It was the fruit of a wide-ranging discussion with all social sectors, including landowners. They had access, they discussed, they made proposals. I spoke to one of them who made suggestions with regard to the decree. So you see it is not a decree born from the will of the executive, it is a decree born of our understanding. We tried to establish the parameters.[56]

There was, in other words, a determined effort to establish some degree of political consensus as the prelude to legislative action; to cover the government's own back before it moved forward. As noted earlier, therefore, registered landowners were being treated as legitimate interlocutors whose concerns were to be taken on board, rather than as mere *grileiros* to be given 66 days notice of eviction.

Significantly, though, Covas did not just concede ground to registered landowners, he also decided to cash in some of his political capital with them.

A truly remarkable list was drawn up for the purpose of targeting devolved properties for reacquisition by the state. Belisário rang the governor for what he describes as 'a very interesting conversation':

> I rang him with a list of the surnames [of registered landowners in the Pontal] and said 'look governor, I am going to read you some surnames', and the surnames were extremely illustrious. They belonged to figures of historical significance in São Paulo, like governors. Others formed a part of Brazilian diplomatic history, a family of ambassadors, there were other older families that had invested in the Pontal, and so on. And the governor said, 'look, criteria are criteria. If we can advance further we will advance'.[57]

Perhaps the most interesting aspect of this, apart from the connections they reveal between political power and land, was the fact that the list had actually been drawn up many years earlier. At that time a row had erupted between the then head of ITESP, Juvenal Boller, and Tânia Andrade, his successor some years later. She explains:

> He was reluctant to give this list to the Fleury government [March 1991 – January 1995] because he believed that it would lack the political conditions to propose legal actions. So this list really was kept locked in the drawer until the Covas government. It was only during the events of the Pontal that we put that list back on the table.[58]

Some years after these events Andrade herself acknowledged that Boller's assessment of the political obstacles to legal action had been right all along.[59]

At long last the list was on the table. Covas not only had the political muscle and capital to work through it, but the political will too. ITESP's proposed legal actions were underwritten with a new authority that went to the highest levels of government. As Belisário notes:

> We coordinated things, but we also acted as a government. It wasn't a plan of a single secretariat that the governor would cynically wait to see if it worked out, and then applaud, or, if it did not work out, sack people. From the beginning the governor took a stance; it was his political will. Thus it wasn't – and isn't – Belisário's plan. It wasn't Tânia's plan. It was a government plan.[60]

Marrying Political and Legal Imperatives

Land was urgently needed. On the basis of past evidence, however, Discriminatory Actions were unlikely to yield useful results fast enough, and Decree Law 42.041/97 (which was specifically designed to overcome some of these limitations by ceding the state's right of discrimination in exchange for quick settlement) would only be introduced two and a half years into Covas' mandate. That left a seemingly unbridgeable gap. There was, however, another category of land that could be targeted for a programme of reform, namely land that had already been judged by the courts to be devolved but, for one reason or another (whether by virtue of the political power of the occupants, or a combination of the impotence, corruption and inertia of the state), had remained illegally occupied. Already, the MST was aggressively targeting this land. To paraphrase the comment made by one militant, it had turned its cannon in that direction and was going in hard. Now it was the state's turn.

Matters came to a head on 4 November 1995 when, to a fanfare of publicity, Mário Covas announced a self-imposed target of settling 1,050 families by 31 December, and a further 1,050 families by June the following year. Although this figure fell well short of the MST's demands, it nevertheless became the litmus test of the government's intentions. The movement reserved the right to suspend negotiations and organise a new round of occupations if the government failed to deliver.

The figure of 1,050 had originally emerged at a meeting between ITESP and the governor. ITESP explained that it had only mapped 23,000 hectares for land reform projects, and that this therefore imposed a technical ceiling of 1,050 on the number of families that could adequately be settled at short notice. It also emphasised that any settlements were contingent upon the definitive acquisition of land through the courts by way of a legal suit known as an *ação reivindicatória*, literally meaning a Reclaiming Action. Yet again a familiar problem arose: the court process was simply too slow. Covas, however, was having none of this, as Belisário explains:

> It was extremely worrying. He gave a deadline and said that we had promised to settle 2,100 families as a first step [notwithstanding the fact that] there were factors that did not depend upon us, like obtaining financial resources for compensation and injunctions. But the governor, who understands quite a bit about social movements, said that the social movement could not survive without a deadline.[61]

Clearly Covas was alive to what the movement could deliver and its internal pressures. He was hoping for concessions from the MST, including a halt to new occupations, and knew that in the absence of immediate results, a credible promise was essential. Future negotiations with the movement depended upon it.

As with Discriminatory Actions, Reclaiming Actions could only be instigated before the courts by state prosecutors, while ITESP remained in the background supplying the relevant documentation. To all intents and purposes the Reclaiming Action was a kind of corrective to the failures associated with Discriminatory Actions. It attempted to go beyond the purely theoretical assertions of state dominion over land routinely associated with successful

Discriminatory Actions, and reassert physical control of devolved land. Legally and politically speaking this was the moment of reckoning between the state and registered landowners. Although its scale was limited, its symbolic significance was considerable.

To the extent that some form of change had been decided upon, it no longer mattered whether occupants were old and powerful families that had dodged longstanding judicial decrees, or were newer commercial entrants that had seeped into the area by buying up land under the state's nose. Armed with copies of judgments declaring the devolved nature of lands, along with technical descriptions of the properties gleaned from land registers, it was now the job of state lawyers – with the governor's backing – to demand the land back, with a view to making it over to land reform projects and meeting the 31 December deadline.

Speed was of the essence. Lawyers at ITESP therefore proposed that recent changes to the Civil Legal Code (Código de Processo Civil) should be used to secure interim control of a portion of the properties pending future negotiations. This was the so-called *tutela antecipada*, of which more in a moment. Unfortunately for ITESP, this thesis was not received favourably by the local state lawyer in Mirante (the district where most of the actions were to be lodged). According to Tânia Andrade, 'he didn't want to present these cases before the court'.[62] Rather than open revolt, however, his opposition was manifested in terms of excessive procedural zeal, an attention to irrelevant detail that embraced 'anything from the location of commas, to whether a document should be included, to requests for further documents, to whether documents had been duly authenticated, even to whether the paper was pink or not'. According to Andrade, 'he created obstacles and suggested that we would lose the legal actions'. As a consequence, by 15 December, and with the deadline fast approaching, no actions had been proposed. The problem was only resolved, and political and legal imperatives favourably realigned, when São Paulo's chief state lawyer, Márcio Sotano Filipe, authorised his deputy, José Roberto de Moraes, to take personal charge of the cases on his behalf. But that still left the question of how to secure interim control of land by means of the *tutela antecipada*. That would be for the judiciary to decide.

Tutela Antecipada

The case eventually came before Judge Catarina Ruybal da Silva Estimo in the judicial district of Mirante do Paranapanema. It was the largest such district in São Paulo state, but also the one with by far the greatest single concentration of devolved lands. The MST had subjected the region to the greatest number of land occupations. The stage was now set for the first test case of *tutela antecipada*, in whose wake dozens of other cases would surely follow.

Although prior to Judge Estimo's arrival in Mirante two *fazendas* had been the subject of successful attempts by the state to reacquire control, these attempts had taken a long time. Part of the reason for this was the vexed question of farming infrastructure. While the law forbade government compensation of registered landowners, because it excluded their acquisition of usucapion[63] rights on devolved land, Article 516 of the Civil Code nevertheless held that any investments subsequently added (e.g. machinery, farm buildings, etc.) needed to be compensated for. This introduced an element of litigation and therefore delays, as registered landowners tried to drive up the prices of their assets by appointing experts, while the state countered with its own experts and the court tried to make sense of the respective claims by appointing experts of its own. Hence *tutela antecipada*: an attempt to get around the problem through a kind of injunctive relief. As Judge Estimo explains: 'The institute of *tutela antecipada* was a law geared towards those situations in which the lags that form part of the functioning of the legal process itself, might risk compromising the rights of the [legal action's] instigator.'[64] The aim was simple: give the state, and by implication the MST, immediate access to the land pending a full and final settlement that would in any case see the land transferred back to the state because its devolved status had already been decided. Government lawyers made a formal request that 30 per cent of the land on several *fazendas* above 500 hectares should be made over to it in advance of any subsequent compensation.

It took two weeks rather than the usual 48 hours for Judge Estimo to reach a decision. Her decision was historic and the explanation for the delay revealing:

> I studied the petition over a relatively long period, because really the fear is of the social repercussions. You see judicial norms exist in order to regulate social life. Often a legal decision of ours ends up producing effects of both a legal and social character. Anyway, having conducted my analysis I granted *tutela antecipada* over a third of the *fazendas*.[65]

When Belisário had first mentioned legal action of this kind to the registered landowners' lawyers, arguing that its merit was that it 'neither attended to the totality of the social problem, nor affected all the property', they had fallen about laughing in disbelief. The general consensus was that although he was a highly accomplished human rights and defence lawyer, he knew little of land law.[66] It is remarkable that it did not matter that Judge Estimo's decision was subsequently – and successfully – appealed to a higher court in São Paulo. For in the meantime she had released the state from its procedural chains, time enough for it to act. In what Tânia Andrade likens to a military campaign, trucks were requisitioned, black plastic sheeting – so much a hallmark of MST encampments – was purchased, landless workers began to assemble, and at 7pm on 31 December 1995, with only five hours to spare, the last of 1,050 families was finally settled on their new land.

Not only had a new social and political dynamic been opened up by Judge Estimo's decision (which included the increasing desire on the part of registered landowners themselves to negotiate their way out of the situation), but a new legal dynamic was opened up, as the majority of first-level judges followed her example, and the state won the overwhelming majority (40 out of 45) of its court actions.[67] The subsequent reversal suffered in São Paulo's High Court, which many put down to its conservative stance on questions involving private property, was subsequently overturned in Brazil's highest court, the High Court of Justice (Superior Tribunal de Justiça – STJ). As part of this case the state not only advanced more traditional legal arguments relating to the sanctity of property, but also brought evidence of the social consequences of its actions following the granting of the *tutela antecipada*, namely the diminution of a major social conflict.

It must be emphasised, however, that whatever the historical import of this decision, the problems in the Pontal do Paranapanema were not resolved at the stroke of a judge's pen. Nor, indeed, should one expect there to have been such an outcome. The state may have unshackled itself from its immediate difficulties, but it could not remove itself from the forces of history. The supposed strength of Belisário's proposal, the notion that it 'neither attended to the totality of the social problem, nor affected all the property', also represented its major weakness, for it left fundamental antagonisms in tact and questions unanswered. It was a workable, even positive fudge, but it was a fudge nonetheless. Indeed it is that inability to confront those antagonisms which largely explains why successive administrations have failed to draw a line under the problem, something the administrations of Geraldo Alckmin and José Serra again attempted to do in 2003 and 2007 respectively.[68] Quite simply, too many powerful people have too much to lose and that is why, even today, the Pontal remains a region of mass occupations and social turmoil.

Conclusion

This chapter has sought to explain the conditions that brought about legal paralysis in the first place, how this situation was partially overcome, and what this says about the contingency of law upon wider social and political processes, including class antagonisms, the role of the state, and the contribution of social movements to change. In order to understand the significance of these contingencies a contextualised discussion has been necessary. To some extent the devil really does lie in the detail: theoretical as well as practical challenges really do have to be grasped in their historical setting, with all the complexities that necessarily entails. It is not necessary to repeat here the vicissitudes of land law, the nature of devolved land, the development of property relations in the Pontal, the layering of an industry of deception with the forces of the market, or the attempt to resolve these contradictions through the instrument of *tutela antecipada*, among others. The point is that despite such complexities, of which there are numerous variants throughout Brazil, some remarkably simple but formidable tendencies do nevertheless emerge. These may be grouped under the broad heading of power relations.

When seen from the perspective of power relations, the Pontal's complexities not only become much clearer, but valuable light is shed upon the extremely problematical nature of legal discourse and practise itself. Evidently, power relations underpin the processes of colonisation with which this chapter began, and their presence is marked in the laws that sought to draw a line under the affair in terms that would, to paraphrase José de Souza Martins, compel non-propertied peasants to work for large estates and thereby hasten the intensification of capitalist relations of production and ownership. However, although landed interests successfully crystallised law in their own interests, the state's writ suffered limitations. São Paulo's Pontal do Paranapanema was one region where its power was actively challenged. Rather than some set piece military confrontation, this took the form of attrition, as webs of corruption were combined with nascent dynamics of capital accumulation. Putative landowners and notaries first 'legalised' remote areas and proceeded to offload these upon buyers either unaware of, or simply unwilling, to abide by the *Lei de Terras*. New relations of power developed that extended back into the state capital. The list of 'illustrious' surnames was never taken from the drawer and presented to the 1991–95 government of Luiz Antônio Fleury.

We will never know for certain whether Juvenal Boller was correct in his diagnosis that there was no point in proposing legal actions against these powerful figures. And in a way it does not matter. The crucial point here is that as a senior legal figure he genuinely thought this to be the case. This is to say nothing of Belisário, the top human rights lawyer and Covas' secretary of state for justice who, before pursuing a legal strategy, first ran the list past the governor himself. Why? For precisely the same reasons as Boller: quite simply, this was political dynamite, and without the governor's full backing it had no chance of success. The law needed certain conditions in place if it was, in the words of José Serra, to 'stick'.[69]

This brings us to the contribution of the MST, because in many respects it was able to provide just those preconditions. The MST's tactic of challenging landowner invasions with occupations by landless workers did more than simply inject a new dimension into the debate; it also shifted the correlation of forces, thereby altering the social, political and, yes, legal dynamic, in a more favourable direction for the movement. There was nothing new in the issues raised by the MST. They had been discussed by lawyers, judges, academics and politicians alike over decades. The point is that the movement raised the issues in a way that really began to matter, and to make the law relevant.

The thesis that underlines this chapter is that that while law (in the shape of Judge Estimo's and the High Court of Justice's decisions) undoubtedly contributed towards the resolution of these – and some of its own – contradictions, political and social factors weighed heavily if not decisively. No matter how inventive the legal imagination of government lawyers, or receptive judges were to new ideas, the fact is that the actions of both groups were socially contingent. Law was the lubricant of change rather than its engine; it was epiphenomenal. At the same time, however, the significance of law in the pursuit of the movement's objectives should not be underestimated. Embracing legal discourse was also a means of unmasking certain realities. With it, the MST could say that pretensions to private property were without foundation, that the emperor had no clothes. But law offered a great deal more besides. Doubtless, a politically minded lawyer like Juvenal Boller will have known this when, in the course of informal conversations with the MST, he first pointed out that the courts had decided that 66,000 hectares in Mirante do Paranapanema were devolved land.[70] After this, to paraphrase Valdemir Rodrigues Chaves, one of the movement's leading militants, the MST turned its cannon in that direction and went in hard.

The devolved nature of land in the Pontal do Paranapanema is a distinctive feature of this land conflict. But a feature it shares in common with the rest of the country is the extent to which law was incapable of effecting change. That it took a social movement with a well founded and deep scepticism of law's intent to provide legal practitioners with their historic opportunity to overcome some of law's own contradictions is deeply ironic but not without precedent.

Politically and ideologically, the impact of the MST was tremendous. It is essential, however, not to get carried away with the movement's contribution and extrapolate its potential – or, indeed, that of social movements in general. On the basis of evidence available, it is clear that the MST made a fundamental contribution to kick-starting a process of land reform in the Pontal, materially affecting political horizons and the progress of legal developments. But throughout the movement's power remained contingent upon the interplay of other factors. Indeed, in some profound structural senses, i.e., those that go beyond these contingent relations and relate to underlying imbalances between landless and landowner groups, its power remained extremely limited. The fact that the MST was able to overcome some of these disparities in the Pontal – putting registered landowners and the state on the defensive, and achieving some significant victories in the process – makes its achievement even more remarkable. As the following chapter will show, though, all this came at a considerable price and real issues remain about both the replicability and sustainability of such interventions. That the Pontal do Paranapanema remains in ferment, even to this day, should make one attentive to these limitations and to the conditionalities of success.

Notes

1 Author interview with Belisário Santos Júnior, 6 December 1999.

2 Ibid. According to Belisário, these comments were made by José Gomes da Silva, a former head of INCRA.

3 Inventário Florestal de São Paulo, cited in Instituto de Terras do Estado de São Paulo, *Cadernos ITESP 2: Pontal Verde: plano de recuperação ambiental nos assentamentos do Pontal do Paranapanema*, 2nd edition, São Paulo: ITESP, February 1999, p. 8.

4 On the early settlement of the region, see José Ferrari Leite, *A ocupação do Pontal do Paranapanema*, São Paulo: Editora Hucitec, 1998.

5 Cited in Carlos Azevedo, 'Pontal: do grande grilo aos sem terra', *Caros Amigos*, no. 2, May 1997, p. 31.

6 Colonel Alfredo Marcondes Cabral cited in Azevedo, 'Pontal: do grande grilo aos sem terra', p. 32.

7 Devolved land is not an easy concept to grasp. Article 3 of the *Lei de Terras* offers a definition telling us what they are *not* rather than what they are:

1. Lands that are not being used by any federal, state or municipal public service...

2. Those lands that, at the time of the law, were private property, that is, corresponded to a legitimate title. (Attention: already at the time of the law the owner had to have a legitimate title.);

3. The *sesmarias*, legitimately conceded by previous governments, and whose owners provided their dimensions [*providenciaram mediação*] registered them and were cultivating the land. Or, in other words, took these three actions within the period and in the form in which the law and its regulations prescribed;

4. The same thing applied to occupations [*posses*] (between 1822 and 1850 occupation was a legal and legitimate means of acquiring land. Article 5 of Law No. 601 notes that peaceful and *mansas posses* are legitimated if acquired by *primaria* occupation).

Source: Miguel Pressburger, 'Terras devolutas. O que fazer com elas?', *Coleção 'Socializando Conhecimentos'*, No. 7, Rio de Janeiro: Instituto Apoio Jurídico Popular & Federação de Órgãos para Assistência Social e Educacional, July 1990, p. 78.

8 José de Souza Martins, *Os camponeses e a política no Brasil*, Petrópolis: Vozes, 1995, p. 42.

9 Miguel Pressburger, 'Terras devolutas. O que fazer com elas?', *Coleção 'Socializando Conhecimentos'*, No. 7, Rio de Janeiro: Instituto Apoio Jurídico Popular & Federação de Órgãos para Assistência Social e Educacional, July 1990, p. 12.

10 The Reserva Florestal do Morro do Diabo was created by Decree 12.279 in October 1941; the Reserva da Lagoa São Paulo was instituted by Decree 13.049 in November 1942; the Grande Reserva do Pontal was created by Decree 13.075 in November 1942.

11 Cited in José Gomes da Silva, *A reforma agrária brasileira na Virada do Milênio*, Campinas: ABRA, 1996, p. 135.

12 Instituto de Terras do Estado de São Paulo, *Cadernos ITESP 4: Terra e cidadãos: aspectos da ação de regularização fundiária no estado de São Paulo*, São Paulo: ITESP, November 1998, p. 99.

13 Author interview with João Pedro Stédile, 18 March 2000.

14 Bernardo Mançano Fernandes, *MST: Formação e territorialização*, São Paulo: Editorial Hucitec, 1996, p. 94, n. 4.

15 Ibid., p. 95.
16 Author interview with José Rainha, 20 March 2000.
17 Author interview with Zelitro Luz da Silva, 20 March 2000.
18 Ibid.
19 Ibid.
20 Founded in December 1963 the core of CONTAG was and remains unionised rural workers (part time and full time), but also includes family farmers and even beneficiaries of land reform settlements. In this latter area, then, there is an element of overlap with the MST. Currently CONTAG represents some 20 million workers grouped among 27 federations and 4,000 rural unions.
21 Leonilde Sérvolo de Medeiros, *História dos Movimentos Sociais no Campo*, Rio de Janeiro: FASE, 1989, p. 92, my emphasis.
22 Ibid.
23 Ibid., pp. 92–4.
24 Rudá Ricci, 'A Contag no governo de transição: um ator à procura de um texto', *Caderno CEDEC No. 15*, São Paulo: CEDEC, 1990, p. 10, cited in Bernardo Mançano Fernandes, *MST: Formação e territorialização*, São Paulo: Editoral Hucitec, 1996, p. 98.
25 Leonilde Sérvolo de Medeiros, *História dos Movimentos Sociais no Campo*, Rio de Janeiro: FASE, 1989, p. 92.
26 Author interview with José Rainha, 20 March 2000.
27 Leonilde Sérvolo de Medeiros, *História dos Movimentos Sociais no Campo*, Rio de Janeiro: FASE, 1989, p. 92.
28 Author interview with José Rainha, 20 March 2000.
29 See for instance Juvenal Boller de Souza Filho, 'Instrumentos jurídicos de uso e alienação de terras públicas', in Raymundo Larangeira, ed., *Direito agrário brasileiro*, São Paulo: Editora LTR, 1999, pp. 35–64. He notes (pp. 35–6) that while Fernando Sodero, a leading commentator, suggests, 'agrarian reform is conducted on private land', public land is in fact one of the key vectors of agrarian reform, that the social function of property includes public as well as private land, with the duties for reform that entails and that every time a property is expropriated by the state it first assumes a public form being passed onto the final beneficiaries. In short, categories like devolved land cannot and should not be excluded from any reform programme.
30 Author interview with José Rainha, 20 March 2000.
31 Author interview with Valdemir Rodrigues Chaves, 1 September 1999.
32 Author interview with Juvenal Boller, 19 April 2000.
33 Article 9. A full text of the law is reproduced in Instituto de Terras do Estado de São Paulo, *Cadernos ITESP 6: Mediação campo: estratégias ação em stuações de conflito fundiário,* São Paulo: ITESP, December 1998, pp. 87–9.
34 Author interview with Juvenal Boller, 19 April 2000.
35 Boller became INCRA's chief lawyer in the mid-1980s, the period of the ill-fated National Plan of Agrarian Reform (Plano Nacional de Reforma Agraria); in the 1990s he became head of the State of São Paulo Land Institute, ITESP.
36 Author interview with Juvenal Boller, 19 April 2000.
37 Author collective interview with six lawyers from the Pontal, 8 September 1999.
38 Instituto de Terras do Estado de São Paulo, *Cadernos ITESP 4: Terra e cidadãos: aspectos da ação de regularização Fundiária no Estado de São Paulo*, São Paulo: ITESP, November 1998, p. 18.

39 Author interview with Miguel Pressburger, 31 March 2000. Leonel Brizola was governor of Rio Grande do Sul once and Rio de Janeiro state twice: 1959–63, 1983–87 and 1991–94 respectively. Pressburger is referring to his first terms as Rio's governor.

40 Author interview with Belisário Santos Júnior, 6 December 1999.

41 Author interview with Bernardo Fernando Mançano, 7 September 1999. For some years before he became one of its fiercest critics, Zander Navarro was closely involved with the MST's research section, the area with which Bernardo Mançano Fernandes subsequently came to be closely associated.

42 Bernardo Mançano Fernandes, MST: Formação e territorialização, São Paulo: Editoral Hucitec, 1996, p. 190.

43 Mimeo, Grupo Especial de Trabalho sobre Assuntos Fundiário do Oeste Paulista, Relatório de Atividades e Conclusões, Ministério Público Procuradoria Geral de Justiça, São Paulo, 20 February 1997, p. 9.

44 For a full discussion of this issue see subsection of the present chapter entitled 'Tutela Antecipada'.

45 Author interview with Tânia Andrade, 3 December 1999.

46 This body drew up Brazil's constitution in 1988. The National Constituent Assembly (Assembléia Nacional Constituinte) was controversial. Many had favoured the election of a separate assembly, less tainted by party allegiances, instead of what actually happened, the election of a National Congress in 1986 with overlapping constitution-making powers. For a detailed account of its deliberations in the area of land reform see José Gomes da Silva, Buraco Negro: a reforma agrária na Constituinte de 1987/88, São Paulo: Editora Paz e Terra, 1989.

47 Author interview with Tânia Andrade, 3 December 1999.

48 Ibid.

49 The favourable nature of these relations is exemplified by Belisário's comment that 'From the beginning [of our government], in each and every meeting with the social movement … strengthening the Institute was amongst the list of demands.' Author interview with Belisário Santos Júnior, 6 December 1999.

50 'Líder dos sem-terra faz desafio ao governo', Jornal do Brasil, 9 October 1995.

51 Author interview with Belisário Santos Júnior, 6 December 1999.

52 Ibid.

53 Ibid.

54 Author interview with Juvenal Boller, 19 April 2000.

55 Author interview with Belisário Santos Júnior, 6 December 1999.

56 Author interview with Benedito Macielo, 3 December 1999.

57 Author interview with Belisário Santos Júnior, 6 December 1999.

58 Author interview with Tânia Andrade, 3 December 1999.

59 Ibid.

60 Author interview with Belisário Santos Júnior, 6 December 1999.

61 Ibid.

62 Author interview with Tânia Andrade, 3 December 1999.

63 Usucapion essentially refers to the acquisition of the title or right to property by its uninterrupted possession for a certain term prescribed by law.

64 Author interview with Judge Catarina Ruybal da Silva Estimo, 17 March 2000.

65 Ibid.

66 Author interview with Belisário Santos Júnior, 6 December 1999.
67 In fact the procedures were a little more complex than this account suggests. It was not simply a question of the judge emerging from her chamber and the state either winning or losing. The concession of *tutela antecipada* was made by means of conciliatory audiences with the judge. This had been a quite deliberate choice on her part. Like the Covas government, Judge Estimo had no desire to inflict a defeat on the registered landowners.
68 Governors Serra, Alckmin and Covas all came from the same political party, the PSDB. In June 2007 Serra put forward legislation proposing the legalisation of disputed lands above holdings of 500 hectares. Both registered landowners and the MST opposed it. Speaking of Alckmin's attempt in 2003 to enact law 11,600, Serra said: 'The previous law was good, but it never stuck. In practise it did not work. We learnt from this.' (Cristiano Machado, 'Serra apresenta projeto para pôr fim a conflito fundiário no Pontal', *Folhaonline*, 16 June 2007.)
69 Ibid.
70 Author interview with Valdemir Rodrigues Chaves, 1 September 1999.

Chapter 2

To Criminalise or Not to Criminalise?

Conflicting Legal Responses to Social Movement Pressure

Is there a right to resistance? Don't we have in the Brazilian Constitution, as in other foreign statues, explicitly, the right to resistance? Do subjects have the right to rebel against a sovereign who is not acting on behalf of the people?
Judge Adhemar Maciel, Brazilian High Court of Justice[1]

The problem is not, essentially, legal in nature, even though, of course, it involves a gamut of legislation. It is a question of politics, in the widest sense of the term, and it is as such that it must be understood.
Clovis Rossi, journalist, *Folha de São Paulo*[2]

This chapter shifts the emphasis away from civil aspects of land conflict in the Pontal do Paranapanema, towards criminal aspects. The role of the state government and the State of São Paulo Land Institute (Instituto de Terras do Estado de São Paulo –ITESP) recede from the discussion while those played by the judiciary and the Public Ministry (prosecutors) become more central. The reality, though, is that the interaction between the civil and criminal spheres underpins developments. Progress on the civil front discussed in the previous chapter (such as the breaking of the log jam surrounding devolved land, and the dramatic, even if patchy, acceleration of land reform initiatives) would have been inconceivable without the pressure of conflicts that became the subject of criminal proceedings, the subject of this chapter. Ultimately it was the pressure of these conflicts that gave newfound urgency to ITESP's, the government's and Judge Estimo's search for creative legal solutions in the civil sphere, as well food for thought for Brazil's High Court of Justice (Supremo Tribunal de Justiça – STJ) in the criminal sphere.

The MST's strategy of intensified land occupation would come at a high price. Not only did the courts sanction the repeated eviction of landless workers from properties – on as many as 23 separate occasions in one case – but the stakes were raised to breaking point when the São Paulo state Public Ministry weighed in by seeking the arrest, imprisonment and trial of leading MST militants under charges of criminal conspiracy. In effect, the movement was put on trial.

While this created dilemmas for the movement (especially regarding the sustainability of direct action), it also led to some positive outcomes, notably a groundbreaking decision by the STJ, whose impact rippled outwards (albeit unevenly) towards other sectors of the Brazilian judiciary. Inside the MST itself it helped to consolidate the existing tendency towards the professionalisation of its in-house legal advice and further development and reliance upon outside legal support networks.

The MST was not the only organisation put on trial by the actions of the Public Ministry. Ironically, so too was the Public Ministry itself, a fact that the media did not readily pick up on at the time. Instead journalists concentrated on the more sensationalist aspects of the Public Ministry's actions, including the acquiescence of one prosecutor to proposals to bypass the legal process entirely by exchanging militants in custody for militants on the run. While this chapter discusses these events, it does so in the broader context of an assessment of the causes behind and adequacy of the Public Ministry's responses to land conflicts in the Pontal.

The issue is important because São Paulo's Public Ministry is widely regarded as the intellectual powerhouse behind the whole movement for the creation of an effective legal organ that with the return to democracy would at long last bridge the gap between constitutional rhetoric and social justice – especially in the sphere of so-called collective rights. Allied to the fact that prosecutors here possessed the best material resources anywhere in Brazil, this raised a tantalising scenario: could they deal with a problem as basic as land reform in a meaningful fashion, i.e., by addressing some of its constitutive elements, or did this sort of issue lie beyond their methodological, intellectual and institutional horizons? As this chapter will show, the question would arise in an even more pointed fashion for the judiciary, which was asked to rule directly upon it.

Part I: The Dynamics of Land Occupations in the Pontal do Paranapanema

By 1995 the MST had organised thousands of landless workers into a wave of opposition against landed interests. That wave finally engulfed dozens of *fazendas*, irrevocably converting them from bastions of landed power into islands of reform. Most of the region, however, would remain dominated by privately controlled devolved land and unresolved contradictions. That said, the changes were significant and ever since have rightly been the subject of extensive discussion.

For those actually involved in land occupations of the 1990s, risk and uncertainty was the dominant concern, not the judgment of posterity. From their perspective the commencement of a socially transformative project was a daunting task. Even the Catholic Church, from which the MST had drawn so much ideological and practical sustenance over the years, expressed major reservations. As Neuri Rosetto, one of the MST's leading national figures, recalls:

> At the beginning the Church said that we would lead the people to violence; 'You will be responsible', they said. When we proposed occupations it was not easy to break the resistance from groups of ours, be they of the left or the Church. They said that 'You are taking these people on a crazy adventure.' Even today they say this: 'Isn't going for an occupation leading to the risk of violence, exposing families, women and children?'[3]

The Pontal do Paranapanema's first major occupation, at the Fazenda Nova do Pontal on 13 July 1990, exemplified the challenge. Roughly 700 families (3,500 men, women and children) were involved. They were initially met with a hail of bullets, but somehow they maintained a presence for a time. Against the wishes of the local bishop, one priest would regularly travel from Mirante do Paranapanema (see Chapter 1, Figure 3) to celebrate mass, baptize children and bring basic foodstuffs. He was subsequently transferred from the region because of his actions. The principal obstacle, however, was the state, headed by governor Orestes Quércia (1987–91). According to Alcides Gomes dos Santos, a veteran of the occupation who had gone in accompanied by his wife and three children, 'Quércia sent a very large battalion of troops – you know, dogs, horses, infantry and the riot squad. This was like a preparation for war.'[4] In the light of this aggressive stance many families felt overexposed:

> So we decided to leave the area because we could see that there was no other way. ... So we retreated, we left. During the night of our exit ... the repression was very strong. It was a very rapid situation, and the families were not prepared. We lost around 400 families that night. Three hundred remained.[5]

Given the ferociousness of the onslaught, it is at first sight surprising that 300 families chose to maintain the struggle by transferring to another site. However, when seen in the context of the daily exploitation, unemployment, underemployment, malnutrition and high rates of infant mortality – in other words the chronic rather than convulsive forms of violence to which these families were daily subjected – their choice and tenacity can more readily be understood. For many, including Gomes dos Santos, the MST's alternative – to take a stand and fight and seek a modicum of autonomy and dignity through the cultivation of land proved a more attractive proposition. Indeed, it would eventually provide his children with the kind of education he had been denied. At the time Gomes dos Santos did not have to persuade his partner, Esmeralda, to follow suit – 'she was a braver fighter than I.'[6] Like so many women in the movement, she was prepared to accept the risks and sacrifices associated with raising young children at the side of a road or in a field because the dangers were outweighed by the chronic risks and poor prospects that came with the status quo.

That night, however, 400 families came to a different conclusion and left. They may have found employment in the labour market as casual or contract labourers, or migrated to the cities in search of work, or moved to more distant regions of the country, or even re-established links with the MST and gravitated towards subsequent MST occupations. We simply do not know. The key point is that on the night in question the MST failed to provide a credible political and organisational alternative around which the 400 could mobilise. To be sure, the operation had never been simply an end in itself but was an integral part of a wider process of building an effective opposition. Nevertheless, while losses might be an accepted part of struggle, attrition rates like these were unsustainable and as such represented a defeat both for the individuals involved and the movement as a whole.

A new method: cat and mouse tactics

When José Rainha came down from the northeast of the country in 1991 to take charge of the situation, he took an extremely critical view of the MST's actions and relayed this back to the national executive:

> The workers were planning an occupation of Fazenda São Bento and I went in to join them. [But] the method was wrong for the reality. They had a method of resistance towards the police and had already suffered the eviction of 700 families which had been reduced to 100. I asked myself what could be done. Then the police surrounded the occupation and I appeared. I saw that it was a situation in which a massacre could occur and I was less than happy with the method that was leading to confrontation. I took the microphone at the meeting and held a robust discussion. I suggested another method: to withdraw the families, negotiate with the police, and encamp by the roadside and analyse the situation. ... As the police were surrounding the encampment I could not say much to the people, but when the police left I said we will recamp and then we'll see what we can do. The people accepted and in this way the police were neutralised, not knowing what to do. I asked the commander to withdraw his troops if he didn't want to soil his hands with the blood of famished and defenceless people, which for him would be the worst thing that could possibly happen. 'No, we are not here for this', he said, 'since you have abided by the order.' And he withdrew the troops. From that day people began to seek me out.[7]

Thus, instead of engaging in unwinnable – and potentially disastrous – confrontations with the state, the movement opted for cat and mouse tactics. As one activist explains:

You see it was a process, it was a method, of winning through the exhaustion [of one's opponents] without causing attrition, because that spread fear amongst the families and weakened the MST. With these tactics of non-confrontation the movement became a mass movement.[8]

The occupation of Fazenda São Bento is a prime example of this. INCRA had classified 3,000 acres subject to expropriation back in 1986. Over a period of just over three years before it was finally taken over in 1994 by the government and made over to land settlements the *fazenda* became the subject of 23 separate occupations and 22 evictions.[9] Only a mass movement, especially one with a strong political, tactical and organisational consciousness, as well as self-discipline, could maintain such a sustained and intensive pattern of struggle.

Multiplier effects

The previous chapter has already shown how the devolved status of the Pontal do Paranapanema's lands could offer legal leverage among the courts, state and land reform administrators, as well as political and ideological leverage (legitimacy) among politicians, intellectuals, journalists and the wider public. The question was how these legal advantages would be crystallised in practise.

Experience elsewhere had taught the movement that one way of transforming the terms of the political debate on an intractable problem was through well-coordinated mass actions, which had a disproportionately powerful impact. This had been apparent during the earliest days of the MST in Rio Grande do Sul when, in October 1985, 6,500 workers from 50 municipalities occupied the Fazenda Anoni and two years later when five agricultural research centres hundreds of kilometers apart were simultaneously occupied. Bold acts like these had succeeded in capturing the public imagination and in raising the movement's political profile.

Valuable political leverage was also gained by inserting these mass struggles within a national perspective. As Gilmar Mauro, a member of the MST's national executive explains in relation to another movement:

> The struggle for housing is a huge social problem in Brazil, and they carry out more radical struggles than us: radical occupations, conflicts with the police, etc. It is even more mass based than us. At the same time, however, it is so compartmentalised, so regionalised, so municipalised. So you end up with the problem of municipalisation or regionalisation that is unable to acquire national unity. So although it is a great social problem, it is unable to transform itself into a political problem.[10]

While the MST's struggle in the Pontal was partly that of a movement attempting to overcome internal fragilities besetting any radical social organisation, it

did so free from the externally imposed legislative constraints that had bedevilled trade union organisation throughout Brazil. These laws, first introduced
by the Vargas regime in 1931 and consolidated in 1941 through a series of
laws governing all aspects of union formation, were inspired by Mussolini's
fascist legislation of the 1930s. The legislation was deliberately structured to
prevent horizonal alliances of labour, with municipal units acting as both the
building blocks but also maximum horizons of trade union action.
Representative structures were imposed from above rather than developed
from below as organic manifestations of popular will. Crucially, solidarity
actions that transcended these arbitrarily and artificially imposed limits were
a priori ruled out of order.

In this regard the MST enjoyed a distinct advantage, namely the possibility of regional and national struggles, which it was keen to exploit from the
outset. Disparate local struggles were plucked from relative obscurity and
imbued with wider social and political significance. As Bernardo Mançano
Fernandes notes:

> The Landless Workers Movement never takes a problem and discusses it
> in itself. It establishes the problem on a national scale. So that a group of
> families which is fighting in Caconé in Mato Grosso state, or in Ogiminá
> in Amazonas, or Cabodró in Pernambuco, are all integrated in a national
> network. At the same time they are fighting in their localities, there is
> someone who they don't know who is struggling on their behalf in
> Brasília, with INCRA. Local movements, on the other hand, spend years
> to get out of the municipality and get as far as the head of INCRA in the
> state capital.[11]

Paradoxically, another multiplier effect the MST would exploit in the Pontal
arose from the spatial concentration of conservative political power itself. The
MST judged the municipality of Mirante do Paranapanema to be the Achilles'
heel of the region's registered landowners. To be sure, this was partly because
the legal cards were stacked in its favour with the 1958 court decision declaring the lands in Mirante do Paranapanema to be devolved. But this did not
mean the movement went for the line of least resistance. On the contrary, it
also chose one of the most difficult problems to crack, the Fazenda São Bento.
This decision would demand all the movement's energies and tenacity.

São Bento was the largest property in the region (5,240 hectares) and could
therefore accommodate more families. It also had more water than available
alternatives. Above all else though, it was politically significant. The *fazenda*
belonged to Sandoval Neto, a former mayor of Presidente Prudente, the centre
of regional power. He retained close ties with one of the most reactionary and
violent of landowner organisations, the Rural Democratic Union (União
Democrática Ruralista – UDR[12]). The MST picked this fight: 'Fazenda São
Bento was considered the principal pillar of the landowners. So we decided to

fight it out there because to the extent that we could get the Fazenda São Bento, the others would follow suit in a domino effect.'[13] Thus, the stage was set for a long and drawn-out struggle.

Hindsight tells us that the movement's domino theory was correct. At the time, however, it was faced with the obvious difficulty that these dominos were hard to push and took years to fall. In the face of this uncertainty conditions had to be created that could sustain a momentum. This occasionally took the form of peaks of activity. For example, on 1 April 1995 landless workers occupied not one but three *fazendas* in Mirante do Paranapanema: Haroldina, Arco-Iris and Rancho 4. This collective act was designed to draw attention to the peculiarities and injustices of land tenure in the Pontal do Paranapanema. The arresting sight of fences being torn down, chains being cut, mass camps springing up overnight and land being cultivated by previously landless families received increasing media coverage. The MST also proved skillful in putting forward its case. Within a week of these occupations, the Mirante do Paranapanema Association of Rural Property Owners (Associação dos Proprietários de Mirante do Paranapanema) acknowledged that land in the municipality was devolved, but that registered landowners wanted compensation for infrastructure. Events, however, were not as neat as this chronology would suggest. Despite the cogency of its arguments and the extensive media interest, the movement was forced on 18 April to leave the Fazenda Arco Iris. The health and vitality of the organisation lay not with metropolitan perceptions or the relatively favourable coverage accorded it by the media,[14] but in its own grassroots. This was the motor of change. It was essential to maintain pressure in the locality. So, on 26 August 1995, yet another cycle of struggle began as 3,000 landless workers occupied three more *fazendas* in Mirante: Santa Cruz, Washington Luiz and Flor Roxa. On the same day, even the Arco Iris was retaken. This pattern of intensive exchanges and overlapping cycles would continue for several years until, one by one, *fazendas* were taken over by the state and permanent land reform settlements were established.

Part 2: Legal Responses to Occupations

Battle – for that is how it felt to all sides concerned – commenced on 8 March 1991. Fazenda São Bento's owner was reputed to be well armed, with between 15 and 20 hired gunmen. The movement's strength, on the other hand, lay in numbers. Rather than a suicidal set piece confrontation, the battle was transformed into one of nerves and stamina. When, at 3 a.m. on the first day, the MST broke the chains sealing the gates of the *fazenda* and entered with 180 families it was greeted with gunfire. The 20 trucks that had been used to transport the families to the site faced towards the *fazenda*'s headquarters with their headlights blazing 'to intimidate [the gunmen] and show them that we were present in great numbers'.[15] The gunmen stopped firing and the movement began to unload the trucks and construct its makeshift encampment. Over the next few months, the registered landowners would repeatedly seek eviction orders from the courts. So began the familiar game of cat and mouse between the MST, putative owners and state authorities.

As noted in the previous chapter, the 1958 court ruling regarding the status of devolved lands in Mirante do Paranapanema remained a moot point until the 1995 decision on *tutela antecipada*. This finally offered an interim mechanism for accelerated land acquisition. The net began to tighten around registered landowners. In response they argued that the parallel problem of occupations – 'invasions' to use their preferred terminology – was an altogether separate issue. They sensed the MST's vulnerability and sought to make it criminally accountable using the courts and full force of the law.

This section explores how prosecutors, police, judges and other legal officials responded to the problem of occupations, beginning with the actions of Paulo Sérgio Ribeiro da Silva, the prosecutor from the São Paulo state Public Ministry who sought the imprisonment of MST militants in October 1995. He is significant because although his conduct came to be seen as inept by some, he is not a mere straw man. He offers a robust and articulate defence of his actions that is consistent with the mindset of substantial sections of the legal establishment. Speaking some years after the events, da Silva argued: 'I would still maintain what I did in exactly the same way. I still believe that my attitude was correct, and is correct. I do not speak of regret or of reconsidering anything because I believe that my action was correct. I'll go further: the facts demonstrate that it was!'[16]

Da Silva entered the legal profession in 1992 as a young man in his early twenties. Like the majority of prosecutors (and judges) in outlying districts, his training was largely on-the-job. In October 1993, he began work in the judicial district of Pirapozinho, quite a large area, stretching some 110 kilometers from the town of Pirapozinho in the north, to Caravari, Narandiba, Estrela do Norte, Sandovalina and Tororó do Paranapanema in the south, on the border with Paraná state. As da Silva explains:

> When I went to Pirapozinho we still didn't have the problem of the Landless Workers in the area. The problem of the Landless Workers was centred more in Mirante do Paranapanema and a little bit in Teodoro Sampaio. The problems begin two years later in October 1995. Until then there was nothing.[17]

Things changed in October 1995 when the MST carried out 'a monstrous invasion':

> I decided, we [the judge and I] decided in truth, that we were going to act. The MST were invading the Mirante do Paranapanema, they were invading properties constantly, burning crops, killing cattle, burning

tractors and even using language from a western. 'They are not going to do this in our backyard. We are not going to let this happen in Sandovalina and the Pirapozinho area. We will not let this happen.' So as soon as they invaded, the local police inspector set up an inquiry, forwarded it to us, and then I formulated charges based upon this inquiry.[18]

Da Silva's approach is striking in several respects. Firstly, from an historical perspective it contrasts with the hitherto leisurely pace of legal activity on devolved land in the Pontal. Now prosecutor, judge and police readied themselves to repel 'invasions' as quickly and forcefully as possible. Secondly, theirs was a systemic reading of the issues at hand, not a piecemeal case-by-case response. This was joined-up, proactive justice, based on a highly selective reading of events as a mere criminal conspiracy.

Da Silva's use of the term 'invasion' is interesting. Juridically and ideologically-speaking this is a loaded term. For the most part, those opposed to the MST use the term to describe the movement's entry into land, while those who support the movement's actions tend to use the term 'occupation'. The reasons are complex. They partly reflect an ideological divide, since invasion of private property has connotations of illegality and illegitimacy. However, they also represent a genuine jurisprudential divide. The term 'invasion' gives priority to the notion that an act of force is used to take something from someone else, while the term 'occupation' stresses other aspects like the existence of property's social functions. The exclusion of the social in this context is seen by many as a kind of methodological and ideological sleight of hand. In talking of 'invasions', therefore, da Silva situates himself at a particular end of the jurisprudential and ideological spectrum.

A related point concerns da Silva's wider vision of occupations as being little more than acts of organised vandalism. Although it would be foolish to deny that some of the incidents he cites did occur, the reduction of the MST, with all its social magnitude to peripheral acts is telling. When thousands of men, women and children occupy a given area, a striking physical transformation of the landscape inevitably follows. Fences are cut and locks broken, undergrowth – sometimes even fields – are burnt and ploughed under for replanting, and it is not unusual for cattle to go missing. Wells and latrines are dug, and wooden posts for huts are driven into the ground as a totally new human infrastructure emerges. By the same token, the movement also provides a framework within which many other basic legally enshrined rights, such as housing, education and health, are addressed for the first time. The question that ultimately presents itself is whether, on balance, this is seen as a destructive, predatory and criminal act, or as an essentially creative social, political and legal act.

Da Silva is clear as to where the balance lies:

When a movement invades a property, generally it destroys the fence. A fence costs a lot. Walls and barbed wire cost a lot. The labour involved takes money. Many end up destroying the grazing land. For example, they set fire to it and then plough it to plant a little piece of corn in order to show that it has been planted – in the knowledge that it will not stay there. That is quite apart from the slaughter of animals that exists, that is a more obscure side. In Mirante do Paranapanema there was a lot of this and a little bit in Sandovalina. I prosecuted some members who did this. The property devalues immensely to the point of almost being worthless. After all, who is going to buy a property in a place like that? Nobody![19]

This stout defence of landed property economics is transformed into an absolutist juridical defence.

Our legislators – the law – protect property. So any act against anyone's property is considered a crime … the law also protects rural property. It protects the dominion that people exercise over that area. The law does not question the legitimacy of that possession. That is important, because the MST makes great play of this – 'No, but it's illegitimate; the title was forged!' This depends upon proof, it depends upon a process of judicial recognition. Until this occurs, the law protects that property, it protects that tenure.[20]

Thus the gamut of structural problems underlying the 'great drama' of which Belisário dos Santos Júnior spoke in the previous chapter – including the historical and procedural limitations of the law itself, never mind its immersion in regional power politics – are excluded from consideration. There is no real drama. As far as da Silva was concerned: 'we would never prevent anyone who wanted land from working it, in fact, it is a working right; but what I can't accept is that this is attempted by conflicting with the law. The problem will not be resolved in this way.'[21]

Da Silva's vision is significant because it reflects thinking within much of the legal and political establishment that is more at home with the categorical certainties of an idealised form of the rule of law than the difficulties and realities associated with its numerous contingencies and inequalities. It also underlines a prevalent problem: how legal rectitude often gives way to highly questionable legal practises. These practises are now examined.

The case for the prosecution and its politics

Da Silva describes the steps leading to the Public Ministry's instigation of a criminal prosecution thus:

The formation or constitution of a group to promote these invasions was notorious. We saw newspaper reports. Now according to our legal codes the formation of a group for the purposes of committing crimes is another crime (legal action in this respect does not depend upon the victim[22]). It is the famous crime of forming a gang. The law is called the formation of a gang or band. So I prosecuted them, I denounced them for committing this crime, for forming a gang. ... In fact, it was not just invasions here, crimes also occurred in Mirante do Paranapanema. There they frequently disobeyed the judicial order. They would invade a *fazenda*, the owner would instigate legal action to evict them, the judge would grant the eviction order, and they would leave. Several days later, they would come back. Strictly speaking, this constituted another crime: disobedience of a judicial order.[23]

On 9 October 1995 a police officer in Sandovalina made a formal request for the arrest of José Rainha and 12 other members of the MST. His request was eagerly taken up by da Silva and presented to the court. For his part Judge Darci Lopes Beraldo, of Pirapozinho, acceded to the prosecutor's request — albeit in just four cases. Thus, on 27 October, he issued arrest warrants for the preventive imprisonment of José Rainha, Diolinda Alves de Souza, Márcio Barreto, and Laércio Barbosa on the grounds that they had broken article 288 of the penal code, relating to the formation of criminal gangs. On 30 October de Souza and Barretto were arrested and transferred to São Paulo's notorious Carandiru prison,[24] while Rainha and Barbosa escaped arrest and went into hiding.

There can be no doubt that da Silva's actions forced the MST onto the defensive. In symbolic terms registered landowners attempted to transform Rainha from media darling into public enemy number one, as they produced photographs and 'WANTED' posters with his name printed in bold letters. Interviewed in jail, his wife complained that the imprisonment was 'illegal' and 'political' and that 'this is not the way to resolve the question of agrarian reform'.[25] The MST's leading lawyer, Luiz Eduardo Greenhalgh, was left to argue what seemed like the finer legal points. Why, for instance, had attempts been made to impede his access to the legal process under grounds of secrecy? Why had secrecy been used in an article 288 case when it was normally reserved for cases of sexual abuse of minors? Why had the judge not stipulated on a name by name basis those actions which he considered to be criminal? On 1 November, Greenhalgh's request for habeus corpus was, in no uncertain terms, rejected by Judge Dirceu de Mello of São Paulo's High Court of Justice. The judge's comments included a highly politicised restatement of the status quo. That they were made by a senior figure illustrates the uphill task facing the MST:

Civilised societies exist as a function of a legal order that establishes and limits the actions of its members. Within it we find the constitutional maxim that guarantees the right to property. To accept that third parties may attack the property of others, under the guise of a social question, would be the ruin of the whole legal order of the country. Today rural properties are invaded, in the mould of the famous 'peasant leagues' [*ligas camponesas*] of sad recollection.[26] If impunity under the pretext of social problems is allowed, tomorrow they could invade industries, factories and commercial establishments. This would represent the death of the State and legally organised society and the judiciary cannot admit or tolerate this.[27]

At a time when the region was in ferment and the government was attempting a negotiated settlement, the movement had effectively been deprived of some of its most gifted leaders. In a symbolic wake for the judicial system, complete with flowers and black armbands, held outside the Pirapozinho court house, a leader of the MST underlined how 'the Brazilian judiciary is agile at arresting workers, but incapable of solving questions that involve unproductive land.'[28] Indeed, da Silva was pleased and at pains to point out that 'these imprisonments disarticulated the movement in this region', specifically citing the sharp decline in the number of occupations immediately following his actions as evidence of this and the correctness of his actions.

In a case of this complexity and contentiousness, incalculability and unpredictability were prevalent features. If the intention of registered landowners was to transform Rainha into public enemy number one on the back of the court's findings, then the spectacle of seeing his partner and a fellow militant shackled and imprisoned had entirely the opposite effect. Overnight Diolinda Alves de Souza was transformed into a cause célèbre around which the centre and left gravitated and schisms reminiscent of the military dictatorship reemerged. The leader of the Workers' Party (PT), Luis Inácio Lula da Silva, who as a former trade union leader had experienced political imprisonment, himself,[29] was moved to comment:

> During the time of the military regime on occasions there was a certain shamefacedness when, for example, they sent people to special prisons. What they have done here is to put two political prisoners in a maximum security prison, treating them as if they were bandits.[30]

Moving Alves and Barreto into Carandiru prison may have been designed to forestall MST protests in the Pontal do Paranapanema and change the relations of force in favour of the state. The effect, however, was to place the prisoners in the media and political spotlight, and within reach of anyone who could reach São Paulo – a city of 18 million with the best communications links in Brazil. A procession of federal deputies quickly made its way to the jail, as did members of the Human Rights Commission of the federal Chamber of Deputies and the archbishop of São Paulo, Dom Paulo Evaristo Arns, a leading figure during the dictatorship in the campaign against human rights abuses.[31] So, if containing movement influence was one of the motives for transferring the prisoners to São Paulo, it proved a public relations disaster, even attracting attention from the international media and human rights groups.

As an exercise in Brazilian justice, events left much to be desired and cracks quickly emerged. The use of handcuffs to restrain the detainees was questioned by a number of experts in civil and criminal law from the University of São Paulo on the grounds that excessive and unnecessary force was used, thereby conflicting with laws governing the use of restraints.[32] The conflict between the state's political and legal arms was the subject of commentary by a leading political commentator, Clovis Rossi. He remarked upon how odd it was that on the one hand the state arrested members of the MST for forming a gang with criminal intent, while at the same time leading representatives of the state, including Governor Mario Covas of São Paulo, negotiated with that self-same gang. Should not the politicians therefore be arrested for complicity in the conspiracy? Rossi concluded:

> In a normal country, it is likely that that would happen. But, in Brazil, things are so confused and complicated that the authorities end up being praised for negotiating with the outlaws. ... The worst thing about it is that the praise is deserved. It is difficult to imagine anything more level-headed, logical, coherent and necessary than negotiating with the MST. This shows, in effect, that either the legislation is wrong or it is being applied improperly.[33]

In a telling comment Rossi noted: 'The problem is not, essentially, legal in nature, even though, of course, it involves a gamut of legislation. It is a question of politics, in the widest sense of the term, and it is as such that it must be understood.'[34]

This raises a vital question: could legal practitioners (judges, prosecutors and police officers) understand the problem in other than 'purely' legal terms? Not according to the Paulista Association of Magistrates. On 7 November 1995, the Association took out an advert in the one of the country's leading newspapers, the *Folha de São Paulo*, clarifying its position on the arrests. Stung by criticism from politicians over the MST case, the Association gave a robust defence of the formal separation of powers and its practise, laying the blame for conflict squarely on other parts of the state:

> It is not for the judiciary to take into consideration, at the time it takes its decisions, momentary political interests, ceding to these in detriment to the legal order. It is a shocking fact that some public authorities have declared that the preventive imprisonment led to instability in the Pontal do Paranapanema, prejudicing negotiations concerning agrarian reform. This instability has been present in the region for many years not on account of judicial decisions, but due to the slowness and lack of firmness

with which other competent authorities, installed in other Powers, have conducted the policy of land occupation. ... It is not the task of the judiciary, which is not a political power, to negotiate or seek political solutions for problems. Its task is to engender respect for the laws in force. That is how it acted in the case in question, when violations of public order were announced and evident.[35]

While there is considerable truth to charges that historically speaking government had failed in its duties, the comments not only ignore its ongoing efforts to resolve past injustices, but also sidestep entirely the politics of the judiciary itself. While the magistrates' statement appears to be an attractive reassertion of judicial autonomy and a rejection of the tyranny of the political, they replace it with a form of legal fetishism that fails to stand up to closer scrutiny. They assert a false opposition between a fixed and stable 'legal order' and fluid 'momentary political interests'; ceding space to the latter occurs to the 'detriment' of the former. There is no hint whatsoever that it might enrich it and provide the legal process with some of the legitimacy it lacks or that, conversely, the failure to adapt to social and political pressures might actually undermine the legal system as it becomes marginal to social conflict and is therefore bypassed altogether. Their analysis of the instability of the Pontal do Paranapanema, which they correctly attribute to causes dating well before 1995, eliminates the judiciary from the picture and ascribes the problem of 'slowness' and 'lack of firmness' solely to 'other powers'. This is false. Evidence presented in the previous chapter indicated that Discriminatory Actions, so much a part of the logjam in the Pontal, ended up in 'abeyance' (limbo) in large part because judicial priorities lay elsewhere. One would never guess, furthermore, that reformers had advocated the development of agrarian courts and more specialised training of judges because of systemic failures in the judicial sphere. Back in 1980, for example, the president of the Tribunal de Justiça in São Paulo rejected such proposals out of hand on the grounds that they would 'lead to increased conflict and call more attention to it'.[36] If these reported statements are correct, and they come from a well placed source, then they indicate a profound misreading of the problems. It is ironic that one of the reasons behind the emergence of the MST, a few years after those comments, was precisely the failure of the judicial system to deal with numerous aspects of the land question. Finally, there is the question of whether the judiciary in this case succeeded in its stated goal of *engendering respect for the laws in force*. The political breadth of condemnation which the incarcerations provoked suggests if anything the opposite, that the legal establishment was held in widespread contempt for its combination of partiality and miopia.

On 16 November 1995, Judge Beraldo revoked his orders of preventive imprisonment, thereby permitting the release of all prisoners. Luiz Eduardo Greenhalgh's earlier requests for habeus corpus therefore fell away, while the main case against the defendants, that of criminal conspiracy, made its way through the legal machinery for consideration at a later date. According to Beraldo, the reason for the early release was that 'order had been recovered'. A few days earlier, on 4 November, an accord had been reached between the state government and the MST in which the former committed itself to settling 2,100 families (half by December and the other half by July the following year), while the MST would suspend its occupations in the Pontal. As prosecutor da Silva explains:

> Because they committed themselves to no longer invading lands, we could no longer talk in terms of the risk that they would re-commit crimes. Once this possibility ceased there was no longer a motive to keep them in prison. I myself made the request that they should be released. So the judge released them.[37]

At the 4 November meeting the MST had asked Governor Covas to use his influence to gain the early release of the prisoners and the suspension of the preventive imprisonment order against Rainha. With typical skill, Covas explained that this was a matter for the judiciary, but also that 'the judiciary can conclude that the imprisonments have no sense'.[38] The judiciary concluded thus, and the prisoners were released.

By the end of December, however, relations with the government once again broke down, this time over the question of whether settlements would be provisional or permanent. The MST publicly lamented the fact that its agreement with the government had been verbal rather than written and therefore that it could not hold it to account. In particular, there was doubt over the legal status of the injunctions (*tutela antecipada* (see previous chapter)) granted by Judge Estimo. According to Rainha, settlements on these lands were provisional, while Belisário affirmed that they were irreversible. At the same time, registered landowners were actively exploring the possibility of overturning Estimo's decisions. 'How', said Rainha, 'am I going to explain that to the families?'[39]

Occupations were back on the agenda. On 20 January 1996, 280 families occupied Fazenda Santa Rita in Mirante do Paranapanema. They were led by Diolinda Alves de Souza. On 25 January the third vice-president of the Tribunal de Justiça in São Paulo decided that the owner of one *fazenda*, the Canaã, had not been given sufficient opportunity to demonstrate the legitimacy of his title, suspending the government's injunctions and thereby putting its whole settlement programme in jeopardy. And yet, as the vice-secretary of justice was moved to comment, 'In 1958 that whole area was declared devolved by the courts. There is no way that the *fazendeiro* can legitimate his title.'[40] That the situation was disintegrating rapidly became evident when, on the same day, Diolinda Alves de Souza was re-arrested along with three other MST militants, Laércio Barbosa, Claudemir Cano and Felinto Procopio. On this occasion Márcio Barreto and José Rainha, who were also listed on the arrest warrant, were able to escape imprisonment and went into hiding.

The formal motives for the re-imprisonments were clear. According to prosecutor da Silva, 'In January, it was clear that the government would no longer be able to maintain it [the truce], and they [the MST] had begun to invade again. I requested the imprisonment a second time.'[41] However, matters were more complicated than this, for the distinct impression was created that justice was less than impartial and was, quite literally, gunning for the militants. According to newspaper reports, Marco Antônio Fogolin, the police officer who charged them and constructed numerous cases against the MST with forensic determination, suggested that if a tank was needed in order to go after José Rainha then he could get the *fazendeiros* to provide him with one.[42]

At this point, events took an unexpected turn. The MST's lawyer, Luiz Eduardo Greenhalgh, explains:

> We tried to make all sorts of representations to the court when Diolinda was imprisoned and Zé Rainha in hiding. The judge decided to call a meeting with the Public Ministry and Jovelino [a lawyer from the MST]. Because we knew the sorts of issues that would be discussed I said to Jovelino, 'tape it'. So he took a recorder and taped it. The meeting was like this: the prosecutor, the police inspector, and the judge attempted to negotiate a deal. They would release Diolinda and the others if Zé Rainha gave himself up to the police.[43]

On 8 February the MST released a copy of the tape. In the conversation, police officer Fogolin took the lead, as he had done throughout.

> As an inspector I have undertaken to make a report to the judge and the prosecutor requesting that the detention of the prisoners be revoked. [However] Zé Rainha must present himself to me and I will bring him here in the presence of the judge with the order for imprisonment, because the police and the justice system believe that they must give an answer to society.[44]

Fogolin continued, 'The whole police force is looking for José Rainha. I can no longer guarantee his life ... José Rainha might react to imprisonment.' He was, apparently, offering the MST 'a heck of a deal'. In his view: 'the government lacks political will, it is only complicating matters. We are trying to resolve things here. Everyone released. I will be the intermediary on behalf of the *fazendeiros*, O.K.?'[45]

In the face of this evidence an apolitical system of justice that does not 'negotiate or seek political solutions for problems' seems untenable. Yet no howls of protest were heard from Judge Fernando Florido Marcondes or prosecutor Paulo Sergio Ribeiro da Silva – a notable omission given that the discussion was held in the judge's chamber, in his presence and at his request. According to Greenhalgh, nothing came of any of the negative representations he subsequently made regarding the officers of the law. Nor did the annexation of the tape to further legal submissions on behalf of the detainees make any difference to the São Paulo High Court. The detentions stood.

Clearly, this was a low point for the officials concerned and a masterstroke by Greenhalgh. Although one should not read too much into a single event, no matter how grotesque, it does nonetheless raise questions over how the MST came to be ensnared in a web of legal actions. As numerous observers had noted, how was it that the legal system, which was so effective at pursuing rural workers for comparatively minor infractions, proved totally incapable of putting the most horrendous criminals, i.e., assassins of rural workers and their paymasters, behind bars? The massacre of 19 landless workers at Eldorado dos Carajás (17 April 1996) is a well documented case in point. Landless workers protesting at the long delay in expropriating land for land reform had blocked a major highway in northern state of Pará. The response of the military police was to shoot them at close range. The manner in which the massacre was subsequently dealt with came to be seen as a litmus test of the justice system itself. Ten years on Amnesty International noted that 'not one of those involved have been imprisoned. Inept police investigation, woefully inadequate forensic research, and the failure to offer protection to witnesses who received threats have dogged the judicial process at every step along the way. ... Inadequacies at every level of the criminal justice system, undue influence of wealthy landowners, and a failure of political will to address root problems are entrenched'.[46] While the treatment of landless workers in the Pontal was clearly of a different order, the harsh line contrasted with the scope the courts were willing to offer a landowner in an area that four decades earlier they had decided was stolen from the state.

The institutional response of the prosecution service

The Public Ministry had undergone an intensive process of self-renewal in the 1980s and had been an intellectual mainstay in the drive towards wider legal reforms. Where did events in the Pontal leave Brazil's largest, most powerful and well-resourced public prosecution service and its much vaunted project of institutional modernisation? The answer, it would turn out, was in the hands of a lone prosecutor and in almost total disarray.

A number of factors lay behind the implosion of the Public Ministry's grand intellectual horizons. In contrast to other areas, such as consumer rights or environment issues, which enjoyed longstanding organisational standing within São Paulo's Public Ministry,[47] there was no corresponding intellectual or institutional framework capable of identifying, let alone integrating, the diffuse or collective dimensions associated with land questions. The issue lay beyond the Public Ministry's conceptual horizons – it could only deal with associated manifestations on an ad hoc basis. There were no special internal support groups or operational centres.

The absence of theoretical insight may have been due to São Paulo's indus-
trialised and urbanised character (despite the prominent role played by agriculture within the economy). It was probably no coincidence that issues close
to urban problems, like consumer, environmental and planning law, should
have found intellectual and organisational expression. Those setting the intellectual agenda within the Public Ministry tended to come from its higher
ranks, which almost invariably meant from within urban centres and middle
classes. Perhaps more than any other state, São Paulo suffered from the errone-
ous but widespread perception that land conflicts belonged to other more
'backward' northern states, rather than to the country's industrial and agro-
industrial powerhouse. To many, not just within the Public Ministry but also
the wider population, the eruption of conflict in the Pontal therefore came as
a rude awakening.

Finally there is the issue of the Public Ministry's internal division of labour
and competencies. For constitutional reasons there is a built-in tendency
towards fragmentation rather than integration, as different aspects of the land
question are deliberately parcelled out between different branches of the
Public Ministry according to whether the issues are deemed to be federal or
local ones. As noted in the Introduction, land reform is primarily regarded as
a federal matter and therefore the preserve of the Federal Public Ministry. For
the related issue of land occupations, however, no such delimitation exists: it
is a local matter. One leading federal prosecutor suggested that as far as the
right of intervention by the Federal Public Ministry in local conflict situations was concerned, 'our competence is not absolutely clear, but it can be
deduced from our function as an ombudsman'.[48] No such ambiguity exists as
far as the Public Ministry within individual states is concerned. Almost invariably it is the local prosecutor who is called upon to intervene at the point
of conflict. Institutionally speaking, land occupations are treated as isolated
episodes of conflict rather than as components in a broader and more complex
picture.

The factor that most sharply defined the Public Ministry's profile in the
Pontal do Paranapanema, therefore, was the conduct of Paulo Sérgio Ribeiro
da Silva himself. To all intents and purposes he was the Public Ministry.
A marked feature of Brazil's prosecutorial system is the autonomy, or 'functional independence' it accords prosecutors, a principle which, as one leading
lawyer notes 'opposes itself precisely to the principle of hierarchy.'[49] This was
one of the prized cornerstones of the process of redemocratisation. At the
height of the military dictatorship in 1971 protection from hierarchical intervention was limited. Thus, for example, pressure was brought to bear upon
one prosecutor, Helio Bicudo, to cease his investigations into police involvement in death squads. Those attempting to force him out of the job (with
success) not only included the government of São Paulo, but the head of
the Public Ministry itself. Not surprisingly, therefore, with the transition to
civilian rule, autonomy was highly prized among prosecutors across the

political spectrum.[50] At the same time, though, this helped to underpin the power of the individual as one of the fundamental variables in the legal system. Even if the head of the Public Ministry had wanted to there was little in the short term that could he have done to alter da Silva's conduct. Indeed, it would widely have been perceived as an assault upon the class of prosecutors as a whole.

Eventually, though, a shift in the posture of the Public Ministry did take place. This was marked by a number of important changes including the departure of da Silva, the election of a new attorney general in São Paulo who was sympathetic to agrarian reform issues, and the creation, at his behest, of a special group of prosecutors to work on land questions in the Pontal. These changes would offer scope for the creation of a slightly more adequate framework of action. Before they could take effect, however, an altogether more decisive shift – decisive in terms of its legal and social ramifications – occurred in an unexpected quarter: at the Supreme Court (Supremo Tribunal de Justiça – STJ) in Brasília.

The response of the judges

Surprisingly, for all the conservatism of the Brazilian judiciary on land matters and the radicalism of São Paulo's Public Ministry, it was the senior judges who made the running and spelt out with greatest precision – and authority – the imperative for radical change. On 12 March 1996 they were asked to rule on the merits of the application for habeus corpus of the four MST militants imprisoned since 25 January.[51] It will be recalled that the MST had failed some weeks earlier in a similar request at São Paulo's High Court, which had referred to the 'death of the state' if the MST's 'impunity' was allowed to persist. A failure in Brasília would mean that the militants would respond to the principal charges (of forming a gang and forced dispossession) in captivity, while the two militants on the run would remain so. The issue for the court to decide was whether the preventive imprisonment of the defendants was essential in this case.

Although the essence of the court's ruling was simple – preventive imprisonment was unnecessary and therefore habeus corpus could be granted – the reasoning that lay behind it was subtle and sophisticated. The judges gave differing emphases to the legal issues at stake. Judge William Patterson asked perhaps the most basic legal question: was preventive imprisonment absolutely necessary under these circumstances? He concluded that preventive imprisonment in this case had been based 'totally upon the maintenance of public order' when 'greater control of the denounced activities' could have been achieved by the bail regime rather than imprisonment. There had been a failure to give due consideration to this issue.[52] Judge Vicente Leal took a similar line, noting that when the requisite conditions are met, bail is 'a citizen's right'. He was not so keen to enter into the merits of land reform: 'they are themes that touch us but cannot be the object of debate on the occasion of this judgement.'[53] His colleague, Judge Adhemar Maciel, felt less constrained, recalling that one of the failures of Brazil in relation to Japan and Taiwan was 'precisely the lack of an opportune agrarian reform'. In this context he raised the following questions: 'Is there a right to resistance? Don't we have in the Brazilian Constitution, as in other foreign statues, explicitly, the right to resistance? Do subjects have the right to rebel against a sovereign who is not acting on behalf of the people?' As far as the more narrow legalities were concerned, the judge concurred with his colleague, William Patterson, that 'from a formal point of view' the indictment was 'a beautiful piece of work. But in its substantial aspect, the facts do not coincide well.' He did not recognise the situation of public outcry, alleged by the prosecution, which in his view would indeed have necessitated preventive imprisonment.[54]

Of all the judgments, the most wide ranging and eloquent was that provided by Judge Luiz Vicente Cernicchiaro. In less than 1,000 words he gave the overall verdict its incisive tone and intellectual depth. He began by setting the scene. The instrument of preventive imprisonment was an exceptional measure under the Brazilian legal order because it deprived the subjects their liberty. It was clearly defined and its use had to conform to certain legal requisites. They might include indications of serious penal infractions, and questions related to the preservation of public order. They could also include the sustainability of the legal process itself, i.e., the practical conditions under which any conviction might be secured. Insubordination of the accused towards legal rules had been alleged. The judge accepted that 'from a formal point of view', this had happened, but he found no grounds for the charge of forced possession (*esbulho possessório*). 'The fact must be analysed in its context, relating it to its motivation', he said.[55]

At this point he shifted the terms of the debate by importing constitutional articles governing a land reform programme.[56] In contrast to Judge Leal's reluctance, Cernicchiaro argued it was evident that these provisions had an object and that:

> The delay (justified or unjustified) of their enactment generates reactions, not always captured within the extent of legal norms. ... The conduct of the agent engaged in forced possession is *substantively distinct* from the conduct of a person with interests in agrarian reform.[57]

Indeed, he noted, the general theory of delict (the general theory underlying criminal law) increasingly invoked culpability, such that its varying degrees could reach proportions whereby their characterisation as a penal infraction was ruled out. So, in this case there were vital qualitative distinctions to be made. It was one thing simply to make use of another person's land, or to change existing boundaries 'for the purposes of personal enrichment without just cause' – so-called forced possession; but it was quite another when the issue was one of 'social pressure for the concretisation of a right (or at least an interest)'. In the former case there was a coincidence, or overlap, of the formal and substantive illegalities. In the latter case, however, there was no such coincidence, for in substantive terms there was 'no illegality whatsoever', while formally, 'and only on this level', could one debate the *modus faciendi*.

Turning to the question of 'public order', Cernicchiaro delivered a broadside at the host of assumptions underlying this notion. Like the actions of people, it had to be understood 'in its historical context'.

> Public order or outcries must be received with caution. They can be generated artificially, so as to give the impression of disquiet within society. In fact public outcry is not to be confused with reactions (occasionally organised) of landowners in areas that may come to be expropriated by the state for the purposes of agrarian reform.

Finally, there was the fact that upon their previous release the prisoners had not fled from the Pontal, and there was no indication that they would do so if released once more.

By any standard Judge Cernicchiaro's findings were remarkable. Although he referred to being 'unhappily constrained within the procedural limits', and the necessity of confining his comments and any remedial measures, his horizons clearly lay beyond narrowly constructed legal paradigms. In fact, his comments were loaded with historical, philosophical and sociological insight. He referred, for instance, to a programme of agrarian reform that long predated the 1988 constitution, he noted the class injustices of Brazil's legal system whereby 'if (formally) the law is equal for all, not all are equal before the law', and he even spoke of the whole question of land reform and conflict as underpinned by a dialectical logic of development. These comments were all the more significant because they were made by a top insider – a member of the High Court of Justice – a leading intellectual in penal affairs, and the chair of the committee looking into the reform of the penal code itself.

The implications of the decision

Measuring the impact of a judicial decision is notoriously difficult, especially if one tries to go beyond the parties directly involved and explore wider social or political ramifications. Put simply, the causal connections become more complex, to say nothing of the dynamic nature of the processes involved. For Rainha and his comrades, who were at the epicentre of the conflict, the links were clear. The decision meant liberty – no small achievement given the aforementioned decapitation of the movement. For the movement as a whole, it was a notable victory, giving it something rarely seen in the legal arena: legitimacy. Indeed, some months later the MST produced a document referring to the judgment with the title 'The occupations of land are constitutional, legitimate and necessary.'[58] The judgment also indicated that significant legal victories were possible and that this was an avenue worth continuing to explore. The decision would bolster the existing tendency towards the development of in-house legal advice and external legal support networks, and underlined the political importance of sustained activity in this arena. This was much more than simply a get out of jail free card. For Luiz Eduardo Greenhalgh, 'this *habeus corpus* changed the jurisprudence of the Superior Tribunal of Justice in Brasília on the MST. The thesis that the MST is not a gang and that its action is not forced possession, was consolidated.'[59]

The legal novelty of the judges' findings should not be underestimated either. As Judge Cernicchiaro later confirmed:

> Without doubt it constituted a pioneering decision in the Brazilian courts. For 10 years this distinction had not been made between acting in order to impose, or demand, or call upon the government to concretise projects of a social order that appeared in the Brazilian constitution.[60]

This was, in other words, a throw back to more optimistic debates during the drafting of the 1988 constitution and, indeed, the strengthening of the Public Ministry as an instrument of constitutional and social change.

Did the decision reflect more deep-seated changes within the judiciary? According to Judge Cernicchiaro:

> Yes, I believe so. The judiciary, like all institutions, has its history and its phases. For a long time the interpretation was made according to the Napoleonic Code, where there was an interest in the protection of a determinate social category. Today, in general, Brazilian judicial culture is undergoing a reformulation. In other words, the interpretation of legal norms looks to the concretisation of social interests, not merely individual ones.[61]

What the eminent judge could not speak of with any precision was the rate of change or its distribution. Even from a privileged viewpoint, at the very apex of the system, his comments were impressionistic as, indeed, was the case with every legal practitioner interviewed in the course of this study. And yet impressions, even if they are by definition a partial view, are no less valuable for it. Thus, although the *habeus corpus* decision highlighted an underlying historical tendency towards a more socially aware judiciary, it simultaneously highlighted the continued – in many ways dominant – presence of countertendencies. In typically diplomatic fashion, Judge Cernicchiaro acknowleged that 'I have not had news that the lower courts have given the same treatment or the same interpretation.'[62] Luiz Eduardo Greenhalgh was more direct: 'amongst the first instance and regional court judges this thesis [of the STJ] is rejected.'[63] Indeed, Greenhalgh's way around the problem powerfully highlights the major conflict within the judiciary:

> All of us, the lawyers of the MST, are engaged in a race against time because we know that the judiciary in the Pontal do Paranapanema is against the thesis, and that the Regional Tribunal is against it. So we have got to move as quickly as possible in order to get to Brasília.[64]

Judge Cernicchiaro's inability to speak with any precision about the rate of change or its distribution is not surprising. The difficulty of criticising such a closed profession and suggesting that the defence of 'determinate social categories' (a coded expression for class) might be a contemporary rather than an historical phenomenon, may be one reason for this together with the genuine complexity, patchiness and unevenness of the phenomenon itself. There is no blanket opposition between STJ, regional courts and first instance judges per se. Although to some extent it applies in São Paulo over this issue, elsewhere, for example in the state Rio Grande do Sul, a number of important decisions favourable to the MST were taken by lower courts.

Thus the STJ's verdict must be seen for what it was: a small – albeit highly significant – move in the right direction, a move that, for all its value, was neither about to rewrite contradictions within the judiciary, let alone social contradictions outside. Its short-term impact was mixed. There was a shift in tone. The MST could hold up the decision as a partial vindication of its strategy, while progressive members of the Public Ministry could hold it up as the kind of direction in which their own institution should be going. The Federal Public Ministry, which had not opposed the application for *habeus corpus*, now grasped the decision with open arms. In his 21 February 1997 report on the situation in the Pontal do Paranapanema, Brazil's deputy attorney general in charge of human rights referred extensively to the decision. That over half of Judge Cernicchiaro's comments were cited verbatim (occupying two pages in the prosecutor's 16-page report), underlines the importance that he attached to them.[65] The deputy attorney general was firmly of the view that the concept of forced possession demanded a far more sophisticated reading than it had hitherto received (prior to 12 March 1996). His report was passed to senior figures including the governor of São Paulo, the minister of justice, and the minister of agrarian reform. Perhaps more importantly, given the power of local prosecutors, it was also forwarded to all levels of São Paulo's Public Ministry – from the chief prosecutor, to prosecutors in the judicial district of Presidente Prudente.

Changes in the Public Ministry

The MST's trial led to a trial of sorts of the Public Ministry from which it did not emerge particularly well. Rather than the proactive defender of the constitutional or public interest, the impression created was of a flat footed and reactive – if not reactionary – institution. Judges hundreds of miles away in the capital Brasília seemed better attuned to the social realities of agrarian reform than prosecutors on the ground.

The flaw was recognised by the newly appointed (March 1996) head of São Paulo's Public Ministry, Luiz Antonio Marrey. He came from the left of the political spectrum and had family connections with Plínio de Arruda Sampaio, a politician who had played a leading role in the reform of the Public Ministry under the 1988 constitution, and remained a central figure in the agrarian reform movement.[66] Shortly before his appointment, in a clear signal of his own institutional leanings, Marrey had joined the most radical of the reform groups within the Public Ministry, the Movement of the Democratic Public Ministry (Movimento do Ministério Público Democrático – MMPD).

Ironically Marrey, who came second in the election, was appointed to his post by Governor Covas rather than by the popular acclaim of his fellow prosecutors. Charges of a loss of independence quickly followed from more conservative groupings of prosecutors within the Public Ministry, like the Association of the Public Ministry (Associação do Ministério Público – AMP). While Marrey noted that there was opportunism in these charges, since, in his words, 'in other circumstances when the chief prosecutor was totally tied to the state government the Association supported this situation',[67] he was nevertheless weakened by the charges. As a fellow member of the MMPD acknowledged, this was his 'original sin'.[68] Although Marrey could argue with some reason that Covas had chosen to break with 'clearly corporatist choices in favour of a more popular and democratic vision',[69] this hardly represented the comprehensive demolition of the electoral argument or the expurgation of his own 'sin'. That would only come two years later, when Marrey was re-elected with a substantial majority.

What this excursion into the politics of selection illustrates are some of the pressures under which even the chief prosecutor was working. On the one hand there was the issue of gubernatorial power, resolved in large part by a meeting of minds; on the other, there was a membership base, substantial sections of which were discontented with the selection result, and all of whom enjoyed substantial degrees of autonomy. Reorienting the profile of the Public Ministry was not going to be easy. The administrative powers of the new attorney general were limited and politically his authority was hardly in the ascendant. Given that the ideological divide within the Public Ministry on the land issue was so profound, it was hardly the easiest issue around which to unite prosecutors. To that extent it remained on the back burner. Its integration under a Human Rights Secretariat, developed during Marrey's tenure as head of São Paulo's Public Ministry, would help reverse this trend.

Externally, though, events began to impose themselves. When Marrey took office the Pontal do Paranapanema conflict constantly appeared on newspaper front pages and in television reports. The land question could not so easily be marginalised by the Public Ministry, and it was clear (and Marrey needed no persuading in this respect), that to date the Public Ministry had not acquitted itself particularly well having been author of a failed legal action in Brazil's highest court, and co-author of actions of dubious legality in the chambers of a local judge. In the light of these events a Special Working Group on Land Issues in Western São Paulo (Grupo Especial de Trabalho sobre Assuntos Fundiários do Oeste Paulista – GETAF)[70] was created on 18 February 1997.

The foundation of GETAF

GETAF's foundation represented the closest the Public Ministry would come to developing a coherent strategy on land questions. However, as the name suggested, it was a strictly regional rather than a statewide initiative – a response to an immediate situation, rather than a model to be replicated elsewhere. GETAF's founding articles referred to 'defining common and uniform strategies of Public Ministry intervention in the region, maintaining contacts with the authorities, groups and people involved in the [land] question, [and] searching for peaceful and legal solutions for the conflicts.'[71] The preamble emphasised that local prosecutors had requested 'the creation of a commission with a view to uniform and co-ordinated actions and a more in depth study of the theme'.[72] As an interview with these prosecutors later confirmed, one of the problems faced by Paulo Sergio Ribeiro da Silva had been precisely his isolation, under immense pressure, and with comparatively little institutional support. Even he welcomed GETAF, albeit because he felt it would 'represent a division of responsibilities, and once a decision had been taken everyone would sign it.'[73]

GETAF also represented a carefully calculated response on the part of the highest echelons within the Public Ministry to changes that had occurred at the federal level a few months earlier. As Paulo Afonso Garrido de Paula, the prosecutor appointed by Marrey to liaise on his behalf with GETAF, explains.

> The intervention of the Public Ministry came by way of an alteration that occurred on 23 December 1996, with Law 9.415 … making intervention obligatory in cases that involve struggles over rural land ownership or in other cases in which there is a public interest. So with this change we began to discuss internally the necessity, or rather the form, in which the intervention of the Public Ministry in these types of actions would occur.[74]

GETAF was a result of those discussions.

A brief note should be made in passing of the origins of federal Law 9.415. This law, introduced by President Fernando Henrique Cardoso's administration, was highly circumstantial in origin. The political process had proved incapable of enacting legislation of this kind, much as it had been incapable of enacting a more progressive constitutional land settlement in 1988. Only a cruel twist of fate, itself the product a stagnated legal and political process in the north of the country, tipped the balance and paved the way towards the emergence of a new correlation of political, and with them legislative, forces.

As the Minister of Agrarian Reform himself noted: 'The impetus behind the major legal changes of this government occur in the period 96/97 very much under the impact of the events in Eldorado dos Carajás.'[75]

Nobody could have foreseen that the massacre at Eldorado dos Carajás of 19 MST militants in April 1996 at the hands of the military police would have had an impact of this kind, putting landowning interests on the back foot. Likewise, far from originating in a legal vacuum or at the whim of Attorney General Marrey and his associates, changes in the Public Ministry were in fact part of a complex – at times ugly – birth process. GETAF owed its existence to a combination of factors including the pressure of events in the Pontal, the requests of local prosecutor, the strategy adopted by Marrey, and even events thousands of kilometers away in Pará state and Brasília. Nobody wanted another Eldorado, least of all in São Paulo's backyard. GETAF was partly conceived as a way of forestalling armed conflict – which remained a distinct possibility.

Immediately following the meeting, at which the creation of a commission of eight prosecutors was agreed, Marrey noted that 'a straightforward and formal application of the law will not resolve the extra-legal situation. It is a social problem that will not be resolved by repression.'[76] His language bore echoes of Judge Cernicchiaro's comments almost a year earlier. It was a clear invitation for prosecutors to use their extra-institutional powers, to engage, for instance, in mediation between the parties, the intent of Law 9.415. Marrey also understood the limits of such actions: 'One must bear in mind that the Public Ministry can't do everything. The resolution of the problems is subject to the action of various authorities of public order'.[77]

Marrey's appointment of Afonso Garrido de Paula as liaison with GETAF represented another positive step. At the Second State Congress of the São Paulo Public Ministry in May 1997, de Paula had defended the thesis that if rural property failed to fulfill its 'social function' (a function defined in the 1988 constitution), then corresponding judicial protections, like eviction orders, could not reasonably be invoked because they had lost their force in law.[78] This line of reasoning was not dissimilar to that pursued by MST lawyers.

The limits of the attorney general's powers also become clear. While respecting de Paula's intellectual abilities, prosecutors in the Pontal do Paranapanema took a different approach. At the beginning of March 1998, a year after the submission by the federal deputy attorney general of his report on the Pontal and the formation of GETAF, several prosecutors from the group provided a collective submission on the alleged crimes of the MST dating back to 1995.[79] A striking feature of their submission (a 38-page document that included copious citations from numerous legal authorities), was the total absence of any substantive reference to the 12 March 1996 *habeus corpus* decision. Instead, no less than four pages were devoted to a verbatim citation of a 10 August 1997 decision by Judge Oliveira Passos of São Paulo's High Court. That judgment, concerning forced possession, had included references to nothing less than 'the death of the state'[80] if the MST had its way. Instead of editing out this dubious ideological excursus, GETAF prosecutors gave his comments the status of legal wisdom by underlining them.

Some subtle shifts were perceptible on the ground. One prosecutor suggested that 'we hit *both* sides very hard, very hard indeed',[81] citing as an example the arrest and imprisonment of a landowner's son on charges of attempted homicide. Despite criticism of the Public Ministry and judiciary for this act, prosecutors were pleased that by the time the suspect was released on bail, the tension had largely been defused. Other examples included Marrey nurturing prosecutors, offering suggestions and being kept informed of developments. In one instance, he was advised of an impending occupation to which the local police commander was reluctant to deploy his forces. Acting on this information Marrey rang the secretary of public security, who ordered the deployment. Similarly, Tânia Andrade, the head of ITESP confirmed the creation of a more proactive and cooperative dynamic between her organisation and the Public Ministry. GETAF was instrumental in enabling the Public Ministry to embrace informal behind-the-scenes work more actively and thereby go beyond issues of crime and punishment. In Andrade's case that informal work meant:

> They alerted me to certain situations in time so I could take action; or called me to meetings so I could explain certain details, or proposed audiences of conciliation between landowners and the state, or audiences of conciliation between the landless and the landowner.[82]

It sounds mundane, but such interventions, the use of personal contacts at times of heightened tension, could weigh heavily upon the immediate outcome even if not upon the underlying structural conflicts themselves.

Conclusion

The previous chapter established that the MST's mass occupations had effectively kick-started a process of land reform in the Pontal do Paranapanema by reconfiguring relations of power in its favour. This chapter examined not only some of the mechanics involved, but also how the movement adapted its broader objectives to the reality of the situation. With more than a quarter of a century of experience behind it, it is tempting to see that model of action as an unqualified success. Certainly the model has proved more than capable of reproducing itself (even if not, as yet, of achieving the strategic goal of a genuinely far reaching land reform). What the case of the Pontal illustrates (although any region could be chosen for this purpose) is just how difficult the process is. Reproduction may not be what it is all about, but it is an achievement whose magnitude should not be underestimated. It is the difference between a movement that had initially begun by haemorraging members, and one that subsequently developed the strength to occupy a *fazenda* 23 times (finally taking it over). It is the difference between success and failure.

The other issue considered in this chapter was the reaction of the legal establishment to the MST's calculated acts of civil disobedience. The law was powerless to compartmentalise and fetter MST struggles in the way legislation had done for many years with urban and rural trade unions (until rebellions of the 70s and 80s challenged the validity of that legislation). Without the fear of government intervention the movement was free to organise itself and conduct struggle as it saw fit. Indeed, for the movement to have any real chance of success, it had to take isolated events and struggles nationwide. The presence of such a large legal blind spot is the background against which the heightened significance of the criminal justice process should be seen. A major question that underlines this chapter is the extent to which that system is transformed into an instrument of repressive social control. Does it criminalise a mass movement struggling for social justice?

What is interesting about the evidence presented in this chapter is not that the answer to this question is both yes and no, as one might expect, but what those different conclusions begin to tell us about the system's operation. It makes uncomfortable reading. Take the example of the Public Ministry. Its grand constitutional vision, forged partly in response to the repressive weight of the dictatorship, collapsed into the actions of a lone prosecutor which bordered on the farsical. Institutionally speaking he was perfectly entitled to take an independent position. More problematically, his position, which can be crudely summarised as a defence of property rights at all costs, is shared by substantial sectors of the legal establishment. The High Court in São Paulo was similarly inclined.

While the evaporation of the Public Ministry's credibility was partly the consequence of the autonomy and discretion accorded individual prosecutors, the evidence of this chapter also reveals quite a conservative institution. The deep dissatisfaction with which Attorney General Marrey, a progressive, was imposed upon the wider membership by Governor Covas arose not so much from the principle of imposition per se, which was the governor's prerogative, as from the fact many prosecutors did not like Marrey's politics.

Turning to the actions of Marrey himself, the deeply divided nature of the field yet again becomes apparent. On the issue of land he was clear: 'a straightforward and formal application of the law will not resolve the extra-legal situation. It is a social problem that will not be resolved by repression.'[83] This was a refreshing change, but one that had its limits. Marrey clearly felt he had to go with the grain as well as cut across it. For present purposes the extent to which he failed or succeeded in exercising his power aggressively enough is not as important as the fact that he rightly perceived its deeply divided and ideological character and felt compelled to act accordingly. As Chapter 5 will show, these divisions over land would directly affect relations between his Public Ministry and President Cardoso's Ministry of Justice, led by Nelson Jobim.

What of the judiciary? Ideological divisions and their impact on practise is a feature that even more open-minded judges are reluctant to discuss. Judge Cernicchiaro, for instance, refers to phases in judicial institutions rather than to their politics, or to the 'interest in the protection of a determinate social category' rather than class interests. Be that as it may, it is evident that his reading in the STJ's *habeus corpus* decision gives the lie to the notion that the law is somehow methodologically constrained to arrive at the sorts of conclusions reached by the lower court, or that, as the Paulista Association of Magistrates suggested, engendering respect for the rule of law was essentially an issue confined to the violation of rules of law and order, rather than inclusive of other wider constitutional determinations, like property's social function and distribution. This is to say nothing of the contributions which the judicary in São Paulo had made to the perpetuation of land conflicts through painfully slow and pedantic decision-making processes.

Where does all the above leave the Landless Workers' Movement? Much of the time the answer is with a membership that is criminalised. Legally speaking the answer should, at the very least be with an arguable case, but that case is largely ignored by the lower courts. This means that the movement simply has to find ways of catapulting cases as quickly as possible to the STJ. This rather negative outlook also leaves the movement where it began, prioritising the social over legal struggle, but that is far from the end of the story. As the following chapters will show, there are vital spaces with which it can engage. These include engagement with institutionalised political power, development of informal legal networks as a means of leveraging movement power, and engagement with progressive judges and prosecutors whose autonomy, coupled with social commitment, offers valuable opportunities for reshaping legal and social discourse.

Notes

1 Reference HC-4399 SP 96/0008845-4.
2 'Quadrilheiros', *Folha de São Paulo*, 5 November 1995.
3 Author interview with Neuri Rosetto of the MST national executive, 6 June 1997.
4 Author interview with Alcides Gomes dos Santos, 21 March 2000.
5 Ibid.
6 Ibid.
7 Author interview with José Rainha, 20 March 2000.
8 Author interview with Zelitro Luz da Silva, 20 March 2000.
9 For details of the struggle and final settlement see Bernardo Mançano Fernandes, *MST: Formação e territorialização*, São Paulo: Editoral Hucitec, 1996. Fernandes notes that while no money was paid by the government to the putative owner, because of its devolved status, the 'owners' capital investments (buildings, machinery, etc.) were nevertheless assessed by ITSEP and compensated for to the tune of R$5,400,000 (Fernandes, p. 183). The issue of whether they were deliberately overcompensated, i.e., bought off, remains a sore point.

10 Author interview with Gilmar Mauro, 10 August 2000.
11 Author interview with Bernardo Mançano Fernandes, 7 September 1999.
12 The Rural Democratic Union (União Democrática Ruralista, UDR) was at that
    time a powerful far right grouping of landed interests operating throughout
    Brazil. The UDR had proved a formidable political force during the run up to the
    1988 constitution, garnering the support of landed interests against land reform
    and activities of the MST. A self-styled defender of property and associated laws,
    its history is intertwined with violent paramilitary activity. See 'The Brazilian
    Democratic Union' in Leigh A. Payne's *Uncivil Movements: The Armed Right Wing
    and Democracy in Latin America*, Baltimore, MD: John Hopkins University Press,
    2000, pp. 101–61.
13 Author interview with Zelitro Luz da Silva, 20 March 2000.
14 Rede Globo's prime time *telenovela* (television drama series), *O Rei do Gado* (*King
    of Cattle*), which appeared between June 1996 and February 1997, touched exten-
    sively, and for the most part favourably, on the plight of the landless.
15 Author interview with Alcides Gomes dos Santos, 20 March 2000.
16 Author interview with Paulo Sérgio Ribeiro da Silva, 9 September 1999.
17 Ibid.
18 Ibid.
19 Ibid.
20 Ibid.
21 Ibid.
22 By this Paulo Sérgio Ribeiro da Silva simply means that in many instances the
    state (i.e., courts) can only seek to punish an alleged offender if the alleged victim
    wishes to instigate criminal proceedings. That applies in the case of land occupa-
    tions. Criminal proceedings in such cases lies beyond the power of the Public
    Ministry and lie with the affected party instead. Hence the action is known as a
    Private Penal Suit (*Ação Penal Privada*), in contrast to a Public Civil Suit (*Ação
    Civil Publico*) promoted by the Public Ministry.
23 Author interview with Paulo Sérgio Ribeiro da Silva, 9 September 1999.
24 Between 1956 and 2002 hundreds of inmates met a violent end. In 1992 alone,
    111 prisoners were killed mostly at the hands of military police in what came to
    be known as the Carandiru Massacre. Conditions at the prison were characterised
    by overcrowding, disease and extreme violence of drug related and other kinds.
    The facility was largely demolished by the São Paulo authorities in 2002.
25 'Justiça serve aos fazendeiros, diz sem-terra', *Folha de São Paulo*, 1 November
    1995.
26 Many would say of much sadder recollection was the military coup of 1964 which
    repressed this movement and forced its leader, Fransisco Julião, into exile and
    partly as a consequence, a meaningful agrarian reform off the political agenda. For
    an introduction to this movement see João Pedro Stédile, ed., *A questão agrária no
    Brasil: História e natureza das Ligas Camponesas – 1954–1964*, São Paulo: Editora
    Expressão Popular, 2006.
27 Reproduced in the discourse of Judge William Patterson, HC No. 4.399-SP, reg-
    istro No. 96/0008845-4, p. 3.
28 Gilmar Mauro cited in 'MST protesta em Pirapozinho', *Folha de São Paulo*,
    3 November 1995.

29 In 1980, as leader of a strike wave, he was imprisoned with fellow union leaders under national security legislation. The strike wave is commonly seen as a significant factor in hastening the demise of the military dictatorship. In this respect some striking parallels may be drawn between events here and in Poland, where the Solidarity union, led by Lech Walesa, would have a devastating impact on the prospects of the communist regime. Not only did both leaders subsequently become presidents of their respective countries, but a significant oppositional/mobilising role was played by the Catholic Church. In Poland's case conservative theology was dominant, while in Brazil liberation theology played a crucial role, transforming President Lula da Silva's hitherto sceptical view of the Church. See George Mészáros, *The Catholic Church and trade unions in Brazil: a case study of the relationship between the dioceses of São Paulo and Santo André and the Metalworkers of Greater Sao Paulo, 1970–1986*, PhD thesis, London School of Economics, 1991.

30 'Deputados visitam Deolinda na Prisão', *Jornal do Brasil*, 3 November 1995.

31 See his moving introduction to the report cataloguing human rights abuses between 1964 and 1979, *Brasil nunca mais*, Petrópolis: Vozes, 1987.

32 'Advogados condenam prisão de Diolinda', *Folha de São Paulo*, 4 November 1995.

33 Clovis Rossi, 'Quadrilheiros', *Folha de São Paulo*, 5 November 1995.

34 Ibid.

35 'Prisão de líderes do Movimento dos Sem Terra – Nota da Associação Paulista de Magistrados', *Folha de São Paulo*, 5 November 1995.

36 This is according to recollections by Juvenal Boller in an interview with the author, 19 April 2000. As well as noting the general reluctance of federal judges to see any specialisation, Boller notes how he was personally admonished by one senior judge when he delivered a petition by rural workers requesting that cases of land expropriation running through the federal courts be accelerated.

37 Author interview with Paulo Sérgio Ribeiro da Silva, 9 September 1999.

38 'Acordo garante sem-terra no Pontal', *Jornal do Brasil*, 5 November 1995.

39 'Covas esfria 'janeiro quente' dos sem-terra', *Folha de São Paulo*, 4 January 1996.

40 'Governo perde área no Pontal', *Folha de São Paulo*, 26 January 1996.

41 Author interview with Paulo Sérgio Ribeiro da Silva, 9 September 1999.

42 'Segurança é segredo', *Jornal do Brasil*, 5 November 1995.

43 Author interview with Luiz Eduardo Greenhalgh, 3 September 1999.

44 'MST apresenta gravação contra delegado', *Folha de São Paulo*, 9 February 1996.

45 Ibid.

46 Source: 'The Eldorado dos Carajás Massacre 10 Years On', Brazil: Amnesty International, 18 April 2006, available at www-secure.amnesty.org/en/library/asset/AMR19/019/2006/en/caf956a4-d43b-11dd-8743-d305bea2b2c7/amr190192006en.html Although some convictions were eventually secured, it is also clear that left to its own devices the criminal justice system was incapable of securing a result. It therefore took external pressure (mass protests, active federal government involvement) to tilt the balance the other way.

47 In December 1982, for example, Lei Complementar 304 was introduced in São Paulo. This gave emphasis to consumer and environmental issues as well as the cultural and natural heritage of the state. By mid-1983 the law was taking institutional effect with the creation of *curadorias*, curatorships, in these areas.

48 Author interview with Ela Wolkmer de Castilo, 13 June 1997.

49 Hugo Nigro Mazzilli, *O acesso à justiça e o Ministério Público*, São Paulo: Editora Saraiva, 1998, p. 151.
50 For a full account of the death squads see Hélio Pereira Bicudo, *Meu Depoimento Sobre o Esquadrão da Morte*, 7th edition, São Paulo: Pontifícia Comissão de Justiça e Paz de São Paulo, 1978.
51 Reference HC-4399 SP 96/0008845-4.
52 Ibid.
53 Ibid.
54 Ibid.
55 Ibid.
56 Chapter 7, on the economic and financial order; Chapter 2, articles 184–91.
57 Reference HC-4399 SP 96/0008845-4. My emphasis.
58 Setor de Direitos Humanos – MST, 'As ocupaçcões de terras são constitucionais, legítimas e necessárias', São Paulo, April 1997.
59 Author interview with Luiz Eduardo Greenhalgh, 3 September 1999.
60 Author interview with Ministro Luiz Vicente Cernicchiaro, 22 October 1999.
61 Ibid.
62 Ibid.
63 Author interview with Luiz Eduardo Greenhalgh, 3 September 1999.
64 Ibid.
65 Ministério Público Federal, Procuradoria dos Direitos do Cidadão, 'Relatório da Viagem ao Pontal do Paranapanema', prepared by Wagner Gonçalves, Subprocurador-Gerla da República, Brasília, 21 February 1996, pp. 13–14. (Document is dated 1996 but was produced in 1997.)
66 As well as heading the Associação Brasileira de Reforma Agrária (Brazilian Association of Agrarian Reform, ABRA) for many years, in 2003 he was responsible for drawing up the President Lula da Silva's proposals for a National Plan of Agrarian Reform. These proposals, which included the resettlement of one million families between 2004 and 2007, were subsequently diluted (to the annoyance of Sampaio and his colleagues) into the actual Plan itself which hoped to resettle 400,000 families.
67 Author interview with Luiz Antonio Marrey, 17 March 2000.
68 Author interview with Dra Ines do Amaral Buschel, 6 June 1997.
69 Author interview with Luiz Antonio Marrey, 17 March 2000.
70 This was by way of Act 011/97 of the Procurador Geral de Justiça (Pt. No. 10.427/97).
71 Mimeo Ato No. 011/97 – PGJ de 18 fevereiro de 1997 (Pt. No. 10.427/97), article 2, subsection V.
72 Ibid., preamble.
73 Author interview with Paulo Sérgio Ribeiro da Silva, 9 September 1999.
74 Author interview with Paulo Afonso Garrido de Paula, 17 April 2000.
75 Author interview with Raul Jungmann, 5 April 2000. For a collection that brings together most of these laws see Gabinete do Ministro Extraordinário de Política Fundiária, Instituto Nacional de Colonização e Reforma Agrária, *Mudanças legais que melhoraram as ações da reforma agrária*, Brasília, 1998.
76 Luiz Antônio Marrey cited in 'Promotores criam comissão', *Oeste Notícias*, 5 February 1997.

77 Ibid.

78 Paulo Afonso Garrido de Paula, *A intervenção do Ministério Público nas ações possessórias envolvendo conflitos coletivos pela posse de terra rural*, São Paulo: Mimeo, May 1997.

79 Mimeo Processo Crime No. 598/95 Comarca Presidente Prudente, São Paulo, 2 March 1998.

80 Acórdão No. 189.369-3/4 da Comarca de Mirante Paranapanema, 10 August 1997, cited in Processo Crime No. 598/95 Comarca Presidente Prudente, São Paulo: Mimeo, p. 34.

81 Author interview with prosecutors André Felício, Marcos Vizusaki and Mário Coimbra, 6 September 1999.

82 Author interview with Tânia Andrade, 3 December 1999.

83 Luiz Antônio Marrey cited in 'Promotores criam comissão', *Oeste Notícias*, 5 February 1997.

Chapter 3

Why Law Fails

The Administration of Land Law in the Context of Power Relations

> Despite the fact that Brazil must improve a lot, it nevertheless has good legislation – be it environmental, indigenous, agrarian. It is sufficient for the state to be able to carry out structural changes. The lack of laws isn't the issue.
>
> Rolf Hackbart, President of INCRA[1]

> The perspective of the Public Ministry ... is that it is all a question of the law – that I have to carry out the law. Look, the law emerges from a complex of relations. Sure, you have to carry out the law, that's right, but it is folly to go into combat on the terrain of the adversary because he wins – and there, with the relation of forces, they [landowners] always win.
>
> Raul Jungmann, Minister of Agrarian Reform[2]

This chapter looks at attempts by INCRA, the national land reform agency, to carry out legally prescribed land audits in the far south of the country, in the Bagé region of Rio Grande do Sul state. As we shall see, the legal system here would conform more closely to more positive stereotypes of the South noted in the Introduction. Far from exhibiting passivity or omission so common in other parts of the country, the legal apparatus (courts, Federal Public Ministry and police) proved proactive in their defence of land reform laws, as indeed was INCRA.

The significance of these events arises from the fact that despite a high degree of institutional convergence and good intentions, especially the desire to uphold the rule of law in general and land reform law in particular, the net result was total failure. The events discussed in this chapter are symptomatic of more deep-seated problems and failures – among which one may count President Lula da Silva's inability to update land productivity indices throughout his two terms in office.

The events discussed cannot be captured within crude discourses (so prevalent among academics, aid and donor agencies) that relate problems of development to 'corruption' while eschewing questions of class. This case study explains some of the complexities behind the lack of progress on land reform under the administration of Fernando Henrique Cardoso and is useful to understand issues facing other reforming governments. It typifies the dynamics prevalent in so many countries, the centrality of power relations to the operation of law itself or, expressed more narrowly, law's contingency in the face of landed interests. That is a lesson worth learning (and relearning) because, among other things, it puts discussions of law reform into much needed perspective. As Hackbart rightly puts it: 'The lack of laws isn't the issue.' For solutions one must think about the social construction of law.

Bringing Land Reform to Bagé

The town of Bagé lies in the extreme south of Brazil, some 400 kilometres southwest of Porto Alegre, Rio Grande do Sul's state capital, near the border with Uruguay (see Figure 4). Despite its rather remote location, Bagé is far

Figure 4 Map of Rio Grande do Sul including Bagé

from being a political backwater. One of its sons, Emílio Médici became Brazil's president (1969–74) and presided over both the 'economic miracle', growth rates of up to 14 per cent, and the military dictatorship's most brutal phase of repression. Landed groups here are among the most assertive in Brazil. Notwithstanding a series of election results testifying to the diminution of their power, their reach continues to extend into the heart of Rio Grande do Sul's politics and beyond. As well as its political reputation, Bagé enjoys a formidable economic weight. For many years it was the undisputed capital to Brazil's highly-mechanised rice sector (accounting for 46 per cent of total rice production in 1992–93).[3] The sector, still one of the most productive in Latin America, helped Brazil become the world's tenth largest rice exporter in 2008. Rice yields in this region have maintained a sharp upward trend, more than doubling in the last 20 years.[4]

In stark contrast, the Bagé region has long possessed a significant cattle ranching sector where there was serious room for doubt over productivity levels. Productivity was (and remains) important because although Brazil's 1988 constitution makes it clear that 'productive property' is a legal defence against expropriation (article 185 stated that expropriation of such properties was 'not permitted'), it also makes it clear that low productivity levels potentially open the way to state expropriation. Thus when the region was targeted by INCRA for productivity studies in the late 1990s as a possible prelude to expropriations, a head-on conflict ensued between the cattle sector on the one hand, and a variety of legal and administrative institutions (including INCRA) on the other.

Land audit powers: vistorias

Whatever the complexity of the legal cases that subsequently arose, one thing is clear, in seeking to conduct land audits the land agency was acting well within its powers. These may be briefly stated in the following terms. By law, INCRA is the body charged with deciding whether a property is productive or not. It does so on the basis of standard formulae, calculated by agricultural economists and tailored to the specific characteristics of the land in question, such as its fertility, chemical composition, topography, susceptibility to flooding, accessibility and areas of environmental preservation.[5] In order to make these tailored assessments, a wide range of data are needed. In the case of cattle ranches, for instance, they may include satellite photos, vaccination certificates, tax returns, sales figures, etc. However, given the notoriously precarious nature of much documentation, for example tax returns based on self-assessment, an indispensable source is the onsite inspection, or *vistoria*. It is a particularly useful means of crosschecking data.

Crucially, implementation of on-site inspections is backed up by force of law authorising INCRA 'to enter the private property, in order to gather data and information'.[6] If at the end of this procedure the land is held to be sufficiently productive that is an end to the matter. If, on the other hand, it is deemed unproductive, then it is for the agency to propose expropriation and either pay compensation by consent or, if necessary, contest the matter in court and, if successful, pay a sum fixed by the courts.

Far from a definitive knockout blow to unproductive properties *vistorias* are merely part of an exploratory administrative mechanism whose conclusions can ultimately be challenged in a court of law. According to one leading study, the prices paid for expropriated land throughout Brazil are substantially inflated by those courts. Taking INCRA's land settlements (approximately 1,600) created between 1986 and 1994 as their sampling universe, Shiki *et al.* concluded that: 'The disparity of costs between regions cannot merely be explained by differentials in the price of land and may be being determined by specific relations of power between INCRA, the large landowners and the legal system.' More specifically, they concluded that 'In obtaining land, it was the compensatory elements of judicial sentences that most influenced the final price.' They find that, depending upon the region, the legal system multiplies the cost of land by a factor of anywhere between one and 14 times, and that for Brazil as a whole the average figure is a factor of 5.01.[7]

Evidence suggests that the legal system provides numerous points of intervention and offers real opportunities for vitiating prospects of land reform, even rendering expropriation a profitable business for the expropriated. Yet in Bagé landowners took the unusual step of seeking to disarm the process of *vistorias* using tactics of mass direct action more commonly associated with the MST. Why?

The roots of conflict

Two key elements stand out: the emergence of the perception that vital interests were at stake, that events might not go their way; and the view that the threat bore a mass character, that is the capacity to swallow up literally hundreds of properties in one go.

Although many factors were involved in the escalation of conflict, such as the contribution of the União Democrática Ruralista (UDR) and associated landowners' organisations to the solidification of opposition to the *vistorias*, the development of a unified front was made that much easier by the prospect of more than 400 properties entering the inspection process. The UDR and others could raise the spectre of Bagé and surrounding areas as becoming the next Pontal do Paranapanema, an anathema to these producers. There was more than a grain of truth to their fears at least insofar as the MST had its sights on the region and had openly called for INCRA to audit these properties. Thus the overriding objective of landowners became the prevention of INCRA from getting its foot in the door either on its own terms or on a large scale.

INCRA's apparently provocative decision to go for mass surveys as opposed to a less combative and more gradualist policy needs to be seen in the context of past failures. Put simply, gradualism had run its course. Land reform was moving forward at a snail's pace. A perception had even grown within INCRA itself that it might represent a significant obstacle to change insofar as its failure to update productivity indices (see next section) effectively guaranteed the status quo and stymied the prospects of land reform. Bagé was significant because it held out the prospect of providing a long overdue impetus to the reform process.

The problem of productivity

Within the context of highly polarised and politicised land distribution, the National Constituent Assembly's adoption of productive property as a constitutional defence against expropriation represented a veritable hostage to fortune. Bagé graphically illustrates the consequences of that Assembly's decision, since events in Bagé would hinge upon the question of precisely what was, or was not, a productive property.

Rising productivity trends have long been observed in agriculture, as well as industry, as various forms of capital intensification and new production techniques have been introduced. The term 'green revolution', however problematic, captured a sense of those leaps in agricultural productivity. Given the contextually determined nature of productivity, it is no surprise that benchmark indices should move upwards to reflect technological and other developments. And yet, in Rio Grande do Sul's rice sector, for instance, it was well known that INCRA's indices of 3.4 thousand kilos per hectare were far behind actual rates of production of 5.1 thousand kilos per hectare.[8] As one INCRA technician put it: 'Technology has doubled land's productive capacity, but the requirement of kilos per hectare stopped at the beginning of the 1970s.'[9]

Who might benefit from this state of affairs? Clearly the answer was anyone who failed to produce at or above an updated figure, and whose land might therefore be reclassified as unproductive and subject to expropriation. In the case of cattle farmers, the divergence between producers and the agency were deemed unacceptable by landowners. On the basis of information (such as vaccination certificates) provided by landowners, INCRA calculated that each hectare could sustain 360 kilos of live animals, in other words 80 per cent, or 0.8 of what is termed an Animal Unit (AU) of 450 kilos. For their part, the ranchers proposed an AU of 0.6, in other words, of 270 kilos per annum.

The landowners respond

Landowners not only felt that their immediate interests were at stake, but that so too was the future modality of the land reform programme within Rio Grande do Sul, if not beyond. Knock the policy off course here and it would have a destabilising impact elsewhere. They were, however, faced with one major difficulty. Initially, at least, there was little they could do to stop

INCRA from adopting 0.8 of an AU as its chosen unit of measure. Drawing lines on paper was something the agency was good at and, in this particular instance, was its exclusive prerogative. Ranchers responded by highlighting any study or statistic that would cast doubt on the INCRA findings,[10] however this was unlikely to deliver a mortal blow to its work. Instead of meeting the agency exclusively on its terms, therefore, they tried to shift the terms of engagement away from university and agricultural institutes towards the corridors of power, courtrooms and even streets in the belief (correct as it turned out) that this was the best way of stopping the agency in its tracks.

The Unfolding Dynamics of Conflict: Phase One

In August 1997 farmers officially presented a document contesting INCRA's productivity indices. However it was only February 1998, when INCRA began to send out notices of intent to audit properties and farmers were obliged to take a position, that events really took off.

Various factors led to the creation of a mindset of resistance. The agricultural sector in Rio Grande do Sul was suffering an economic crisis stimulated by liberalisation, including the development of the South American trading alliance of Mercosul and the loss of competitiveness to other regions within Brazil. The persistence of unfavourable exchange rates over a four-year period, followed by elevated interest rates, ate into profits and contributed to an increasingly indebted agricultural sector. Farmers felt threatened and some were selling up.

Politically the region was predisposed to resistance given its intense dislike of the MST and deep suspicion of a state agency devoted to land reform. In Santana do Livramento, a municipality close to Bagé, the local council had just passed a law authorising the creation of a militia to deal with land occupations, and on local radio stations men were being called to arms.[11] In Bagé, the mayor articulated the hostility felt towards INCRA. Standing on top of a truck during a demonstration outside the hotel where INCRA technicians were staying, he declared: 'INCRA has no morals for anything. While I am mayor they will not do anything here!'[12]

More pragmatic reasons for resisting the *vistorias* arose from the claimed capacity of any subsequent land settlements to permanently alter the local balance of power – 'large scale settlements in a region lead to the social, political and economic disintegration of the municipality'.[13] In the specific case of Bagé, the mayor will doubtless have had in mind the loss of the nearby municipality of Hulha Negra to the Partido dos Trabalhadores (Workers' Party – PT) in 1997 by a margin of 12 votes. Not only were there seven nearby settlements with a substantial demographic/electoral potential, but also the MST campaigned hard for the PT candidate. It could be argued that the mayor's worst fears were realised in the November 2000 elections, when the PT succeeded in securing the election of its candidate as mayor of Bagé.

Such associations between the MST electoral power should be treated with caution. The connections are complex and contradictory. Whatever the MST's other mass characteristics electoral homogeneity is not one of them. In any case, the movement's presence needs to be seen in the context of other electoral dynamics. Only in this way can one begin to explain why, for example, the November 2000 elections that saw Bagé fall to the PT also saw Hulha Negra slip from its grasp into the hands of the Democratic Labour Party (Partido Trabalhista Democratico – PDT) – notwithstanding the continued presence of MST settlements. Other factors in these elections included overcoming the divisions that had beset Hulha Negra's rightwing during the 1997 vote, and the catastrophic record of Bagé's administration (which had failed to pay its workers for almost a year) prior to the 2000 result.

By the middle of February the UDR suggested to sympathisers that they should not countersign INCRA's notices of intent. On the 19th, at a mass gathering of more than 400 farmers from around Bagé, the Agricultural Federation of Rio Grande do Sul (Federação da Agricultura do Rio Grande do Sul – FARSUL), formalised the position on a range of issues. No farmer would countersign notices of intent until the productivity indices were altered, FARSUL would make an official request at the highest levels (in Brasília) that the audits be suspended pending the calculation of new more farmer-friendly indices, and INCRA would be questioned over its 'real motives'. In addition, through its legal advisor, FARSUL gave farmers guidance about techniques and the legal implications of resistance.[14]

INCRA snatches defeat from the jaws of victory

Landowners had a powerful local ally in the governor of Rio Grande do Sul: Antônio Britto (1995–98). During his re-election campaign he had made all the right noises. INCRA, he said:

> …labours under a number of illusions. The first one is that whoever invades land has the right to it. This is the first place in the world where the agency of land reform stimulates invasions … Yes, there must be land reform, but with seriousness and serenity.[15]

Britto made these comments at the beginning of May 1998. The governor's problem, however, was that events were closing in on him. Just as INCRA had forced the hand of the farmers, who had opted for the tactic of civil disobedience, so too INCRA had been forced to consider the legal options. Having found their way blocked by more than 150 protestors and 50 vehicles on 7 April,[16] lawyers for inspectors from INCRA sought, and obtained, an injunction five days later. One clause of Judge Picarelli's decision stated 'if the need arises I authorise the requisition of police reinforcements to accompany workers from INCRA in the land inspection duties'.[17] While Britto might have sympathised with the protestors, his deputy, Vicente Bogo, who was acting governor during the electoral campaign, would soon be faced with the dilemma of whether to send in the troops, as the judicial decree required. If he did, it would be the first time in Brazil's history that the military police were used in large numbers to enforce a land audit. The stakes were high and all sides were now set on a collision course.

Incredibly, in what was to become one of many retreats, INCRA climbed down. A day after the judge's decision became public, INCRA, finding itself newly empowered, announced that it would, after all, suspend its land audits in Bagé. One newspaper suggested '[t]he insistence and vitality of the Bagé rural producers' actions against the criteria used by INCRA in its *vistorias* of the region achieved its first victory.'[18] It certainly was a remarkable victory, snatched from the jaws of a legal defeat. For the governor it brought welcome relief.

The official reason given for suspension was the pending discussions between Raul Jungmann (the Minister for Agrarian Reform), Gedeão Pereira (leader of the Bagé farmers union) and Carlos Sperotto (leader of FARSUL). While it has to be said that the suspension of 'hostilities' is a common tactic pending talks, it was equally clear to most observers that INCRA's overall strategy was veering dramatically off course. Further evidence of this came a day later, in Brasília, with proposals by the head of INCRA, Milton Seligmann, that a commission be created to re-examine the indices in Bagé. For the land-owners, one of whose goals had been reconsideration, this represented a major concession. They had forced their foot in the door and, emboldened, were determined to open it wider. Continuing their offensive, they pushed to expand the commission's remit to include indices for the whole of Rio Grande do Sul, rather than the municipalities of Bagé, Candiota and Hulha Negra, as INCRA had proposed. Seligman was left to paper over the cracks and reconcile the irreconcilable. 'The negotiations', he said, 'are continuing in order to guarantee the tranquillity of the producers and, at the same time, to maintain the process of agrarian reform.'[19] Shortly after, Administrative Decree 170 of the Ministry for Agrarian Reform officially created the commission. As one newspaper headline put it, 'The government gives way to the pressures of the producers'.[20] However, tension remained on the ground as the agency pushed ahead with audits in a spasmodic fashion.

In Brasília, the landowners lobbied with all forces at their disposal, including federal deputies associated with their cause – the so-called '*bancada rural-ista*', or ruralist block. A month after the meeting with Seligman, members of the ruralist block from the Agriculture Commission of the Chamber of Deputies, met with the Minister for Agrarian Reform, Raul Jungmann, to press their cause.[21] As well as discussing productivity indices and the progress of the commission, they suggested that the minister buy rather than expropriate land, an issue that we return to in some detail later on. Although these activities of national coordination were significant, and this was the level at which many of the key decisions would ultimately be taken, leverage came from the capacity to maintain the pace and pressure of events on the ground. In this respect, the ranchers were not found wanting.

Alongside avenues of institutional politics and street protests, landowners sought to wrong-foot INCRA in the courts. Several tactics were employed in this legal offensive. One was to request a judicial suspension of INCRA's work. This failed on two occasions; the agency was deemed legally entitled to go about its business. Another tactic entailed owners absenting themselves from properties, despite prior notification by INCRA, in the hope that if the audit went ahead without their presence it would be considered an invasion of property and therefore illegal. This led to limited success, since the judge only suspended audits pending the presentation of a comprehensive timetable of visits by INCRA to the Bagé producers association. Finally, in August 1998, towards the end of the first phase of the dispute, in a move coordinated through the farmers' organisation, the National Confederation of Agriculture (Confederação Nacional da Agricultura – CNA), the legality of the administrative instruments governing the implementation of indices was called into question. The CNA suggested that the relevant statutory instrument, INCRA's Normativa 08 of 1993, had neither been approved by the competent authorities, nor published in the official digest, the *Diario Oficial*. As a consequence, it held no legal force and therefore could not be applied.[22] If this was indeed the case, then there was a real possibility that land audits would unravel at the seams – not just in Bagé or Rio Grande do Sul, but throughout Brazil. While an interesting strategy with potentially far reaching implications, the judicial scrutiny of Normativa 08 never came about, eventually being overtaken by other unexpected developments discussed below.

Surprisingly, perhaps, the courts afforded the landowners little succour during the dispute. Perhaps this also had something to do with the more progressive stance of the judiciary in the south, although that should not be exaggerated. INCRA was on very strong legal ground. In the event, however, INCRA chose to relinquish that advantage altogether. This says much about its internal contradictions, the fragility of the organisation in the sphere of institutional politics and the countervailing power of extra-institutional social mobilisation.[23] These developments left the agency facing two ways. In the federal capital, Brasília, the core of INCRA policy (the indices) was at risk of a partial meltdown, while in Rio Grande do Sul the method of enforcement, *vistorias*, was beginning to gather a momentum of its own.

Landowners and legal institutions collide

The Federal Public Ministry and courts became involved with events in Bagé because they raised issues about the failure of a federal institution (INCRA) to carry out its legally appointed tasks. While the independence of federal agencies from local influence should not be overstated, they were, nevertheless, at one remove from the dispute. This may partly explain the Federal Public Ministry's willingness to commence investigating the legality of Mayor Azambuja's declaration that '[w]hile I am mayor they will not do anything here'[24] – a clear incitement to non-compliance. It may also explain the willingness of Judge Picarelli to cite powerful local figures like Azambuja and Gedeão Pereira in his injunction of 12 April. The facts of the case also spoke for themselves, so it is difficult to see how, on purely legal grounds alone, he could have rejected the petition. As Judge Picarelli notes:

> In this case, INCRA is engaged in the legitimate exercise of administrative powers of policing, for it is carrying out *vistorias* in conformity with the constitutional obligations set out in Art 5, XXIII and XXIV, which establish the limitations to the right to property in favour of the collectivity ... the right of rural producers to demonstrate not only collides with the right of technicians to move freely, but it impedes the Administration from exercising the power of administrative policing and, as a consequence, executing the public service determined by the federal constitution and by law number 8.629/93.[25]

Whether due to the independent-mindedness of the individuals concerned, the facts and dynamics of the case, or the institutional setting, decision after decision began to go in INCRA's favour. In August, for example, as an indirect consequence of the court's decision to authorise the use of federal police reinforcements, the lawyer to the Bagé rural producers' association was arrested in the course of an extremely tense confrontation in which shots were fired and a member of the Federal Public Ministry and technicians from INCRA were barred entry to an inspection site.[26] On 25 August Judge Picarelli was asked to consider a request from the Federal Public Ministry for the 'preventive imprisonment' of a list of leading representatives from the leading producers' organisation, FARSUL, including its head, Carlos Sperotto.[27]

The symbolic significance of this last act is hard to overestimate. Charges of this kind, including resistance, incitement and the formation of gangs, were routinely laid at the door of the MST, not landowners. And on those rare occasions when they did stand accused, it was hired hands who usually stood in the dock. The idea that powerbrokers should be charged and, by implication, that collective political groupings be placed in the dock, was unheard of.

Pressure began to mount upon the justice system itself. The court, but more especially the Federal Public Ministry, became issues in their own right. 'We have', said the judge in reference to the landowners, 'tried to conciliate, but now they are in the realm of illegality. There is a lack of good sense.'[28] He noted his participation in five meetings since April with INCRA and landowners, and how the latter had employed every legal artifice to impede land audits. As for the Federal Public Ministry, one prosecutor in particular, Marcos Vinicius Aguiar Macedo, came to be seen as a threat to ranchers and 'out to get them'. Rio Grande do Sul's leading daily newspaper, *Zero Hora*, branded him 'the tormentor of rural producers'.[29] Recognising these difficulties, the Federal Public Ministry placed a newspaper advert clarifying the situation. Among other things, the advertisement stated that the actions of the Public Ministry were carried out in strict conformity with its legal obligations and that the prosecutor had intervened personally to try and render the law effective while leaving the search for precise solutions to the contending parties.[30] The Public Ministry's head in Rio Grande do Sul, João Carlos de Carvalho Rocha, similarly felt obliged to make a public statement. 'Prosecutor Macedo', he said, 'was not, and is not, the tormentor of rural producers. He merely carried out his duty of mediating the situation in an attempt to find a solution via legal means ... Indeed, the Public Ministry has nothing against the producers. At the same time, however, we will not allow citizens, be they rural producers or not, to carry out civil disobedience.'[31]

The politics of mediation and prosecution

Despite occasional protestations to the contrary, the work of prosecutors is necessarily political. The gravity of the problems encountered in developing countries like Brazil, and manifest inability to meet the scale of legal obligations, put subsequent choices into sharp relief. A considerable degree of discretion also left prosecutors 'free' to define their agenda in the realms of investigation, prosecution and mediation or combination thereof. Mediation would prove crucial to the Federal Public Ministry's profile in Bagé.

Theoretically speaking, mediation offered scope for resolution of the conflict beyond the courts. The Federal Public Ministry had to reconcile several conflicting imperatives, principal among these being the desire to seek a negotiated settlement within a timeframe that would allow it to vindicate the rule of law. These factors, combined with the lack of time, high degree of polarisation and volatility of the situation clearly demanded a political rather than technical reading of events.

Powerful evidence of this comes from internal INCRA documents. A report produced in May 1998 by INCRA's re-registration arm, RECAD (an abbreviation of the word *recadastramento*, re-registration), makes clear how external intervention came about, with the mediatory rather than condemnatory role of the legal system, and finally, the sustained nature of that intervention:

> Feeling itself impeded from maintaining the rate of work initially foreseen, and fearing for the physical safety of its members, INCRA's technical team in Bagé decided to request the mediation of the Federal Justice in order to guarantee its land audit activities. After all, the alternative that faced the team was either to reach an agreement with the landowners, or to go ahead with the land audits but accompanied by a police force of colossal proportions, involving both the federal police and the army...

Through the Federal Courts in Bagé, and with the presence of the [Federal] Public Ministry, three meetings between the leaders of the landowners in Bagé and the leadership of RECAD were held, the aim of which was to arrive at a proposal with regard to INCRA activities in Bagé that could attend to the minimum requirements of both parties.[32]

The report goes on to detail their positions, irreconcilable differences, and their joint memorandum of understanding of 5 May 1998, to which both the Federal Public Ministry and federal courts were signatories. Indeed the report notes that the agreement 'was only possible as a function of mediation'.[33] The terms of this accord allowed INCRA to audit those properties whose owners consented, provided that the number of audits was scaled down from three to one per working day. In return, landowners would guarantee that INCRA inspectors would achieve at least 16 unimpeded audits by 25 May.

Despite representing a breakthrough of sorts, events within Judge Picarelli's office lacked the potential to stimulate a broader dynamic of conciliation. Like the eye of the storm, this haven of relative calm was subject to the swirl of forces outside. It was an illusory calm. All sides, knew this. The only conceivable way of reversing the situation would have been to send in a police force, something INCRA was unwilling to countenance. A revealing passage of the RECAD document shows that the federal courts and Public Ministry were not entirely happy with the situation:

Both expressed some concern to coordinators from RECAD regarding manifestations of indecision and weakness shown by leaders of INCRA from the beginning of RECAD's work. Amongst these manifestations they included the very decision to revise the indices and the hesitant and extremely slow attitude with regard to the use of police powers as prescribed in law. According to them, successive displays of indecision and the failure to take clear measures that would guarantee the work of RECAD progressively strengthened the landowners' movement and its sense of power while demonstrating the institutional weakness of INCRA.

The Public Ministry also manifested its concern that, while INCRA planned a strategy of implementation involving significant human, material and financial resources, it did not foresee the level of political support necessary to guarantee the execution of those activities, leaving its technical team exposed.[34]

Even if it did not go into much detail, the Federal Public Ministry's analysis of INCRA was, in many respects, faultless – drawing attention to the contingent nature of administrative action and the question of its political preconditions and sustainability in the face of an onslaught from landowners.

While this situation undoubtedly represented a problem for INCRA, since it was failing in its legal obligations, it also posed difficulties for the Federal Public

Ministry. Functions specifically attributed to it by the Brazilian constitution included 'to ensure effective respect by the public authorities and by the services of public relevance for the rights guaranteed in this constitution, taking the action required to guarantee such rights'; and 'to institute civil investigation and public civil suit to protect public and social property, the environment and other diffuse and collective interests.'[35] Evidently these issues were germane to the present conflict.

Rather than a triumph, then, it could be argued that the accord brokered by the Federal Public Ministry on 5 May represented a conscious shelving of that duty (from three audits per day to one) with the consequent knock-on effects upon INCRA's resettlement strategy in Rio Grande do Sul. This reinforces the notion that events were generating a political reading of events.

That INCRA lurched from crisis to crisis was hardly surprising given its organisational and ideological divisions. The agency had tentacles spreading from Bagé back to Brasília and nationwide. From a merely technical point of view, coordinating these instances was a complicated task, one made all the more difficult by ideological divisions. But whatever the stark realities in Bagé, once transferred to Brasília issues were mediated by a quite different set of considerations and dynamics, including the tug of national policies and constituencies. Among very powerful circles within INCRA and the Ministry of Agrarian Reform (see following section), it was felt that enforcing the law, with all that this course of action entailed, constituted a political problem and costly luxury the agency could ill afford. Perhaps the conflict could be resolved by jettisoning an expropriatory model in favour of a more market-oriented approach, i.e., buying up land by consent.

This highly controversial proposition was not widely accepted, especially in Rio Grande do Sul, but because these differences were never resolved they manifested themselves as mixed messages regarding enforcement. An internal document signed by all departmental heads in Rio Grande do Sul effectively acknowledges this fact. In June 1998 they requested clear guidance from INCRA nationally, as well as political support, noting that, 'The formation of the Commission [to revise the agricultural indices for the state of Rio Grande do Sul], in the face of the pressure of landowners in Bagé and of FARSUL, was seen by society and the employees of this agency as an act of fragility on the part of INCRA.'[36] They went on to argue that in addition to the failure to meet their own targets, repositioning the indices might even lead to the unravelling of other cases that had already been decided by the courts, since new indices would 'transform properties hitherto classified as unproductive into productive ones.'[37] Other legal ramifications cited included 'relinquishing a provision made in law that determines that indices must be fixed "in such a way as to take into account the scientific and technological progress of cattle rearing and regional development".'[38] More seriously, they expressed the fear that 'ceding to the pressure of the landowners implies relinquishing articles of the constitution relating to the expropriation of rural properties that are not fulfilling their social function.'[39] Their concerns underlined from within the powerlessness of the state's legal and administrative agencies and, seemingly, the worthlessness of the constitution itself.

The termination of phase one

It is difficult to provide a precise date at which the Bagé episode concluded. As with the legal proceedings, one must talk instead of the emergence of a trend that culminated towards the end of August 1998, with strands postdating this time. Regarding the proceedings, for example, it was only in late October that the Federal Regional Court (Tribunal Regional Federal) would adjudicate on the principle of whether associations and federations such as FARSUL could be held legally and financially responsible over their actions in support of blockades. Indeed, this response arose as a consequence of Judge Picarelli's September decision to grant INCRA's injunction request.[40] There is, however, no question about how the conflict ended. A decision was taken at the highest levels to end it and that ultimately meant that once again INCRA had to shift its position, quite literally ceding ground. For the governor, the timing was not quite as fortuitous as INCRA's decision to step back from the brink in April. Some weeks later, on 25 August, the deputy governor, Vicente Bogo, was obliged to provide more than 400 troops (a sizeable contingent) in order to guarantee the audit of the Fazenda Rodeio Colorado. On the following day, the head of INCRA, Milton Seligmann reached an agreement with landowners that foresaw the termination of two judicially sanctioned audits as well as the abandonment of 24 other previously agreed audits. A cooling off period of 30 days was also put into place.

These actions were coordinated with the Ministry of Agriculture, the traditional bastion of support for landed interests, and were announced by the Minister of Agriculture himself, Francisco Turra. He said that, 'From the moment landowners acknowledge respect for the law and the institute has conducted its role [terminating a handful of judicially sanctioned audits], lands will be bought from those who want to sell them. The question is resolved.'[41] Although he went on to suggest that 'It is a decision that does not inflict a major defeat on anyone',[42] it is notable that the leader of FARSUL, Carlos Sperotto pronounced himself well satisfied with the deal while INCRA in Rio Grande do Sul remained conspicuously silent.

Signalling the shift in policy, the Minister of Agrarian Reform, Raul Jungmann, announced a personal visit to the state the following week with the express intention of buying substantial quantities of land (up to 30,000 hectares) via the local stock exchange.[43] He offered the intellectual justification for this shift in an article for the leading daily *Folha de São Paulo*.

> The legal framework of expropriation [*instituto de desapropriação*] is hardly compatible with land settlement en mass; its efficacy in regions like the

South and Southeast is declining. The cost benefit ratio is falling inexorably while the fiscal costs of the programme are rising.[44]

Post-mortem

The policy of *vistorias* was effectively dead in this part of Brazil. Official confirmation would come in the form of a hastily arranged ceremony in Brasília, where the deceased was laid to rest. On 17 September, Milton Seligmann, the head of INCRA, announced that due to the need to make financial savings of nine per cent, re-registrations of *all* property throughout Brazil would be postponed until 1999. Seligmann was at pains to point out that this global halt also meant an end to audits in Bagé. Not surprisingly, the leader of Bagé's landowners celebrated the occasion. 'What lovely news', he said, 'peace has returned to Bagé'.[45] The following day INCRA's inspectors packed their bags and went home.

Perhaps it was hoped that the extra three months would lead to the emergence of another dynamic altogether, or that the purchase of land would resolve the problem, or perhaps all that really mattered at this stage was the diminution of conflict and re-election prospects of President Fernando Henrique Cardoso. As one journalist noted, 'the order for the Minister of Agrarian Reform and INCRA to avoid radicalising the situation with the landowners of Bagé came from him. Fernando Henrique wants their [the landowners'] votes in October.'[46] Whatever the factors leading to a 'solution', its strictly temporary nature became all too apparent in the course of 1999 in the second phase of the dispute.

Phase Two of the Bagé Conflict

Early in this chapter it was suggested that developments in Bagé typify patterns and dynamics prevalent throughout Brazil. They highlight certain types of power relations and disposition of forces over sustained periods of time. The well-delineated nature of these forces lends events a depressingly predictable quality. All parties would largely act according to type, whether it was Minister Jungmann administering the conflict, landowners defending their interests, the state of Rio Grande do Sul forwarding its policies, or judges and the Federal Public Ministry acceding to INCRA's requests. Phase two of the conflict would turn upon broadly the same issue, namely the setting of productivity indices and whether INCRA would be permitted to carry out land audits. Although the various parties acted predictably, they did so in the context of new political circumstances. Fernando Henrique Cardoso had succeeded in his November presidential re-election bid, and Raul Jungmann was reappointed to his old office, but the national and local correlation of forces had shifted considerably.

Dealing with the national picture first, by early July 1999, as part of his coalition balancing act, Cardoso announced a number of ministerial changes.

These included the replacement of the Minister of Agriculture, Francisco Turra (a thorn in the side of certain now more powerful allies), with Marcus Vinícius Pratini de Moraes. The latter was a member of the right-wing Brazilian Popular Party (Partido Popular Brasileiro – PPB) and was on very good terms with the president of another right-wing party and coalition ally, the Party of the Liberal Front (Partido da Frente Liberal – PFL). Ostensibly brought on board to strengthen Brazil's agricultural exports at a time of increasing global protectionism, Pratini de Moraes brought with him not just his much vaunted skills as an economist, but a curriculum vitae that symbolised Brazil's authoritarian military past and limitations of its democratic present.

While Cardoso, Jungmann and other 'left' allies were busy reinventing themselves and shifting social democracy to the political right,[47] Pratini de Moraes had maintained a remarkably even keel. During a 30-year period spanning the transition to democracy, Pratini de Moraes assembled an impressive array of top federal ministerial offices including Planning, Industry and Commerce, Mines and Energy and now Agriculture. These were held during the military governments of Marechal Costa e Silva (1967–69), Emílio Médici (1970–74), and, albeit briefly, the civilian administration of Fernando Collor de Mello (1990–92). Furthermore, although the Planning and Mines and Energy portfolios were held for relatively short periods, these were supplemented by his non-ministerial appointments and role at the nerve centre of the authoritarian project, as head of General Costa e Silva's special advisors, and as cabinet secretary. His reappearance in the second Cardoso administration is therefore revealing, suggesting that he was there to shore up the president's fortunes in the face of a changed electoral conjuncture. By cementing Cardoso's right-wing alliance, Pratini de Moraes' inclusion simultaneously made that government more responsive to certain class interests and undermined the more liberal aspects of social policy. Nowhere is this more evident than in relation to the question of land reform, an area that theoretically, at least, lay at the periphery of his ministry, but which Pratini de Moraes increasingly sought to subordinate to his will. Those interests soon became apparent in the Bagé.

Dealing with the second concern here (the regional situation), this had changed beyond recognition. Rio Grande do Sul now had a new governor. Out went Antônio Britto, and with him the best hope landowners had of a political alliance, and in came Olivio Dutra (1999–2003) of the Workers' Party (PT). For Carlos Sperotto (a member of Pratini de Moraes' PPB) and other landowners, the distinct improvement of the national picture was offset by the electoral defeat suffered at the state level. A new state government had emerged that was firmly committed to land reform. This was graphically symbolised by the setting up of the Extraordinary Land Reform Secretariat (Secretaria Extraordinária da Reforma Agrária) within the government (although its powers were legally and financially circumscribed when compared to those of INCRA). The appointment of Frei Sérgio Görgen, a leading land activist with close ties to the MST, as its head seemed to confirm the landowners' worst fears. Görgen had been closely involved in the genesis of the MST and, only a year before his appointment, was targeted by state police over the occupation of the Guabiju ranch in the northeastern part of the state. At the time, March 1998, state police had placed his name at the top of a list requesting his preventive imprisonment along with 13 other MST suspects. Personally and politically Görgen's appointment therefore represented a dramatic reversal of fortunes.

Compounding the shift in land reform strategies was a shift in policing and security policies. The new state Secretary for Security and Justice saw land conflicts as a social rather than police matter, a policy that would inevitably generate its own contradictions, but which for the MST nevertheless represented a positive step forward.

The above changes also affected INCRA. Although the policy of land audits had been buried in 1998, a great deal of business had been left outstanding and the land settlement timetable had slipped badly. Now, with the election of Governor Dutra, the appointment of Görgen, and the strengthening of the MST's hand in Rio Grande do Sul, a new head of steam was building up. This included suggestions that if INCRA could not do its job, then the state government would go it alone, outflanking federal initiatives by settling 10,000 families within four years.

Although the political impact of this posture was substantial, practically speaking there was never a real possibility (or necessity) of going it entirely alone. In national terms INCRA's resources dwarfed those of the state, and by law the land agency held the legal monopoly on land expropriation. A state policy of cash land purchases that deliberately marginalised INCRA would undermine that other cherished objective, the acquisition of land through expropriation rather than market forces. All sides were aware of this. What the local state possessed in terms of political willpower and not insubstantial economic resources, the agency made up for in terms of human, material and legal resources. Rather than competing or duplicating efforts, it made sense for both sides to seek an understanding. This is precisely what happened later when partnership agreements were signed between the government of Rio Grande do Sul, INCRA and the Ministry of Agrarian Reform.

The last major change to affect the region was in the leadership of INCRA itself. Unlike the appointment of Pratini de Moraes, or election of Governor Dutra, however, the full implications of Paulo Emílio Barbosa's nomination as head of INCRA in Rio Grande do Sul only became apparent as events unfolded.

The build-up to phase two of the dispute

With the formal suspension of land audits in September 1998, INCRA and progressive forces pushing for land reform had suffered a major defeat. The changed electoral circumstances of November 1998, however, meant that it was therefore only a matter of time before the issue was revisited. As is so often the case, the MST provided the catalyst. It had long been frustrated by the absence of progress shown by INCRA. João Pedro Stédile described events as 'testimony to the incompetence of INCRA'.[48] The MST was also facing pressure from its own grassroots. Almost at the same time as INCRA was privately acknowledging its own failings, landless workers encamped not far from Porto Alegre were burying their fourth child as a direct result of respiratory complications associated with malnutrition.[49] Neither INCRA's explanations, nor the landowner arguments that lower productivity ratios needed to be maintained or lowered further in order to maintain the succulence of beef[50] sat well with these stark social realities. By August 1999 the MST decided to put land audits back on the agenda. Enough was enough.

On 12 August 1999, 380 families linked to the movement occupied a ranch known as the Fazenda Capivara in Hulha Negra, a municipality on the border with Bagé. Landowners obtained an eviction order (albeit one that was subsequently overturned by a higher tribunal). Sensing and fearing the strategic implications of a successful occupation in this part of the country, the mood of landowners was uncompromising. Their view, according to the new head of INCRA, Paulo Emílio Barbosa, was that, '[w]e have a judicial order and it will be carried out at whatever cost. We will remove the people from there, whatever it takes.'[51]

In the light of newspaper reports suggesting that a conflict was 'imminent'[52] and that 200 landowners were massing to confront 1,000 landless and both sides were heavily armed, Barbosa was guided by two imperatives. Firstly the withdrawal of landless workers from the ranch, and secondly the avoidance of any direct conflict between the two parties. His unsuccessful negotiations with landowners over this and other issues ('all doors were slammed in our faces'[53]) finally led Barbosa to switch tack and concentrate efforts on a trilateral solution with the MST and Olivio Dutra's government. This finally came on 19 August. Given the significance of these negotiations, Barbosa's account merits detailed consideration:

> In the light of the failure of all attempts to set up a meeting of conciliation between the parties over the Fazenda Capivara eviction order we drew up an agreement. It was between Secretary of State for Agriculture, representing the governor of the state, INCRA and the representative of the Landless Workers' Movement. Accompanying the process was the Bagé section of the Order of Brazilian Lawyers [Ordem dos Advogados do Brasil], the Federal Public Ministry, and the state Public Ministry. We signed up to the following agreement:
>
> The state of Rio Grande do Sul promises to settle 40 families within 30 days. INCRA promises to settle 200 families within 30 days. INCRA promises that within 45 days it will recommence land audits so as to verify that property within Bagé is fulfilling its social function. As soon

as the illegal occupation ceases INCRA promises to immediately notify the landowners of the Fazenda Capivara of its intention to audit the property with a view to assessing whether it is fulfilling its social function. The occupiers of the Fazenda Capivara promise to leave it whereupon they will go to an area designated to this end by the government of the state of Rio Grande do Sul.[54]

Should INCRA ever have agreed to such an accord? Was it not being blackmailed? The prior question, surely, is whether the agency should ever have ceased in its constitutional mandate to audit properties in the first place. In any case, there was the immediate issue that landowners were giving it little choice given their intention to enforce the judicial order come what may. The desperate nature of the situation was underlined by a fax of 19 August sent by the National Agrarian Ombudsman to the local judge in the Bagé district, Antônio Prates Picolli, requesting him to suspend the eviction order and avoid a by then unnecessary conflict with the police.

Quite apart from the strategic implications of the land occupations in this part of the state, one feature that must have reinforced the landowners' determination was the prospect of a PT administration being obliged to supply troops for the purposes of evicting their allies in the MST. Already 60 troops had been provided, but for the express intention of keeping the sides apart rather than enforcing the judicial mandate. For obvious reasons, neither the PT nor the MST wanted to see such a turn of events. The logic propelling them towards a trilateral solution was compelling.

Raul Jungmann has suggested that other factors may have impelled the state government. In particular, due to the events on the Fazenda Capivara, and the reluctance of the state authorities to authorise troops for the purposes of eviction, landowners at this time were openly threatening a boycott of the 99th Expointer agricultural trade fair, the largest such gathering in Latin America, and, as Jungmann put it, 'a symbol of gaúcho[55] pride'. Landowners had made a resolution of the Expointer question contingent upon a resolution of the Capivara situation – which, of course, they were not prepared to defuse. Jungmann continued: 'The state government had already lost Ford,[56] it could not lose Expointer; that would have been terrible in political terms. In some senses, therefore, FARSUL wanted to blackmail the state government.'[57]

On 20 August the MST left the Fazenda Capivara as per the previous day's agreement, and the immediate situation was defused. Although the landowners, who were never party to the agreement, could not complain, since their formal demands had been met (albeit not through the hoped for course of forcible eviction), they maintained the pressure, as the spectre of land audits reappeared on the horizon. According to Minister Jungmann, this led to the strangest of meetings:

It was dramatic, something happened that I never expected to see in my life. I went to a meeting with the governor, with the MST, with the Public Ministry, and with Frei Sérgio, in which all were agreed to suspend the audits. Even the MST agreed to suspend the audits – obviously in the name of governability.[58]

It is public knowledge that Governor Dutra was seeking a way out of the impasse and had even proposed the temporary suspension of land audits.[59] In the light of this, an Interministerial Decree was published on 27 August 1999 in the *Diário Oficial* (the government gazette).[60] It heralded an agreement between ministers Jungmann and Pratini de Moraes to temporarily suspend land audits for 30 days pending the outcome of a new joint ministerial commission that would examine productivity indices in Rio Grande do Sul.

We will never know the tenor of discussions between Jungmann or Pratini de Moraes, nor understandings the latter came to with groups like FARSUL. What is certain is that the Interministerial Decree paved the way to the resumption of Expointer on 28 August.

That the MST might have come to a common understanding with Jungmann should not, in principle, be a surprise. João Pedro Stédile provides a crucial test when he remarks that 'It is necessary to negotiate, but never at the price of demobilising the movement. Otherwise you have nothing to negotiate in the future.'[61] Certainly, the MST negotiates, does deals and signs thousands of contracts with all levels of government (municipal, state and federal) in matters as diverse as the ownership and management of land and plant, the provision of technical assistance, education and even legal advice.[62] Given the MST's ability to sign contracts with international giants like Coca-Cola and Parmalat, it is hardly surprising that it was able to give signals that would benefit a close ally who was being blackmailed by landowners and as a consequence was in great difficulty. In practise, it was inconceivable that Olivio Dutra would have made proposals to suspend land audits pending definition of the indices – especially so early on in his administration – without the informal consent of the MST.

Any notion that the MST had subordinated itself to party political considerations and failed Stédile's test, having demobilised its Capivara occupation, needs to be seen in a wider light. In particular, key promises that had been secured. The state government would settle 40 families, INCRA would settle a further 200 families, and at the end of 45 days land audits in Bagé would be resumed – with the Fazenda Capivara top of the list. Given that the interministerial agreement would run out on 25 September, and that under the agreement of 19 August Bagé audits were in any case projected to start *after* 25 September, the scale of the concession to Dutra was not so great. For the moment at least, it seemed that where the combined might of INCRA and the legal system had failed in 1998, the MST might be about to succeed. The policy of land audits in Bagé was being raised from the dead.

Paulo Emílio Barbosa's appointment and significance of law

Paulo Emílio Barbosa's appointment as president of INCRA on 13 November 1998 would have a major bearing on events that nobody, not even Barbosa himself, would anticipate. Among other things it brought the tense relationship between law and politics to the fore. To many inside INCRA, Barbosa was an unknown quantity. As a ministerial appointee he was seen as a safe pair of hands with links to the outgoing governor's administration. He was a member of Governor Britto's Party of the Brazilian Democratic Movement (Partido do Movimento Democratico Brasileiro – PMDB) and had been head (and later liquidator) of the State Housing Corporation of Rio Grande do Sul (Companhia de Habitação do Estado do Rio Grande do Sul – COHAB).

Barbosa's views of the MST were hardly favourable. Press and personal reports contributed to this as did the fact that on taking office he moved into offices occupied by the MST. 'You could say', recalled Barbosa, 'that I was concerned that I would receive treatment that was not exactly respectful.'[63] He also believed that personal dealings with landowners would be easier given the widespread view that: 'they are men of culture, men of civility and so on. The MST, on the other hand, struck me as that kind of movement – one only has to see the accusations that are made in relation to members of the MST.'[64]

Barbosa was also sympathetic towards Christian social teaching. His uncle, Pedro Montenegro Barbosa, was president of the Institute of Cultural Development (Instituto de Desenvolvimento Cultural), a Christian social teaching think tank that produced its own journal and gave seminars. In an editorial on agrarian reform Pedro Barbosa commented specifically on the occupation of the Fazenda Capivara suggesting: 'It is imprudent and illegitimate attitudes such as those of the MST that have to be defeated in the course of the reform process. Agrarian Reform is not achieved through violent invasions of private property. Above all, it is a technical scientific process.'[65] In keeping with Catholic social doctrine, though, the editorial did acknowledge that property also had to fulfil a social function.

Initially Barbosa's motives for going to INCRA may have been generic: 'I went there precisely in order to help and make a contribution to this question of agrarian reform by means of which I hoped to diminish the great social problems that face our country.'[66] This, however, quickly changed. In many respects law acted as his way into the land question and oriented his subsequent conduct.

Prior to his secondment to Britto's administration and then to INCRA, Barbosa had been a senior prosecutor in the Federal Public Ministry's offices in Rio Grande do Sul. The Federal Public Ministry gave Barbosa permission to join INCRA, and it continued to pay most of his salary costs. According to Barbosa,

> Although I would be carrying out duties for a federal agency, it was felt that given the relevance of the issues – particularly their social and political aspects, and given that agrarian reform is a constitutional issue of great relevance – it would be important to have a representative of the Public Ministry there.[67]

Beyond this, it was felt that the issue lay very much within the Federal Public Ministry's area of interest, as defined, for example, by Article 82 of the Civil Legal Code (Código de Processo Civil) which, among other things, paves the way towards the defence of collective interests. In addition:

> My institution felt that it was convenient and important that one of its representatives, a member of the Public Ministry, should act directly in relation to the problems, in the sense of trying to resolve them one way or another. In other words, acting much more on the causes rather than on the effects.[68]

As Barbosa indicated, the Federal Public Ministry in Rio Grande do Sul often challenged the government over the pace of agrarian reform and in relation to other legal obligations, for example the environmental impact of land settlements, the illegal sale of plots of land, or overpayments of land. One might say, therefore, that for the Federal Public Ministry it represented a golden opportunity to push forward its constitutional mandate.

It comes as no surprise, therefore, that when as head of INCRA in Rio Grande do Sul Barbosa received requests from the Federal Public Ministry, he took these extremely seriously. Furthermore, when it came to the activation of INCRA's legal machinery over the question of land audits, it was logical that Barbosa would take a proactive legal approach.

The conflict begins in earnest

The Expointer agricultural fair had taken place and a second inter-ministerial agreement was signed on 24 September.[69] It superseded the first agreement in two key respects. Article one extended by 30 days the deadline set for the joint committee to develop new productivity indices. Article two, however, revoked article three of the first agreement that had suspended land audits and had made them contingent upon the committee's findings. In other words, a de-coupling took place that finally allowed land audits in Rio Grande do Sul to go ahead irrespective of the committee's deliberations.

Aside from its content, one feature that stands out from the agreement is the manner in which it was presented to the public. The moment it was signed attempts were made to qualify its significance. On the day of its publication, the executive secretary of the Ministry of Agrarian Reform, José Abrão, was at pains to point out that while technically the audits could be recommenced, in the absence of new indices audits would have no practical effect for the purposes of expropriation. He also pointed out that for technical reasons 'there was no alternative but to re-edit the suspension [clause]'.[70] The commission had needed more time and if the first inter-ministerial agreement had not been re-edited, then the way would have been opened to full scale audits – which was not the federal government's objective.

Carlos Sperotto put it differently: 'We believe that, independently of the possibility of land audits being conducted, good sense will prevail. We are giving a vote of confidence in the government and we will follow developments, hoping that before long the new indices will be defined.'[71]

What neither José Abrão nor Carlos Sperotto had counted upon, was the presence of Paulo Emílio Barbosa. The latter had already been questioned by the Federal Public Ministry over INCRA's settlement targets in general and the suspension of land audits in particular. In an August 27 letter of reply to the Federal Public Ministry, Barbosa admitted that INCRA would be unable to carry out its settlement targets. This was because, among other things, a federal court injunction preventing INCRA from notifying landowners of impending audits in the absence of productivity indices had only just been revoked. Land owners had refused to countersign notifications, and in any case the first inter-ministerial agreement had just suspended the prospect of land audits throughout the state for 30 days.[72]

Interestingly, Barbosa also referred to the fact that the much vaunted method of land purchase was not going ahead as planned. It will be recalled that with his announcement of the agreement that foresaw the end of audits, almost exactly a year to the day earlier, the then Minister of Agriculture, Francisco Turra, had said that: 'lands will be bought from those who want to sell them. The question is resolved.'[73] Barbosa's letter indicated the opposite. Buying land was proving to be an extremely problematic proposition. Much of the land being offered at the time was in frontier regions and therefore of dubious legal provenance.[74] Thus, when negotiations were underway over the 30,000 hectares suggested at the time of Minister Jungmann's 1998 visit, it became apparent that the vast majority (988 out of 1,309 families) would have been settled in these precarious frontier regions. Thus, it was not simply a question of how much land was available, but also where it was located – its legal provenance. Another issue raised was the price being demanded. Apparently this exceeded INCRA offers by a factor of between 10 and 100 per cent – well beyond negotiable limits.[75]

Quite apart from the slippage in INCRA's timetable and difficult questions being raised by the Federal Public Ministry, there was, of course, the issue of the agreement that had been made between INCRA, the MST and the state government immediately prior to the withdrawal of the landless workers from the Fazenda Capivara. That agreement foresaw the recommencement of land audits in Bagé within 45 days. Nothing in the second inter-ministerial agreement either altered that fact or, in any legal or administrative sense, superseded it. Carlos Sperotto, Marcio Portes de Almeida and Barbosa all knew this. The question, therefore, was would INCRA keep its word?

On 4 October, as per schedule of the agreement drawn up on 19 August, INCRA in Rio Grande do Sul announced its intention to start the process of land audits in Bagé, commencing with the Fazenda Capivara. 'I cannot avoid carrying out my legal obligations', said Barbosa. 'We are following institutional and legal criteria.'[76] The view of FARSUL was forthright. According to one of its spokespersons: 'land audits are worse than land occupations because with the former one risks losing the property'.[77] In any case, it was suggested, it was important to wait for the definition of the indices. This contrasted with the view of Governor Dutra's Agriculture Secretary, José Hermeto Hoffmann. 'Better late than never!'[78] 'Land reform', said Hoffman, 'must be carried out on the basis of land audits and expropriation. There is no other way.'[79]

Finally, on 5 October, the views of the Minister of Agriculture, Pratini de Moraes, became clear. He de-authorised the audits suggesting, as FARSUL had, that audits should not begin without a definition of new land productivity indices, and that in any event he had an agreement with the landowners (an agreement that never became public) and would not alter 'a single comma' of that arrangement.[80] The issue of indices and land audits, which had been so successfully swept under the carpet in 1998 by an agreement between the Ministry of Agriculture and the Ministry of Agrarian Reform was back on the political agenda.

While Pratini de Moraes went on the offensive with strong declarations, Raul Jungmann, despite close links to President Cardoso, would not be drawn on the issue. Perhaps sensing Jungmann's weakness de Moraes' declarations became more strident, climaxing with a radio interview on 24 November. His views merit extensive citation because they give an indication of the uphill struggle faced by land reformers in Brazil:

> There's no need to expropriate anything. There are plenty of ranches for sale. This business of expropriation is a political manoeuvre. What has to be done, in fact it is our recommendation to INCRA, is that there are loads of ranches for sale in Rio Grande do Sul and that agrarian reform programmes should be carried out by means of the acquisition of ranches. All one has to do is to ring a rural estate agent because there is an enormous number of people wanting to get out of cattle ranching and other agricultural activities, therefore there is no need to expropriate. There is in Brazil today, enough land to carry out an agrarian reform without creating all this trauma. Our recommendation is the following: expropriation should only function and should only be put into practise when there are no alternatives to purchase given, after all, that availability through the market is a lot simpler, far quicker, and creates many fewer problems.[81]

It should be recalled that the Brazilian constitution takes a different position on the issue of land reform, the social function of property and the question of expropriation. Pratini de Moraes' comments were a direct attack on that legal regime and the work of another ministry. In what was, perhaps, an echo of his authoritarian past, he also went on to ascribe to himself a series of administrative powers that he simply did not possess. 'The inspections', he said, 'are suspended, they will not continue, I have already advised the people there [landowners in Rio Grande do Sul] of that ... Until this question of the indices is resolved there will not be any inspections.' He went on to emphasise that, 'these indices of occupation of lands in Rio Grande do Sul are totally obsolete and irrelevant. They just serve as a source of debate and political exploitation'.[82]

It is not necessary here to dwell on the implications of his comments for the prospects of land reform in Brazil (upon which they were an open and calculated assault), or what they imply about the presence of landed interests within the heart of the Cardoso government. Suffice it to say they are reminiscent of tendencies that led to the scuppering of the first National Programme for Agrarian Reform during the transition to democratic rule, and tendencies that had also exerted a regressive impact upon the drafting of the chapter on agrarian reform in Brazil's 1988 constitution.[83]

That the Minister of Agrarian Reform should have kept virtually silent in the face of such a sustained assault from a fellow minister was remarkable. Jungmann himself was wary of the efficacy of the current legal framework and in favour of market-based solutions, albeit for different reasons. He had already gone on record to this effect in his *Folha de São Paulo* article.[84] To this extent the Minister of Agriculture was merely crudely articulating themes that had already been endorsed by Jungmann himself a year earlier. When pressed by the media, Jungmann sidestepped suggestions of a division between ministries and sought to depersonalise the issue with carefully chosen words: 'I am absolutely certain that the President [of the Republic] would veto any attempt to remove basic duties from INCRA. ... Defining what is an unproductive property is fundamental to a programme of expropriation.'[85]

The ensuing vacuum was filled instead by the relatively unknown lawyer from the Federal Public Ministry, Paulo Emílio Barbosa, who openly criticised the Minister of Agriculture in the following terms:

> Expropriation is indispensable and is the principal instrument for agrarian reform. One cannot turn INCRA into a luxury estate agent, of which there is a serious danger. It seems that there is a desire that this should happen. This would lead INCRA to lose its institutional and social function.[86]

Shortly after these comments, Barbosa was sacked.

Raul Jungmann's explanation for his dismissal of Barbosa is revealing:

> Minister Pratini gave a radio interview and Paulo Emílio decided to answer the minister. Upon doing this, he put himself in a position in which a subordinate of mine was attacking a fellow ministerial colleague. This would weaken me in a terrible way. That is to say, if I was already in a weak situation, in which I was already extremely worried, this concern

now reached new heights. 'Look', I said, 'we may meet our Waterloo here. In other words, from a relatively confined space for manoeuvre, from a regional centre, these people will develop leverage and create a problem for me throughout the country.' So I took the decision to dismiss Paulo Emílio.[87]

On the face of it he suggests that chains of command had been broken, thereby leaving him in a vulnerable position, but his comments leave unanswered the question of whether Pratini de Moraes' own actions constituted a far greater violation of ministerial authority. Evidently it does, but Fernando Henrique Cardoso's congressional alliances meant that he was not about to sack Pratini de Moraes. Jungmann's explanation also underlines the magnitude of the potential crisis facing INCRA. He was perfectly aware that Pratini de Moraes' repeated de-authorisations may have left Barbosa in what one newspaper at the time described as an 'uncomfortable position', but Barbosa's response had raised the stakes too high on a terrain where Jungmann felt his ministry was vulnerable. Apparently this was neither the time nor the place for a fight because it threatened to mutate into a national conflict:

> This impasse [over the indices] was dragging on and the situation was becoming ever more disadvantageous for us. I also feared that the situation [in Bagé] would spread to the whole of Brazil, in other words, that other organisations would go to the courts and try and stop the whole business in its tracks.[88]

This is a remarkable statement, locating the source of conflict in the political and legal sphere – precisely the kind of terrain where Barbosa felt invincible. Indeed, following his dismissal, Barbosa was able to claim with some justification that: 'Our legal department overcame ... *all* the legal barriers that the [landowners] placed in front of INCRA.'[89] Both the Federal Public Ministry and the judiciary had largely accepted INCRA's stance, and yet here was the Minister of Agrarian Reform claiming that the process was fraught with *legal* risks.

Provided – and it is a big proviso – one takes the prospect of some kind of legal chain reaction as a genuine possibility (an issue that lies beyond the scope of the present work), there may be a sense in which Jungmann was right. Bagé constituted what was earlier termed a 'best case' scenario in legal terms. By the same token, however, one must question whether the legal apparatus in other parts of Brazil would have been equally as forthcoming in states such as Maranhão, Amazonas, Pernambuco or Bahia? The answer is almost certainly not.

Indeed, even if one discounts the north-south split altogether, there remain questions over the capacity of the legal system as a whole to sustain a wave of mass litigation. Clearly, the legal apparatus would have survived, but the question remains whether land audits and indices would have been severely undermined by getting bogged down in interminable legal actions. That is the clear implication of Jungmann's comments, notwithstanding the fact that, in Bagé at least, 'all the legal obstacles' had been overcome.

Ultimately, though, it was within the realm of political strategy and tactics rather than administrative or legal spheres that Jungmann located Barbosa's downfall. As Jungmann explains:

> You see Bagé is the position on the hill – they [landowners] are up at the top; so the perspective of the Public Ministry, of Paulo Emílio is that it is all a question of the law – that I have to carry out the law. Look, the law emerges from a complex of relations. Sure, you have to carry out the law, that's right, but it is folly to go into combat on the terrain of the adversary because he wins – and there, with the relation of forces, they always win.[90]

On the face of it there was a head-on conflict between two quite distinct rationales: those of law and politics.

A dialectic of law and politics

There is little doubt that Barbosa came to the job with a strong 'legal ethic', but it was not law for its sake. Faced with the numerous contradictions of Brazil's legal regime, he adopted a reading that sought intellectual coherence by emphasising law's social dimension. In one article, for example, he noted that: 'on delimiting the scope of property, and limiting it to its social function, the Constituent Assembly sought to guarantee one of the supreme values of the rule of law, the principle of equality which imposes, before anything else, a just and equitable social policy'.[91] This socio-legal reading was one reason why he had accepted the job at INCRA in the first place.

Perhaps the more significant feature of Barbosa's ethic was the emphasis given to implementation, an approach in keeping with the Federal Public Ministry's constitutional objectives. This desire to implement largely explains why someone lacking any radical sympathies eventually found himself taking up positions with such radical implications.

While the Fazenda Capivara episode and others in which INCRA temporarily suspended land audits indicate that Barbosa was aware of more than purely legal considerations,[92] charges that he lacked sufficient 'jogo de cintura', or political finesse, to stay in place are probably true. According to press reports the kind of 'jogo de cintura' required was one that 'could make agrarian reform progress without entering into conflict with the landowners'.[93] As Barbosa later remarked, 'there is simply no way of conciliating or reconciling agrarian reform with large unproductive estates; either one successfully attends to the demands of one or one attends to the demands of the other'.[94]

That remains as true today, under Presidents Lula da Silva and Dilma Rouseff. Both have balked at the idea of confronting powerful agricultural interests, leaving agrarian reform as a policy of structural change in a state of near paralysis.

Barbosa's dismissal

The announcement of Barbosa's dismissal on 30 November 1999, was posted in the official digest at exactly the same time as the announcement of new productivity indices through Portaria Interministerial no. 3.[95] As Jungmann explains, this was deliberate:

> I took a number of decisions. The first was that Paulo Emílio had to leave. The second was that he departs but that simultaneously the indices would also come out. So I appealed to Minister Pratini. He was not there, he was abroad in Seattle, so I appealed to the Presidency of the Republic. I said 'look, in order to administer the situation Paulo Emílio leaves but the indices come out and I go back to carrying out agrarian reform.' In other words fine, I will concede in one area but I will gain in another and I will remain in charge of the game – exclusively in charge. Thus everything happened on the same day. It was studied in minute detail. It was extremely tense. I was in permanent phone contact. It was a manoeuvre that had to be skilfully accomplished, it had to be precise and it had to work. I could not afford to lose. So on the one hand Paulo Emílio leaves, therefore I regain the principle of authority, while on the other hand by putting the indices on the table I made it clear that I am in charge obviously within the law.[96]

Paulo Emílio Barbosa's reading of events differed. Jungmann had became a 'prisoner' of the Minister of Agriculture as a result of major ministerial changes then under way – in particular the transition from what had hitherto been entitled an Extraordinary Ministry of Agrarian Reform into a permanent ministry.[97] This change also included a major shift of resources (billions of dollars) and responsibilities (for family agriculture[98]) away from the Ministry of Agriculture towards the Ministry of Agrarian Reform. It led to a tacit understanding whereby the state of Rio Grande do Sul was handed over to Pratini de Moraes on a platter while Jungmann was given freer rein over national matters.

Although profound, in one sense these differences of interpretation do not matter, for they confirm a number of more important points. Firstly, that Jungmann was playing the long game. Secondly, that the sustainability of ministerial integrity (both personal and institutional) was the uppermost consideration. Thirdly, that there were real tensions between the ministries such that the sustainability of productivity indices was increasingly called into question. Fourthly, the high degree to which land reform policy and practice was – and remains – bounded by landed interests. And finally, that at the end of the day, Rio Grande do Sul (and Bagé in particular), could be sacrificed on the altar of these wider considerations.

Of course, none of this implies that Rio Grande do Sul was totally abandoned, even if the head of INCRA and his policy of land audits were. In both agricultural and political terms the state was too significant for that. As far as Jungmann was concerned, 'this was not the time for Bagé, it was a Vietnam for us, I had to recommence the [wider] process, one day I would be back to Bagé.'[99] Just like land reform in Brazil, though, that day never seems to come.

In the meantime, therefore, the issue became who would replace Barbosa:

> The situation was extremely delicate with repercussions that could be extremely grave for us. I needed a local player of stature. In other words, if it was a Paulo Emílio, or whoever else, I would not be able to impose the indices. I needed someone of stature who could counterbalance the political system that was opposed and, at the same time, could have relations with the Workers' Party. What was needed was an institutional arrangement. An alliance was needed.[100]

Why was an alliance needed and what was its underlying rationale? Jungmann explains: 'I must always equilibrate. Evidently, I have to walk to the left, but I cannot break, I simply cannot break with the right completely. In that sense it is a process.'[101]

The alliance was eventually crystallised with the candidacy of Vicente Bogo. As a member of Cardoso's PSDB, there was an element (albeit diminishing) of an orientation towards the left. Bogo's forceful defence of agrarian reform during the Constituent Congress reinforced those credentials. At the same time his former role as Governor Britto's deputy underlined a willingness to make alliances with the right. This mix of qualities and tendencies was exemplified in Bogo's decision to send troops in against the landowners. Like the third-way brand of politics he espoused, Bogo could, seemingly, look both ways simultaneously. His stewardship of a newly restructured INCRA, however, marks the beginning of a new set of events and issues that lie beyond the concerns of this chapter.

Conclusion: Putting Bagé into Perspective

This chapter has shown how the power of legal instruments and frameworks are profoundly affected by shifts in the centre of gravity in the political and social fields. These shifts heighten or diminish the 'force of law', if necessary displacing it altogether. More than simply affecting law from without, though, the implicit argument has been that it could never be stripped of these other contextual factors, since its meaning derived from its relationship to these spheres. Bagé lays these connections bare. From its inception the constitutional concept of productive property was problematic (as some of its authors intended), but its real content had to be established. To paraphrase Jungmann, 'the law emerges from a complex of relations' and cannot be set apart from them. Juridically speaking and other things being equal Bagé should have possessed an open and shut quality, but the fact is that things were not equal, and rarely are, particularly under highly polarised social conditions.

Given the establishment of a major set piece conflict, the question was what would prosecutors and judges do about it? In key respects Bagé would live up to expectations as a best case scenario, and all that is best in Brazil's legal system. Phase one of the dispute saw the relentless pursuit of the infractors by the Federal Public Ministry. Its 23rd August request for troop and helicopter reinforcements noted the 'imperative need to make good the canons established in the juridical order and to defeat this veritable insurrection against the law'.[102] It asked 'for how long will the federal judicial authorities have to tolerate excesses of this order?' And it concluded not only that INCRA was engaging in an act of 'crystal clear legality', but that any failure to provide substantial police reinforcements would 'again lead to the loss of prestige in the justice system.'[103] Notwithstanding the legality of the administrative act and the presence of judicially sanctioned, but limited, police reinforcements, there was a 'growing sense amongst the local population that the protestors were immune from punishment' and a real possibility that this would lead to a corresponding 'loss of credibility in the [legal] institutions'.[104] Thus, it was not so much landowners who were on trial, but the legal system itself.

Raul Jungmann was fully aware of those concerns. Indeed, after leaving office he wrote an open letter to President da Silva on the subject:

> President, no democrat can sacrifice the rule of law in name of the combat against poverty and social exclusion. … Normality implies the strict and rigid adherence to the law – whether we like it or not. Mr President, follow the law and make others follow it.[105]

As a minister, however, Jungmann accorded such arguments a lower priority. His nationwide perspective conflicted with what, according to him, was the Federal Public Ministry's more narrow view that 'it is all a question of the law'.[106] In later phases of the dispute Jungmann was concerned with his own ministerial credibility and institutional integrity. In Bagé, on the other hand, the Federal Public Ministry and judiciary were equally if not more concerned with their own institutional integrity and credibility – especially given the 'crystal clear legality' of the issues involved. As with ministerial authority, maintaining the legal order entailed its own brand of politics. From their point of view it was not a question of the rule of law in splendid isolation, or of law at one isolated moment in time, or even of other things being equal and therefore allowing law to take its course. Rather, the issue concerned cumulative damage – both extant and potential – to legal institutions in Bagé and beyond. For this reason the more pragmatic line advocated by Jungmann was never a real option. It entailed major costs, like 'loss of prestige in the justice system', which the Public Ministry and judiciary felt they could ill afford.

Despite the highly favourable legal conjuncture, in which prosecutors, courts and INCRA worked with the grain of land reform rather than against it, land reform was stopped in its tracks. Ironically, it was the Minister for Agrarian Reform himself who dealt the mortal blow because in his view it was proving politically unsustainable and fraught with too many risks.

Perhaps more remarkable, for someone engaged at the highest levels of political power, were Jungmann's repeated references to his own powerlessness – whether this was in regard to the need to walk to the left without breaking with the right, or the more dramatic references he made to the spectre of comprehensive and humiliating defeats. Landowners, on the other hand, were able to operate in two spheres. If political and legal capital could not be secured through the courts, then other instruments, ranging from social mobilisation to intensive lobbying efforts were employed. These extra-legal and extra-parliamentary means allowed landowners to change the rules of the game entirely, thereby leading to the suspension of audits, reconsideration of the indices and with them the total marginalisation of the courts.

The contingency of law in the face of landed power, is starkly underlined by Barbosa's assertion that, 'despite all the efforts that were made, the forces were really great and gave us no chance to carry out audits.'[107] Of course, legal power should not be underestimated. It offers a codified articulation of the land question and frames much of the discussion, as landowners are content to acknowledge and social movements know only too well to their cost. There were instances in Bagé when decisive power was very much within the ambit of the justice system and was used effectively. Thus the landowners' strategy of bogging the dispute down in the courts failed to work, and the Federal Public Ministry was active in dragging the landowners into the courts on its rather than their terms. But Bagé ultimately represents a major defeat. That the MST yet again had to look to direct action alternatives is an indictment of the system's failures. Not surprisingly, the MST's verdict was harsh. The whole event was, 'testimony to the incompetence of INCRA. Nothing, it seems, can stand in the way of *vistorias*, except for incompetence that is.'[108] In the light of this failure the movement confirmed it would occupy lands where audits were impeded. That Barbosa, a member of the Federal Public Ministry and a former MST sceptic, should agree in terms with the MST also underlines the magnitude of the defeat:

When a minister [Pratini de Moraes] puts himself above the democratic rule of law in his country saying that there will be no land audits until the new indices are published; when he interferes in a ministry that is beyond his competence and preaches civil disobedience, what can we expect from the MST if not this: if INCRA does not occupy this institutional vacuum we will occupy all those areas where land audits are opposed? What else can we expect?[109]

Within the context of such powerful forces the idea of a neutral law that takes no account of power relations – both within the legal sphere itself and outside – is an illusion. Indeed it is recognised as such by many practitioners on a daily basis. By way of example it is interesting to note that one aspect of Jungmann's reading of events was reproduced in almost carbon copy format by the Federal Public Ministry but in order to justify maintaining pressure upon landowners, rather than removing it. As Marcelo Beckhausen, one of the federal prosecutors involved put it:

> We understood that the problem of land audits was extremely serious and that it could generate an unsustainable situation as regarded the targets established by the federal government. The [anti-audit] movement could spread to other regions in the state and rural producers might unite in the same way and begin to stop INCRA continuing audits that were within its legal remit ... So a meeting was held and it was agreed that INCRA should continue carrying out audits for the purposes of land reform and the Public Ministry would make itself fully available. ... Several federal prosecutors were drafted into Bagé because at that time there wasn't a fully qualified prosecutor. So a number of prosecutors began to act in that region and all, frankly speaking, were imbued with the same sense of duty.[110]

Making resources available in this way was a calculated political act, albeit one intimately related to INCRA's and the Federal Public Ministry's constitutional duties. Barbosa's error seems to have been his belief in both the pre-eminent validity of legality in relation to other spheres, and his belief in its material sufficiency in relation to other forces. By contrast, Beckhausen made clear the politically bounded nature of legal action even if, like Barbosa, he too wanted to make the law stick.

> The possibility exists that we in the Public Ministry could make recommendations to the effect that INCRA should be made to carry out land audits and expropriations in the region and municipality of Bagé. A possibility exists for instituting a public civil suit in order to oblige INCRA to carry out its duties with regard to agrarian reform. All this depends upon the attitude of the Public Ministry and also depends upon a legal procedural environment. You are not going to institute a public civil suit that you know is then going to run into difficulty and be unfavourably received. I think that you have to exhaust all the extra-judicial lines of

actions before then going on to institute a public civil suit or institute other judicial procedures.[111]

Where does all this leave land reform law? The short answer, at best, is in a state of disrepute and paralysis. Thus Barbosa's valedictory address could do little but make an impassioned plea that things ought to be different:

The indices are there, and now they are trying to stitch up an agreement so that only those properties whose owners consent, or will consent, are audited for the purposes of agrarian reform. But where is the constitution and where are the laws of this country?[112]

The ways and extent to which things might change is the subject of subsequent chapters.

Notes

1 Author interview with Rolf Hackbart, 6 July 2007.
2 Author interview with Raul Jungmann, 5 April 2000.
3 Zander Navarro, Maria Stela Moraes and Raul Menenzes, 'Pequena história dos assentamentos rurais no Rio Grande do Sul: formação e desenvolvimento' in Leonilde Servolo de Medeiros and Sérgio Leite, eds, *A formação dos assentamentos rurais no Brasil*, Porto Alegre: Editora da Universidade, 1999, p. 23.
4 See for example Foreign Agricultural Service, 'Brazil 06/07 Rice update and trip report', *Commodity Intelligence Report*, 30 March 2007, available at www.pecad.fas.usda.gov/highlights/2007/03/brazil_rice_30mar2007/
5 For a full technical discussion and elaboration of these procedures, see Norma de Execução no. 2 of 14 September 1999 in *Diario Oficial*, no. 177, 15 September 1999, pp. 8–14.
6 Lei No. 8.629/93, Paragraph 2, Article 2.
7 Shigeo Shiki, Henrique Dantas Neder, Paulo Henrique Rangel Teixeira, Carlos Guanziroli, *Custo Social da Reforma Agrária*, 1998, available at www.dataterra.org.br/Documentos/FAO-INCRA/shikiframe.htm
8 'A discórdia no campo', *Zero Hora*, 26 April 1998.
9 'Estudo dá razáõ a fazendeiros', *Zero Hora*, 26 April 1998.
10 These included studies by soil specialists from the Federal University of Rio Grande do Sul, the Federal University of Pelotas, and Embrapa (Empresa Brasileira de Pesquisa Agropecuária), the Brazilian Agricultural Research Company that is linked to the Ministry of Agriculture.
11 'OAB contestará lei que cria milícia', *Zero Hora*, 15 April 1998.
12 'Produtores protestam contra inspeçáõ do INCRA em fazendas', *Zero Hora*, 4 April 1998.
13 'Porque não as vistorias do Incra', *Correio do Sul*, 8 April 1998.
14 'Produtores rurais debatem atuaçáõ do INCRA no Municipio', *O Minuano*, 21 February 1998.
15 'Brito anuncia possível arrendamento da CICADE', *O Minuano*, 6 May 1998.

16 See '150 produtores barram vistoria do INCRA', *Correio do Sul*, 8 April 1998.

17 'Justiça cencede liminar ao Incra no caso de vistorias', *Correio do Sul*, 14 April 1998.

18 'Incra anuncia que suspende vistorias em Bagé', *Correio do Sul*, 15 April 1998.

19 'Proprietários rurais rejeitam itens de protaria do Incra', *Zero Hora*, 18 April 1998.

20 'Governo cede a pressões de produtores', *Zero Hora*, 23 April 1998.

21 'Fetter Júnior reúne-se com Raul Jungmann', *O Minuano*, 14 May 1998.

22 'Confederacão questiona índice na justiça', *Zero Hora*, 26 August 1998.

23 On the issue of institutional fragility see pp. 101–102 of present chapter as well as the section dealing with 'Phase Two of the Bagé Conflict'.

24 'Porque não as vistorias do Incra', *Correio do Sul*, 8 April 1998.

25 Mimeo, federal court injunction of 12 April 1998, pp. 5–6 (in author's possession).

26 'Advogado preso em confronto', *Zero Hora*, 14 August 1998.

27 'Procuradoria da República pede a prisão de ruralistas', *Correio do Sul*, 26 August 1998.

28 'O diplomata do conflito', *Zero Hora*, 26 August 1998.

29 'O algoz dos produtores rurais', *Zero Hora*, 26 August 1998.

30 'Ministério Público Federal, nota à imprensa', *O Minuano*, 27 August 1998.

31 'Procuradoria busca uma saída pacífica', *Zero Hora*, 27 August 1998.

32 RECAD, unpublished *Relatório Recad*, Bagé, May 1998, p. 3.

33 Ibid., p. 4.

34 Ibid.

35 Constitution of the Federative Republic of Brazil, 2nd edition, translated and revised by Istvan Vajda, Patrícia de Queiroz Carvalho Zimbres and Vanira Tavares de Souza, Brasília, 2009, Article 129, sections II and III respectively. Available at: www2.camara.gov.br/english/brazilian-constitution-2

36 Mimeo, 'Avaliação do recadastramento de Bagé', 15 June 1998, p. 1.

37 Ibid.

38 Ibid., pp. 2–3

39 Ibid., p. 3.

40 The decision of the Federal Regional Court (Tribunal Regional Federal) held that the associations such as FARSUL could not be held responsible for the actions of third parties. 'Justiça assegura manifestação', *Zero Hora*, 30 October 1998.

41 'Acordo prevê a suspensão das vistorias', *Zero Hora*, 27 August 1998.

42 Ibid.

43 'Jungmann vem ao RS autorizar leilão', *Correio do Povo*, 27 August 1998.

44 Raul Jungmann, 'Um novo mundo rural', *Folha de São Paulo*, 30 August 1998.

45 'Corte de recursos suspende vistorias', *Zero Hora*, 18 September 1998.

46 Ana Amélia Lemos, 'O protesto na Expointer', *Zero Hora*, 29 September 1998. Lemos was one of two journalists who later conducted the explosive interview with Pratini de Moraes, the Minister of Agriculture, that indirectly led to the sacking of Barbosa.

47 In 1967 Cardoso had written a classic Marxist text on dependency theory with Enzo Faletto, *Dependency and Development in Latin America*. He subsequently rejected Marxism and as Brazil's president came to embrace markets as well as privatisating of state assets on a massive scale. Jungmann was a former member of the youth wing of the Brazilian Communist Party (Partido Communista Brasileiro, PCB). As Minister in Cardoso's government he would give considerable

weight to the intrinsic capacity of markets to deliver key land reform objectives, especially through the policy of willing seller willing buyer. Events like these represented a significant shift in the nature of the state as a political and economic actor. Political alliances with the right were a tangible expression of the intellectual shift.

48 'Um atestado de incompetência do Incra', *Zero Hora*, 26 August 1998.
49 'Sem-terra sepultam a 4a criança', *Correio do Povo*, 22 June 1998.
50 As a vet from the Federal University of Rio Grande do Sul whose work was cited by FARSUL explained: 'With greater the amounts of land available, cattle will eat better, fatten more quickly and have a higher pregnancy rate. ... Increasing the weight of animals per hectare diminishes repeat pregnancies of young calves ... If we wait for the cattle to age, it may even acquire more weight, but it will result in meat of lower quality.' José Piva Lobato cited in 'Estudo Contesta índices do INCRA', *Zero Hora*, 26 June 1998.
51 Oral submission by Paulo Emílio Barbosa to the Human Rights and Citizenship Commission of the Legislative Assembly of Rio Grande do Sul, 8 December 1999, mimeo transcript, pp. 14–15.
52 Paulo Emílio Barbosa, 'A qualquer tempo', *Zero Hora*, 9 September 1999.
53 Oral submission by Paulo Emílio Barbosa to the Human Rights and Citizenship Commission of the Legislative Assembly of Rio Grande do Sul, 8 December 1999, mimeo transcript, p. 14.
54 Ibid., p. 15.
55 *Gaúcho* is a term used for persons from Rio Grande do Sul. It has proud historical and cultural overtones.
56 This is a reference to the Ford Motor Company which had just pulled out of a proposed manufacturing investment deal in Rio Grande do Sul. A loan of R$460 million (or US$255 million) and other tax incentives by the state had not proved enough. Instead, exploiting and stoking up the fiscal war between states, the company opted for the more lucrative offer made by Bahia's Governor César Borges of the PFL. The deal was so attractive that the federal government had to change the law on fiscal incentives in order to allow it to go ahead and help its ally. (See 'Governo muda lei para beneficiar Ford', *Folha de São Paulo, Dinheiro*, 30 June 1999.) Dutra's PT was roundly condemned for its 'failure' in the local media.
57 Author interview with Raul Jungmann, 5 April 2000.
58 Ibid.
59 See, for example, 'Farsul mantém boicote', 24 August 1999, ww8.zaz.com.br/rural/1999/08/24/005.htm and 'Governo define com Farsul a realização da expointer', 24 August 1999, ww8.zaz.com.br/rural/1999/08/24/001.htm
60 See Portaria Interministerial no. 1, 25 August 1999 in *Diário Oficial*, no. 165, 27 August 1999, Section 1, p. 39.
61 Cited in James Petras, 'The new revolutionary peasantry: the growth of peasant-led opposition to neoliberalism', *Z Magazine*, www.lbbs.org/zmag/articles/petrasoct98.htm
62 See George Mészáros, 'No ordinary revolution: Brazil's Landless Workers' Movement', *Race and Class*, vol. 42, no. 2, Oct–Dec 2000, p. 9.
63 Author interview with Paulo Emílio Barbosa, 1 February 2000.
64 Ibid.

65 Pedro Montenegro Barbosa, 'Editoria, reforma agraria' in *Cultura e Fé*, ano 22, no. 86, July–September 1999, p. 18.

66 Author interview with Paulo Emílio Barbosa, 1 February 2000.

67 Ibid.

68 Ibid.

69 See the Portaria Interministerial no. 2, 24 September 1999 in *Diário Oficial*, no. 185, 27 September 1999, Section 1, p. 55.

70 'Prorrogado prazo para rever índices', *Zero Hora*, 28 September 1999.

71 Ibid.

72 Mimeo, letter of 27 August 1999 from Paulo Emílio Barbosa (Regional Superintendency of INCRA, Rio Grande do Sul) to the Federal Public Ministry (in author's possession).

73 'Acordo prevê a suspensão das vistorias', *Zero Hora*, 27 August 1998.

74 Because of the clash between state, federal and private land interests in frontier regions, these are among the most complex and legally contentious of areas. This is an issue that is not just relevant to Rio Grande do Sul, but occurs widely across Brazil.

75 Mimeo, letter of 27 August 1999 from Paulo Emílio Barbosa (Regional Superintendency of INCRA, Rio Grande do Sul) to the Federal Public Ministry (in author's possession).

76 'Incra retoma vistoria de propriedades', *Zero Hora*, 5 October 1999.

77 'Ruralistas atacam o governo', *Zero Hora*, 2 October 1999.

78 'Incra vai retomar vistorias', *Zero Hora*, 2 October 1999.

79 'Vistoria de terra começa a ser definida', *Zero Hora*, 4 October 1999.

80 'Ministro da Agricultura desautoriza vistorias', *Zero Hora*, 6 October 1999.

81 Transcript of Rádio Gaúcha interview with Pratini de Moraes on 24 November 1999.

82 Ibid.

83 These issues are raised respectively in the following two highly authoritative works: José Gomes da Silva: *Caindo por terra: Crise da reforma agrária na nova república*, São Paulo: Editora Busca Vida, 1987 and *Buraco negro: A reforma agrária na constituinte de 1987/88*, Rio de Janerio: Paz e Terra, 1989.

84 Raul Jungmann, 'Um novo mundo rural', *Folha de São Paulo*, 30 August 1998. See text referred to in note 44 above.

85 'Ruralistas tentam mudar regras de produtividade em fazendas de gado', *Estado de São Paulo*, 29 November 1999.

86 *Jornal do Brasil*, 29 November 1999 cited on www.agrosoft.softex.br/online/msg00083.html#Inicio

87 Author interview with Raul Jungmann, 5 April 2000.

88 Ibid.

89 Transcript of submission to the Commission of Citizenship and Human Rights, Chamber of Deputies, Rio Grande do Sul, 8 December 1999, pp. 19–22.

90 Author interview with Raul Jungmann, 5 April 2000.

91 Paulo Emílio Barbosa ,'A qualquer tempo', *Zero Hora*, 9 September 1999.

92 On 22 November, shortly before his dismissal, Barbosa announced the temporary suspension of audits 'in order to avoid conflicts'. 'Recuei para evitar conflitos', *Zero Hora*, 23 November 1999.

93 'Superintendente do Incra está no centro da polêmica', *Zero Hora*, 26 November 1999.
94 Transcript of submission to the Commission of Citizenship and Human Rights, Chamber of Deputies, Rio Grande do Sul, 8 December 1999, p. 47.
95 See Portaria Interministerial No. 3, 30 November 1999, in *Diário Oficial*, no. 229, 1 December 1999, Section 1, p. 35. Babosa's dismissal notice appears in Section 2 of the same edition.
96 Author interview with Raul Jungmann, 5 April 2000.
97 Author interview with Paulo Emílio Barbosa, 1 February 2000.
98 Known as the National Programme for the Strengthening of Family Agriculture (Programa Nacional de Fortalecimento da Agricultura Familiar, Pronaf), Pronaf financed individual and collective projects at much lower rates of interest than the private sector. The aim was to generate returns for and assist in the development of family smallholdings and agrarian reform settlements. Financing was available for capital equipment, infrastructural projects and investments in seeds and technology. Supporters of Pronaf note that arrears and failure rates are the lowest of any credit operation within Brazil, comparing extremely well with the private sector.
99 Author interview with Paulo Emílio Barbosa, 1 February 2000.
100 Ibid.
101 Ibid.
102 Mimeo, Ministério Público Federal, Procuradoria da República no Rio Grande do Sul, *Pedido de requisição de reforço policial*, 23 August 1998, p. 5.
103 Ibid.
104 Ibid., p. 4.
105 Raul Jungmann, 'Carta aberta ao Presidente Lula', *Folha de São Paulo*, 15 July 2003.
106 Author interview with Raul Jungmann, 5 April 2000.
107 Transcript of submission to the Commission of Citizenship and Human Rights, Chamber of Deputies, Rio Grande do Sul, 8 December 1999, p. 13.
108 João Pedro Stédile quoted in 'Um atestado de incompetência do Incra', *Zero Hora*, 26 August 1998.
109 Paulo Emílio Barbosa quoted in 'Um atestado de incompetência do Incra', *Zero Hora*, 26 August 1998.
110 Author interview with federal prosecutor Marcelo Beckhausen, 21 January 2000.
111 Ibid.
112 Transcript of submission to the Commission of Citizenship and Human Rights, Chamber of Deputies, Rio Grande do Sul, 8 December 1999, pp. 22–3.

Chapter 4

The Limits of Progressive State Action

[Governor] Requião issued his decree prohibiting the use of police forces in evictions, but this change is not achieved by decree alone.

João Pedro Stédile, Leader of the MST[1]

No superintendent [of INCRA] can survive in a state, and oversee the agrarian conflict, who does not, in some measure, receive support from within the states. It simply doesn't happen any other way. You always have to operate within these parameters...

Raul Jungmann, Minister of Agrarian Reform[2]

This chapter deals with the limits of state policy on land reform but also its potentialities in the context of the state of Paraná between 1991 and 2002, under governors, Roberto Requião (15 March 1991–2 April 1994) and Jaime Lerner (1 January 1995–1 January 1999; 1 January 1999–1 January 2003[3]). Paraná during this period illustrates the sorts of tensions of state power so typical of the dynamics of land reform throughout Brazil. The chapter also explores the impact a favourable political terrain (at the level of the state) can have upon the mediation of land conflicts (between landless workers and landowners), but also the political mediation of judicial power itself, a vital variable in land conflicts.

The contrast between Requião and Lerner on land reform issues could not be more marked and that would have profound implications in the legal sphere. The former was pro-land reform, while the latter presided over a period of extreme violence in the countryside. According to statistics compiled by the Catholic Church's Pastoral Land Commission (Pastoral da Terra), between 1995 and 2002, 16 landless rural workers were assassinated in Paraná, 49 received death threats and there were 134 evictions.[4] Paraná's national share of land occupations put it on a par with highly mobilised areas of the country such as Mato Grosso do Sul and Pernambuco.

As has been noted, agrarian reform should flow from federal initiatives, but for part of the period in question, 15 March 1990 to 29 December 1992,

President Fernando Collor de Mello was in charge of federal policy. Even allowing for the fact that his administration was rudely cut short by impeachment proceedings on the grounds of corruption, his government nevertheless marked a new low point for land reform, be it the low number of areas expropriated, the physical area obtained, or number of families permanently settled.[5] This policy vacuum, combined with active repression of rural movements like the MST, meant that to all intents and purposes land reform was dead in the water. Against this bleak background Roberto Requião's government offered some promising possibilities. The question was whether Requião, like other sympathetically-minded governors, could make a difference within the limited space available. It is a question that constantly arises within Brazil's federal power structure, albeit sometimes in reverse, as federal initiatives outstrip the conservative pretensions of local states. Indeed, that is precisely what would happen with Requião's successor, Jaime Lerner. The chapter also examines INCRA's record in Paraná under the leadership of Maria de Oliveira a close colleague of Raul Jungmann. Like Requião she too proposed some significant reforms and like him her eventual political demise is seen as symptomatic of the limits of legality and progressive state action present throughout Brazil, a fact that underlines the importance of extra institutional social forces like the MST.

One Step Forward: the Requião Administration 1991–94

Horácio Martins de Carvalho, the former head of Paraná's Land, Forest and Cartography Institute (Instituto de Terra, Cartografia e Florestas – ITCF)[6] and later a close advisor to Requião, related how 'a month or so after Requião assumed office there was a meeting in the governor's palace where, for the first time in Paraná's history, he received around 300 workers in the palace's amphitheatre to negotiate demands relating to the land struggle.'[7] It is difficult to convey the impact this meeting had at the time upon both the participants and outside observers. The event signalled a cultural and symbolic break with the authoritarian past and the beginning of a more genuine commitment on the part of Paraná's new government towards land reform.

As far as issues relating to expropriation were concerned, the state government's hands were tied. Like the neighbouring state of São Paulo, there was some scope in Paraná for addressing the complex issue of devolved land, albeit the perceived scale of the problem, and hence the possible benefit, appeared much smaller. Struggles frequently involved conflicts over land title and use, rather than the issue of whether it belonged to the state or not. But there was one key area – a major component in the dynamics of Brazilian land struggle, no less – in relation to which the government of Paraná, like all state governments, could make an almost instant difference: evictions. It was legally responsibile for implementing evictions. Seen from another perpsective, it could regulate key aspects of land conflict.

At first sight the legal principle governing the local state's intervention appears relatively straightforward. Once the judiciary grants an eviction order, it then becomes the duty of the state government to provide the requisite police to execute that order. However, in Paraná, Requião and his administration had grave concerns about this process. These related not so much to the general principle, for which there was no argument, as to the manner of implementation and its profoundly negative social implications. For this reason Governor Requião began to question the precise terms and conditions governing the execution of judicial orders. It would lead to the introduction of a series of buffer mechanisms, some legal/technical, others more informal, within the machinery of the land eviction process itself. The combined effect of these new regulatory mechanisms would be to slow the process down, while dramatically expanding the scope for extra-legal resolutions of conflict. This also implied the opening up of a quite different political and legal dynamic.

Before discussing that dynamic and the specifics of the measures themselves, some brief comments about Carlos Frederico Marés, the man put in charge of framing the new legal infrastructure, are in order. Marés served as the state of Paraná's chief attorney from the very first day of the Requião administration to its last. Strategically speaking, Marés' appointment was highly significant because the administration's project not only required the development of alternative legal mechanisms but, once in place, it would inevitably demand their sustained defence in the face of equally sustained attacks from disgruntled and well organised landowners, judges and politicians.

Marés was eminently well qualified to respond to these challenges and he was clearly sympathetic towards the political project itself. He had a strong and longstanding interest in social affairs (quite independently of the governor) and approached law creatively, very much from a social perspective. This point is an important point. As Luis Edson Fachin, one of the Brazil's leading legal experts on the land question, and a former head of INCRA's legal department confirmed:

> a lawyer who works with the land question inside an institution has a fundamental role. It can be extremely negative, i.e., obstructive, when the lawyer is not culturally prepared to understand that his function there is not a bureaucratic one, but is a function guided by an end, which is to help in the regularisation of land [regularização fundiaria] where necessary, and to assist in the implementation of land reform insofar as is possible. ... In my own experience, many lawyers who locate themselves in these institutions are people who lack sensibility towards these questions and transform their work into a merely bureaucratic existence, i.e., pushing paper, instead of being, as it were, personally implicated in what they are doing.

It seems unimaginable that a FUNAI [National Indian Foundation, Fundação Nacional do Índio] lawyer could be prejudiced against Indians, but they do exist. It sounds inconceivable that an INCRA lawyer could be against agrarian reform, but they exist.[8]

Just as importantly, Marés was technically highly gifted. As one of the country's foremost legal experts on the indigenous question, he would later be appointed by President Fernando Henrique Cardoso to head FUNAI. Whatever political limitations accepting this role may have entailed, it is some measure of Marés' social commitment that he later resigned (April 2000) from the post in protest at the repression of Indians by police at controversial celebrations to mark the 500th anniversary of Brazil's 'discovery'. 'I cannot', he said, 'remain in a government that engages in physical aggression against the organised indigenous movement'.[9] He was opposed to social repression as an instrument of social regulation. It was not his 'project, style or history'.[10] His work in Paraná is a good example of that project, style and history.

Returning to the measures Marés helped to institute, in August 1991 the governor issued a decree, number 643. Its preamble noted first that there was no point in removing a group of squatters if there was nowhere else to put them and second that the state had an obligation to find an alternative. This was then coupled to an injunction upon officers of the military police obliging them to pass all eviction orders up the chain of command to the Secretariat of State for Public Security (Secretaria de Estado da Segurança Pública – SESP[11]). In practise, the idea was to subject implementation to a roundtable discussion among several secretaries of state outside the security apparatus (including, for instance, the Environment and Land Secretariats), with the aim of finding a solution before executing the judicial order. It was a long overdue step.

To say the least, the judges were unhappy with this decree, declaring it unconstitutional. Two features of their actions stand out. On the one hand there is the general constitutional point concerning relations between the executive and judiciary, appropriate lines of demarcation, etc. On the other, there is the issue of underlying political dynamics, namely the extent to which judges were approaching the issues from a 'purely' legal perspective.

Regarding constitutionality and the inherent tensions in the relationship, Marés, who was very much in the eye of the storm, sums up the situation well.

The judges thought that the decree was a justification for failing to carry out judicial mandates. ... It was considered an affront because the judge ordered an eviction, and then the executive would study the situation, would then consider how it would remove, if it would remove, etc. This was an affront because the judicial order had to be carried out – immediately. Requião said no. Sure, judicial orders must be carried out because they are guaranteed, but they have to be carried out within criteria that do not take away other rights, like human rights, the right to life, the right to security of those who are being evicted, etc. That, more or less, was the nature of the conflict. It was a conflict among rights.[12]

The extent to which procedural formalities are imperative or, conversely, subject to other substantive considerations (including human rights) cannot be resolved abstractly but demand a contextual reading. Should there be any doubt as to the weight of the issues at stake Requião gives a graphic instance of these. In one case, the judges handed him an eviction order, this time in an urban setting, in Curitiba, Paraná's capital. The order demanded the immediate eviction of some 20–30,000 squatters from an area that had been occupied and developed over a 30-year period. The judges were insistent. Yet it was precisely this sort of eviction that the governor termed 'socially reprehensible'. It went against the grain. According to him, therefore, in the end he authorised the eviction, 'but on the condition that it would be led by the president of the Tribunal de Justiça.'[13] In effect, the judges had been placed in the front line with all the implications (social, institutional – even personal) which that entailed. Not surprisingly, 'the hypothesis of an eviction suddenly evaporated.'[14]

This leads to the second issue touched upon above, namely the corporate, ideological and political dynamics underlying the judiciary's approach. It is ironic that the decision to declare the governor's decree unconstitutional was itself legally flawed. Instead of waiting for a legal action of unconstitutionality to be initiated in the courts, the judges took it upon themselves to declare the decree unconstitutional. Had they waited, it would have been entirely possible for them to have reached this same conclusion. As it was, they opted for a quick-fix solution, a declaration of unconstitutionality. As Marés notes: 'the declaration was not valid because it was not a judicial declaration, it was an administrative declaration of the court.'[15]

Although formidable issues in their own right, questions of procedural exactitude and constitutionality did not lie at the core of the dispute, at least not at the beginning. Nor, surprisingly, did the land question, however ideologically indisposed certain judges may have been towards urban squatters and landless workers. Requião traces the origins of the problem to corporate interests:

> I noticed that at certain moments of attrition between the judiciary and the executive, especially in regard to the tension that developed over their pay claims, which the executive did not grant, the judges attempted to demoralise the executive by throwing in socially reprehensible evictions.[16]

Thus, it was on the back of a pay dispute that the question of evictions first became an object of localised political friction, and subsequently assumed constitutional proportions, as requests were made for federal intervention and the governor's impeachment on grounds that he failed to implement judicial mandates. In this way, the constitutional dynamics of conflict took over and largely overshadowed the pay dispute.

What of the mechanics of decree 643 itself? How were these conceived, and what impact did they have? As mentioned earlier, the government of Paraná was deeply sceptical of the judiciary's whole approach on both social and legal grounds. It was not just a question of the 'socially reprehensible' nature of evictions; there were significant methodological and doctrinal doubts too. Although Requião's closest advisor on the land question, Horácio Martins de Carvalho, noted the obvious legal point that 'you can only take something back into ownership, if ownership exists in the first place',[17] in practise these sorts of issues did not seem to matter:

> The judges immediately give the repossession order based on the civil code and not on the constitution, nor the land statute, nor the law that regulates the code (in the so-called clauses of the civil code of the defence of property); all of which makes it absolute and not relative – as the constitution mandates.[18]

It is a common problem, deeply ingrained within judicial culture and training. The unusual part was the state government's response.

In contrast to the declared policy of the Covas government in São Paulo (where even the more liberal minded of its members were at pains to emphasise that 'the state has a clear policy on evictions: we carry out all judicial decisions'[19]), Paraná's government felt that 'it was important that the judge be given time to see whether the occupation at hand had occurred on land that might be subject to expropriation, or on an abandoned estate, or on land that had been illegally privatised, etc.'[20] The aim was to avoid 'sending the troops at the speed which the judiciary wanted'.[21]

For the judiciary this represented a violation of the separation of powers doctrine, the subordination of legal to political imperatives; but for the Requião administration it simply represented the vindication of other legal imperatives (human rights) traditionally subordinated to or violated by excessive legal formalism. The net result of the administration's action was to create a delay, typically of a week to 10 days, in which inspection reports on land productivity were prepared and negotiations with the landowner and squatters could begin. In the scheme of things this delay sounds slight, but it opened up a vital space. Given the ability of events to suddenly take on a chaotic and sometimes violent dynamic of their own, the emergence of a buffer period of days offered the possibility for a different political dynamic to emerge.

In some respects the most immediate task was to avoid armed conflict. The figure charged with coordinating the state's response was Horácio Martins de Carvalho. More often than not he was rung at home in the early hours (the most favoured time for occupations because of the tactical advantage and protection the cover of darkness afforded landless workers). He would immediately involve

the governor, the head of public security, the military police, social movements, and groups like the Catholic Church's Pastoral Land Commission.
'Together we would go to the area to avoid an armed conflict and then try and
understand how the situation could be resolved. This happened on numerous
occasions.'[22]

It should be stressed that this was not just any form of mediation, for example one based on notions of value neutrality, or the idea that the parties should
be left to themselves to sort out an agreement. A semi-spontaneous or
bi-partisan resolution of conflict was unlikely given both the high stakes, and
the fact that ultimately a third party (the state) was directly involved –
whether because of the eviction question, or because of the wider federal obligation to institute a programme of land reform. In the specific case of Paraná,
mediation was unashamedly value laden. 'There was firmness on the part of
the governor that people would not be removed by force and that negotiations
would have to take place', remarked de Carvalho. The state's working assumption, he said, was that 'landowners had their rights, but also landless workers
had to be respected because if they did not occupy they would forever remain
landless workers'.[23] It was against this background that agreements could be
forged, either through the negotiated acquisition of disputed land, or, as also
happened on a number of occasions, an agreement by the landless workers to
leave the area. The general presumption, though, was clearly in favour of land
reform. This represented a significant change in the relation of forces.

In and of themselves these developments would have been insufficient.
Delay was a useful tactic but it hardly constituted a strategy. They therefore
had to be complemented by the creation of what amounted to a series of creative legal partnerships. The state had to think laterally if it was to push the
process forward. Because the federal agency had the monopoly of expropriation but was not geared up to the task, Paraná's Land, Forest and Cartography
Institute (ITCF) could intervene by carrying out much of the technical work
(the historical research and on-site land audits) itself. It would then seek what
in effect amounted to the federal agency's stamp of approval on the documentation. Agreements and memorandums of understanding were drawn up
along these lines. In this way, instead of allowing the political process to stall
altogether, because of technical issues (legal limitations upon the local state),
the opposite occurred. A way was found to lift the legal restrictions and
thereby the local state stimulated and strengthened the process of reform.
A multiplier effect was introduced.[24]

Logics of Disintegration: Limitations of Requião's Approach

Among the obvious dangers in concentrating upon the mechanics of state
power, and referring to 'buffer mechanisms', is that the issues come to be seen
as largely technical when in fact they possess other vital dimensions, including

cultural ones. Take the question of the police. This force posed huge challenges for the new administration. While Requião openly acknowledged that 'the police are corrupt in any part of the world',[25] he was faced with the fact that in Paraná, as with many other parts of Brazil, they were known for being particularly corrupt and violent. The connection between police and paramilitary activities – a kind of 'revolving door' syndrome in which serving and former police engage in clandestine activities – was well known to rural activists who were frequently targets for beatings or even assassination. Yet now Requião was in charge of the police which he expected to implement his new and more flexible eviction policy. How would he (and they) respond to this contradiction?

Requião's solution was unusual, to say the least: 'I put a fireman in charge of the military police.'[26] It sounds absurd but the decision had serious implications, for the success of the policy now depended upon this new appointment. In fact the appointment of a firefighter was not so strange. The Brazilian public held the fire services in much higher esteem than the police or military, widely seen as corrupt. In addition, the fire services, like the military and civil police, were organised under the collective umbrella of the Secretariat of State for Public Security (SESP). Requião was candid about the appointment: 'I put a fireman there because he had not been trained to be aggressive.'[27] Not surprisingly, many rank and file police officers were deeply unhappy at the appointment but, according to the governor, the eventual result was that his chosen leader 'helped me avoid unnecessary conflicts. The guidance before the police was to mediate.'[28]

Attempts at altering the culture of the military police took other arguably more unusual forms. The MST's João Pedro Stédile explains.

> Requião issued his decree prohibiting the use of police forces in evictions, but this change is not achieved by decree alone. So he organised a series of debates with the officers to examine these questions. The essence of these debates, which we [the MST] conducted, was to get the officers to understand that police action would not resolve the land question; that the police were there to inhibit the commission of a crime, and that in the case of a land conflict every time the police got involved it would worsen.[29]

By any standard this is remarkable: the leader of the MST was giving lessons in sensitive policing and the wider agrarian question to a repressive police force led by a firefighter. Times truly had changed. Perhaps more remarkable still was the fact that for a time at least, it seemed to work. The only major weakness (a weakness that was by no means unique to Paraná) was that the framework was largely held together by the personal authority of the governor himself, and not as a result of any deeper cultural or institutional shift. In other words, once the administration fell in 1994, so, too, would most of the gains. Indeed, if one looks to the second Lerner administration (1999–2002) the gains were all but wiped out in what increasingly became a scorched earth policy towards the MST.

Before dealing with the Lerner administrations, however, it is important to put the achievements of the Requião administration into perspective. Land conflict in Paraná did not suddenly end by decree. On the contrary, if anything, the deteriorating situation at the federal level left the governor to wrestle with an intensifying series of local contradictions, be they his relationship with the police, with the judiciary, or with the MST itself – whose substantive demands could, from the very outset, only be partially met. In theory, however, the model was sustainable. After all, Requião was in charge of the police, was holding the judges at bay and had, in his words, 'reached an agreement with the Landless Workers' Movement, whereby they would not invade productive areas. If they invaded, the state would react.'[30] Equally, there were clear imperatives for the MST to cooperate. These derived from its own analysis of the state. As Roberto Baggio, the movement's leader in Paraná, and a member of the national executive, notes:

> Throughout all the governments we were quite clear that our main struggle was not against the local state government. The aim was to exert political pressure upon the federal government to resolve the problem. We always worked along the lines that state governments had to be allies in order to pressure the federal government to resolve the issue, because the more the movement struggles the more benefit it brings to the local state: more families are settled, more resources are passed on. Municipalities increase their tax base.[31]

If anything, the simultaneous advent of the Collor and Requião governments, which were moving in two opposing directions on land reform, merely served to reinforce this line of reasoning.

The rationale for cooperation was compelling, but other opposing logics were in play too. On 3 March 1993, these came to a head with bloody consequences for both sides. Back in 1991, as a direct response to one land occupation, Requião had ordered that research be conducted into the origins of a property, which turned out to be on devolved land. He brokered a deal with the 'owner', Olivo Benedelli, a *grilheiro* who had illegally occupied the area over some 30 years, but who had, according to the governor, managed the forest reserves correctly and, by many accounts, his farm productively. The 'owner' agreed to relinquish his claim over half the area, which was made over to land settlements, in exchange for legal recognition of his remaining half.[32] Two years later, however, the conditions for those landless families, who were promised effective resettlement but were still living under canvas, had become unsustainable. They expanded their occupation to some of the land that had been privatised, an act that was deemed unacceptable by the governor:

> They should never have invaded a negotiated area. It was a totally irresponsible attitude by the MST or whoever, because I don't think they were the leaders of the MST because they would not do such a crazy thing.

They would not make an agreement, obtain a huge area and then go and invade another productive area.[33]

In the meantime, undercover military police approached the encampment and three of their number were killed. A climate of war had developed and the military police wanted revenge. Requião explains:

The conflict was transformed into an extremely difficult one. At the time I was being pressured to remove the police from the area and allow the assassins of the three policemen to go away. I did not accept this. If I accepted the death of three police and removed them from the area I would never command the Military Police of Paraná. I would lose. I ordered them to arrest the murderers.[34]

This would prove a fateful decision. Paradoxically, by seeking to maintain his authority over the police Requião had effectively relinquished immediate control, and at a decisive moment. What followed was a mass arrest of people deemed suspects. Many were subjected to torture, including by electric shock and submersion under water. Such practises were reminiscent of the dictatorship and culminated in the singling out of one activist, Diniz Bento da Silva (known as Teixeirinha). After seeing his 13-year-old son kidnapped, he gave himself up to police but was then tortured and killed.

Thus, authority over the police had been re-established, but at a price that not only included the death of Teixeirinha, but a massive split within the administration, and between it and many of its traditional allies in the social movements. The honeymoon was over. As Horácio Martins de Carvalho, who left the government over the issue, notes:

There was a rupture of credibility, or rather political loyalties, that had been established. The government had been loyal to the movement, and the movement to the government. Each respected the other. From then on it became a question of you do your bit and we'll do ours, and if there's a conflict then so be it, and if we have to sit down and talk, then we talk. A very delicate situation had developed.[35]

Even if the old polarities and enmities did not reassert themselves with their customary vigour, Requião's policy had clearly run its course. Its real strength had never lain with legal decrees, no matter how skilfully crafted or enabling, nor in the formal institutional frameworks, but rather in the underlying political dynamics and their associated contradictions. The difficulty was that the latter's root causes (substantive redistribution) could never really be addressed at the level of the local state, given its necessarily limited room for manoeuvre. The policy was innovative and creative, but constrained and always subject to the risks, which eventually emerged in an explosive and tragic fashion.

Two Steps Back (1994–98 and 1998–2002)

With Jaime Lerner's election and then re-election as governor of Paraná, the situation became infinitely worse. An architect, urban planner and former mayor of Curitiba, Lerner was not particularly interested in rural affairs, but would nonetheless collaborate in allowing the police and judges to make the running in repressive tandem. This train of events flowed from Lerner's accept-ance that his political survival depended on entering into electoral alliances with forces of the far right, especially during his second term of office when the electoral arithmetic tilted further in their favour. It was a Faustian pact. All that his allies asked in exchange was that the government should hand over chunks of authority, most notably security policy, to forces like the Rural Democratic Union (União Democrática Ruralista – UDR), with paramilitary connections and strong links to Paraná's landowners. The result was a contra-dictory combination of power, i.e., the trappings of elected office, but increas-ing powerlessness, as expressed in the governor's inability to determine certain cabinet posts. As Maria de Oliveira (who found Lerner to be personally sym-pathetic), the former head of INCRA in Paraná (and later a close advisor to the Minister of Agrarian Development, Raul Jungmann) put it, 'Nomination isn't the will of the governor, it's the will of other interests. The nomination was the UDR's.'[36]

As noted earlier, the UDR was a powerful far-right grouping of landed interests operating throughout Brazil. With the UDR and associated indi-viduals effectively in charge of security policy the outlook was bleak. State authority had not so much been hijacked by the forces of the far right, as handed to them on a plate.

In the wider realm of land policy, a collapse ensued – one characterised by the paralysis of local state initiatives. Such room as there was for manoeuvre was not used and could be traced back to the corridors of power. According to Maria de Oliveira (who found Lerner to be personally sympathetic), the governor sur-rounded himself with advisors who 'were not committed [to land reform] and who had no concept of what a repressed and organised social movement [like the MST] entailed as it pressured the state to change its orientation.'[37]

Correlations of Power

Despite the undoubted differences and seemingly bewildering nature of the twists and turns involved in the Requião and Lerner administrations, both can be understood in part as the product of dynamic, often conflicting, forces attempting to express their power within the political *and* legal realms. To be sure, landed power was more deeply embedded in the Lerner administration, but it also acted as a major constraint during Requião's term of office. However it was not just about landed power. A range of factors were involved. In Requião's case, for instance, the dynamics of eviction increasingly became a function of the judiciary's own corporate interests. At the same time, the mechanics of eviction increasingly became subject to the state government's own land reform policies. And when things fell apart, as they did over the Teixeirinha case, this happened not in splendid isolation, but because the tremendous build-up of pressures could no longer be contained or managed. Some sectors within the MST, for instance, felt that pacts with the government had reached their limit and that constraining localised demands was becoming counter-productive. On the other hand, the governor's policy, following the killing of the police officers, was governed not so much by the individual merits of the case itself, as by Requião's self-confessed desire to maintain control over the system. This was exacerbated by the release of other pent-up demands from right-wing forces within the security forces which quite literally wanted to reassert their authority with a vengeance. A new equilibrium was reached, albeit through a bloody trade-off in which events were allowed to take their course and state policy was effectively knocked off course.

Similar complexities are in evidence from the outset of the Lerner administration. He, too, began with a series of trade-offs which reflected the marked shift in the social and political centre of gravity. His was an administration of the political right. Relations between the governor and the judiciary were reconfigured rapidly. Lerner simply agreed to their pay demand and in this way a major source of tension was eased. However, when it came to rural social movements the strategy was different: containment was the order of the day. Increasingly, pent-up demands were met with a combination of incomprehension from close advisors to Lerner, and a gradually expanding logic of repression. The latter became especially evident in the second Lerner administration. The progressive militarisation of social policy, like all repressive strategies, may ultimately be unworkable and generate its own contradictions, but in the short term it proved viable. It helped relieve tensions between the executive and the police, as the latter was allowed to revert to type. The fact that this occasionally resulted in a public relations headache, for instance a well documented abuse of human rights, was a price that Paraná's governor, one of the most astute managers of public relations in the country, could afford to pay.

Any idea that the legal sphere somehow stood apart from these machinations, that justice was neutral or blind, is untenable. The deployment of legal force was subject to a variety of mediations – political, corporate, cultural, economic and ideological. Likewise, it would be wrong to think of the capture of the security services by the UDR simply as a disintegration or disfigurement of state power, i.e., a deviation from an ideal. The state was never capable of rising above social tensions. On the contrary it expressed them.

At a national level the views and experience of José Gomes da Silva, a former head of INCRA, give an insight into how social tensions are expressed within the state and are all too often resolved in favour of landed interests. Back in 1985 da Silva and his colleagues had painstakingly elaborated a proposal for agrarian reform, the first National Plan of Agrarian Reform (Plano Nacional de Reforma Agrária – PNRA) which was finally handed over to President José Sarney on 27 September that year. What was finally approved by presidential decree (Decree number 91.766) a few days later was a plan disfigured beyond recognition. As da Silva notes, what eventually emerged was the result of:

> concessions to large landholders [*terratenentes*], to their organisations at all levels, to the conservative lobbies, to the pressure groups installed in the major newspapers, in the televised media, in the intimacy of the presidential palace and in decisive positions among the three powers.[38]

Unbeknown to the original drafters of the proposal, Fábio Luchesi, a land lawyer who had made part of his fortune opposing INCRA's attempts at land expropriation, had been secretly ushered into a room at the behest of President Sarney himself and set to work 48 hours before the decree was published. The result took the Minister of Agrarian Reform completely by surprise and left José Gomes da Silva honour bound to hand in his resignation with immediate effect.[39] Incredibly, though, worse was yet to come. A confidential INCRA report on the history of the PNRA would later note that the promised settlement of 1.4 million families between 1985 and 1989 never materialised. In fact the figure achieved, 89,945, represented less than 6.5 per cent of the target. Huge sums of money, R$3.2 billion, were nonetheless expended during this period, much of which ended up in the pockets of ministers and their friends.[40]

To be sure, other social forces, including the MST, also tried to express themselves through state power, a fact that is as true today under the government of President Dilma Rouseff and of President da Silva before her, as it was under the administration of Governor Requião in Paraná. The fundamental problem, of course, is that groups like the MST enjoy relatively limited leverage compared to other social forces, especially those of the right. The latter command extensive veto powers within the state administration, and congress, as well as the extra-parliamentary forms of economic, political and even cultural power witnessed by da Silva above. This is not to deny progress, as the figures in Table 2 from the Introduction clearly illustrate. The appointment of Tarso Genro as Minister for Justice (2007–10) similarly underlines the Lula government's progressive attitude and contrasts starkly with that of Nelson Jobim, the Minister of Justice (1995–97) in Cardoso's government (discussed in the following chapter). Under President Dilma Rouseff there is even a special Secretariat General of the Presidency (Secretaria-Geral da Presidência da República) whose stated aim is to advise the presidency on relations with civil society and develop channels of communication that allow for their participation in policy.[41] But as with mediation strategies under Requião, such frameworks, no matter how valuable, suffer major stuctural limitations and are no substitute for structural changes characteristic of a land reform programme.

The Failure of Reform in Querência do Norte

The case of Querência do Norte, a region in northwestern Paraná bordering the state of Mato Grosso do Sul (see Figure 5) provides further evidence of the significance of power relations in the development and failures of policy and land reform law. During the late 1990s, Querência do Norte exhibited the most intensive new wave of occupation in any part of Paraná (at least 11 ongoing occupations in 1998 alone[42]). To landowners this represented a real challenge. If encampments were not stopped in their tracks then a perceived danger existed that these could be transformed into permanent settlements, with all the negative political and economic implications these had. One only had to look a few kilometres over the border, to the Pontal do Paranapanema, where landed power had suffered significant setbacks, to appreciate the seriousness of the situation. Landowners were not about to give up without a fight.

Figure 5 Map of Parana highlighting Querência do Norte region

On the back of renewed rural worker demands, INCRA in Paraná, under the leadership of Maria de Oliveira, also began to take a keen interest. The logic for its intervention was compelling. The region included unproductive properties, along with depressed socio-economic characteristics similar to those in the Pontal do Paranapanema. Extensive cattle farming had replaced coffee, cotton and fruit cultivation and this had resulted in the collapse of employment. According to Oliveira, this system of production 'ended up excluding the population of the region. The exclusion of labourers was automatic and it generated horrendous levels of poverty. The landowners only arrived by plane, bringing their shopping with them from outside. There was no town, because there weren't people; there was no commerce because there were no buyers. There was no church because there was no priest. There was no school, no children. There was nothing.'[43]

Newspaper reports of the time indicated that much economic activity took place clandestinely through parallel bookkeeping.[44] In order to avoid paying local taxes and maintain a highly lucrative enclave economy, cattle were routinely shipped to market by truck under cover of darkness. To all intents and purposes these animals did not exist, at least not in fiscal terms. As long as INCRA averted its gaze this was a workable – even highly profitable – proposition. The moment it began to take an interest in the question of land productivity in northwestern Paraná, the landowners found themselves faced with a conundrum: how would they be able to assert the productivity of their estates in the absence of tax and vaccination certificates?[45] To claim that they did not have these documents would amount to an admission that they had systematically broken the law. The answer was not to play INCRA at its own game, but to force it to back off altogether or contain its activities. As on so many occasions, power relations were the determining issue rather than the fact that INCRA had the law on its side.

To a considerable extent, INCRA's interest in the region was a direct response to MST pressure. Unlike the government of Jaime Lerner, INCRA was duty bound to respond more positively. However, judicial intervention through the granting of eviction orders for the imprisonment of members could weaken the MST. Such difficulties had faced the movement in the Pontal do Paranapanema. In northwest Paraná though, they were magnified by a singularity: the figure of Judge Elizabeth Khater. A June 1999 article published in *Caros Amigos* magazine outlined her activities.[46] She had been responsible for the production of no fewer than 45 eviction orders and granted 17 preventive imprisonment orders relating to individuals (including Paulo Expedito Demarchi, the regional leader of the MST), encamped upon four ranches: the Bandeirantes, Rio Novo, Transval and Porangabinha. On 14 May 1999 she widened the net to include a further 13 individuals.[47]

There was no doubt that a generalised crisis was developing (especially the militarisation of conflict) to which the judiciary would eventually have to respond one way or another. On 1 February 1998, for instance, a landless worker had been executed at point blank range in an extra-judicial eviction involving some 50 hired gunmen.[48] His death, which came about despite explicit warnings to the police, was widely condemned, and formed part of a more ominous picture. Ranchers were open about the fact that they were continuing to arm themselves. 'Protecting our properties with whatever means at our disposal,' said one, 'is a constitutional right'.[49] 'We are', he went on, 'prepared to defend our property at whatever price.'

Judge Khater weighed into the debate with a May 1997 newspaper interview[50] in which she suggested that unless Jaime Lerner's government acted to enforce judicial mandates with more conviction, it would end in disaster. The landowners had told her they were arming in order to secure evictions themselves. Interestingly, though, far from condemning their actions, or calling into question their legality, she merely underlined her concerns over the state's failure to evict workers from the Dois Córregos ranch, 100 kilometers to the east of Querência do Norte. 'The state is disobeying a judicial order'.

Once again, the old conflict that had bedevilled Requião's administration appeared to be reasserting itself, except this time under Governor Lerner. Because the judiciary had granted numerous eviction orders, and a reservoir of these had built up throughout the state of Paraná under the Requião government, the social implications of breaking the legal logjam were extremely serious. A press report of the time suggested that at one stage Governor Lerner even 'begged' landowners not to instigate legal actions for federal intervention. That report went on:

> In order to contain MST invasions, and oblige the state government to carry out eviction orders that have been decreed by the judiciary, the tactic of the UDR from now on is to request federal intervention in Paraná. 'Lerner is terrified at the prospect of federal intervention', said a member of the UDR.[51]

Was Judge Khater a willing accomplice to landowner pretensions or merely attempting to 'reintroduce' the rule of law in a region historically characterised by the chronic evasion of legal obligations and systematic abuse of fundamental social and economic rights? It is difficult to know for certain, but on 7 May 1999, immediately after a particularly brutal eviction by police, when spirits in some quarters were running high, the judge went to a restaurant in the town of Loanda and was found celebrating the success of the operation with landowner friends. By chance a reporter from the *Folha de São Paulo*, happened to be there.

> During the meal, a reporter approached her. The judge mistook him for a policeman and praised him. 'Congratulations on your work! I was just praising the work of you all to all my rancher friends. We are here celebrating. This could be the beginning of a union between landowners and

the military police.' Upon perceiving her mistake, the judge became white as a sheet and tried to explain herself. 'But friendship did not influence' (in the judicial decisions).[52]

Far more serious than Khater's public exposure was the fact that other judges, with more circumspect views, were handing out similar sentences every day, in a pattern repeated not just in Querência do Norte or elsewhere in Paraná, but throughout Brazil. The collective capacity of the legal system to grant eviction orders (and even institute bogus cases against human rights advocates[53]) was infinitely greater than its capacity to convict police officers, hired gunmen or their paymasters. A 2010 bulletin from the MST lamented the fact that despite the assassination of 1,600 rural workers since 1985 only 80 have resulted in judicial processes, 16 people were found guilty and only eight are currently in prison.[54]

Of course arrests, prosecutions and convictions of landowners did take place. Even Judge Khater herself ordered the detention of a security officer from the Água da Prata plantation following his alleged assassination of a landless worker in November 2000. However, the overwhelming bias of the system, the comprehensiveness of its failure to live up to its own claims, in contrast to the marked capacity of landowners to assert theirs within it, made it the latter's weapon of choice and object of deep suspicion among landless workers.

For the regional head of the UDR, Marcos Prochet, 'The response of the state to the eviction request at the Dois Córregos ranch ... amounts to an authorization for the owners to arm themselves.'[55] Khater's interventions therefore must have come as music to his ears. Apparently she had even attempted to push the process forward with approaches to the Secretariat of Public Security, hoping 'the government would acknowledge the gravity of the situation and carry out the eviction order. Before it is too late.'[56]

One cannot tease out precisely how much these and other multiple pressures (including the fear of federal intervention) weighed upon the state government, but by 1999 the latter began to unleash its repressive power against the MST and receive plaudits from landowners. In May 1999 landowner organisations from Paraná sent dozens of letters to Governor Lerner and his Secretary of Public Security, Cândido Martins de Oliveira, congratulating them for their firm action on evictions. These had, in the words of one correspondent, helped 're-establish peace, law and order and the right to property in the region'.[57] The Catholic Church's Pastoral Land Commission (in a joint report with the MST) concluded the opposite. 'Today Paraná can be characterised as the principal point of tension in the struggle for land in Brazil. In the state of Paraná in 1999 alone there have been 137 imprisonments of landless workers, 29 violent evictions involving about 2,000 families.'[58]

After a brief period of relaxation under the Requião government, the legal system had reverted to its more familiar line of containment and criminalisation.

The MST had geared up its occupations, and landowners had geared up their response in the political and legal spheres. Even if the judiciary denied the connections in public, landowners were only too well aware of their importance and the value of a multi-pronged strategy.

Where did these oscillating correlations of force leave the government agency whose job it was to give practical effect to constitutional injunctions on land reform? Speaking in February 1998, José Carlos de Araújo, the chief advisor on land issues to the Lerner government and later a head of INCRA in Paraná, was damning. 'INCRA', he said, 'has been extremely slow in the process of agrarian reform in Paraná and this has generated the conflicts we are now witnessing.'[59] The view (which historically speaking was largely correct) is ironic not only because his own tenure as head of the organisation a year later would represent an even greater failure, but also because the political will, which is a prerequisite to any form of change, was present within INCRA at the time he made his comment. This latter point merits some explanation.

Under Maria de Oliveira's leadership, between 1996 and 1998, INCRA took some bold decisions. In particular, in July 1997, it began to roll out a plan in the northwest of the state under which 670 properties, each over 450 hectares in size, would be re-registered. The idea was to resettle 1,500 families in private properties in the region. To this end, any acquisition would be effected either through the discovery and expropriation of unproductive properties, or through the consensual purchase of productive properties.[60] Although these actions were in accordance with the law, the UDR immediately condemned them. A trial of strength ensued between the two organisations. It was not a confrontation that INCRA was keen on.

Recognising that the core of UDR activities for both the south of the country and the state of Paraná itself lay in the town of Paranavaí, the agency decided to set up a provisional unit there. According to Oliveira, the aim was 'not to confront the UDR, but to be able to converse better with it, to be alongside it every day, to call it into INCRA in order to explain to it the nature of our work. To give transparency to the process in order to avoid that they should become enemies of the programme.'[61] This kind of approach had worked in the course of ITESP's negotiations with landowners in the Pontal do Paranapanema. Crucially, though, it was under different conditions, in particular with the firm backing of the state government, which immeasurably strengthened that agency's hand. The correlation of political forces in Paraná, let alone the legal setting (which did not involve devolved land) differed markedly, and at the state level it was landowners, not the governor, who were increasingly in charge of land and security policy. To a large extent, therefore, the agency went into battle with one arm tied behind its back.

When Oliveira's team went into Paranavaí it was initially met with widespread hostility and working conditions were virtually impossible. Verbal threats were made against employees. 'We couldn't even buy a pen in the town!' Oliveira noted.[62] Eventually, however, the mayor and the UDR did agree to meet INCRA. Prior to this Oliveira had initiated a media offensive to explain her case. Now she threw open the books for detailed inspection. The overall strategy was spelt out as were the methods of analysis – from satellite plotting, searching local land record offices and, via the Ministry of Agriculture, accessing data on the movement of cattle. Oliveira suggests that within certain limits some 'enthusiasm' was generated within the ranks of the UDR, partly because all the costs of gathering the technical and legal data (drawing maps, preparing productivity reports, updating land registrations, etc.) would be borne by INCRA. It was providing productive landowners with a free service.

Given her acknowledgement that 30 per cent of the properties INCRA was able to investigate were unproductive, it seems understandable that many landowners were not so keen on this free service. It begs the question how would those with unproductive properties respond. As one of the country's most effective lobbies, there were clear reasons for landowners sticking together in spite of their differences. Matters would depend upon how the overall sample would have eventually unfolded.

In the event, though, Oliveira never found out. Her policy of transparency backfired spectacularly. Instead of separating landowning interests into different factions she was removed from her job at the behest of those same interests. At a meeting in the town of Ponta Grossa, in central Paraná, federal and state deputies allied to landowning interests were given a taste of Oliveira's plans to roll out her programme throughout the state. She later acknowledged this was a grave tactical error which led to the intensification of efforts to remove her. Raul Jungmann, the Minister for Agrarian Reform, later summed up the episode in the following terms: 'she was eviscerated'.[63]

Oliveira's removal is important because yet again it illustrates the limits of change. For all INCRA's federal characteristics, the minister himself was at pains to point out that Maria de Oliveira's case demonstrated that:

> No superintendent can survive in a state, and oversee the agrarian conflict, who does not, in some measure, receive support from within the states. It simply doesn't happen any other way. You always have to operate within these parameters and that's what happened.[64]

In saying this, Jungmann was not condemning Oliveira (indeed he gave her a job in his personal office as a chief advisor immediately after her removal). Rather, he was stating the facts as he saw them. It should be borne in mind, however, that the contingent nature of power and the federal agency's apparent weaknesses was not simply the result of the need to do business in the states. It also went to the heart of the federal administration and internal compromises it had made with conservative allies. Those compromises included bringing figures like Pratini de Moraes into prominent positions of power, resulting in attempts to stymie the prospects of land reform from within the administration itself.

Conclusion

Much of the evidence presented in this chapter is deeply troubling because it appears to suggest that often it does not matter who is actually or nominally in charge because the power of landed interests is so overwhelming. One need not delve into the thorny question of whether politicians like President José Sarney were actually or nominally in charge, whether in his case he was a willing or unwilling accomplice. All that matters is that he served land reform on a platter to its opponents. A not dissimilar situation applied to Jaime Lerner's state governments, where electoral politics and a conservative disposition played their part. But the same cannot be said for Roberto Requião in Paraná. There then arises the difficult question of what his regime amounted to and its wider implications.

The view set out in this chapter is that Requião's government did indeed represent a step forward and that who is in charge does make a difference. The more pertinent question, therefore, is how much of a difference? The political and, one might add, legal space created by the Requião administration should be regarded as a victory for landless interests in an otherwise bleak national landscape. This, along with symbolic changes, should not be belittled. At the same time, though, his government was never going to bring about structural change. That would have required much stronger (including federal) forces in play when in fact the reverse – federal opposition – was the case.

Ironically it was the MST (whose members had not been properly resettled) that blinked first. Through an occupation it set off a chain of events that would culminate in the killings of three police officers and one of its own militants, and the implosion of its pact with the state government. But this was merely the trigger. The state government was already embattled. Legally speaking it was on the defensive even if Requião's chief legal officer was absolutely correct in asserting not merely that 'it was a conflict among rights',[65] but that for once the human rights of the most exploited sectors of society should take precedence over legal formalism. The state government also found itself cornered in financial terms because President Fernando Collor's federal government was opposed to land reform and was hardly likely to offer the sort of support that Mário Covas and ITESP in São Paulo subsequently enjoyed with President Fernando Henrique Cardoso's government (a political ally). Such differences meant that Paraná's room for manoeuvre was extremely limited. Although its engagement in the mediation of land conflicts offered useful tactical advantages, in the last analysis this merely postponed the inevitable. The margin of action was diminishing for all sides. Only more substantive political changes at a national level (or a greatly empowered landless movement) could have altered matters. Meanwhile local tensions were bound to play themselves out.

All this makes the election of Lula da Silva as president in 2002 and 2006 that much more significant. Potentially at least, the pro-land reform stance of his administrations constituted a vital part of the puzzle that had been missing for decades. Indirectly, the experience of Paraná gives some insight into the limitations upon progressive action at the level of the national state. These limitations are not of the constitutional variety expected of all federal power systems (in which competencies are formally divided), but relate to how the pieces fit together and actually work in practise, to relations of power, not paper formulations. Legally speaking the federal administration may have been in the driving seat, but it was the Minister of Agrarian Reform himself who stressed the importance of support within the states. His assertion in this and other chapters, amounts to an acknowledgement that the sheer force of countervailing pressures within states constitutes a critical variable governing the effectiveness of INCRA's actions. Inevitably these forces will vary from state to state depending upon the precise correlation of forces. This is not an iron law of rural oligarchy. There is nothing inevitable or predetermined about the outcomes. On the contrary, these issues are historically determined, a fact that makes the contribution of movements like the MST to rural struggles so important. In the specific case of Maria de Oliveira, however, the sheer strength of landed power meant that to a large extent it did not matter that the law was behind INCRA's initiatives. Her demise is symptomatic of the limits of legality and progressive state action present throughout the country.

Notes

1 Author interview with João Stédile, 18 March 2000.
2 Author interview with Raul Jungmann, 5 April 2000.
3 Technically three were in command since Mário Pereira, Requião's vice-governor, assumed office between 2 April 1994 and 1 January 1995. Requião had resigned in order to pursue elections as a senator for Paraná.
4 Cited in 'Especial Júri Anghinoni: A impunidade nas terras do Paraná', 20 July 2011, available at http://terradedireitos.org.br/biblioteca/especial-juri-anghinoni-a-impunidade-nas-terras-do-parana/
5 See Table 2 in the Introduction.
6 The Land Institute was in many respects directly comparable to ITESP in São Paulo. It was crucial in carrying out land audits which INCRA then put its name to for legal reasons.
7 Author interview with Horácio Martins de Carvalho, 27 November 1999.
8 Author interview with Luis Edson Fachin, 25 November 1999. In Chapter 1 we also saw how a relatively junior state lawyer could obstruct the work of São Paulo's land agency, ITESP, on ostensibly technical, but in reality ideological grounds, and how this resistance eventually led ITESP to call in the state's chief attorney to do the job.

 9 'Presidente da Funai sai e critica repressão', *Folha de São Paulo*, 23 April 2000.
10 Ibid.
11 The SESP incorporated the civil and military police as well as fire brigade and transport department under its jurisdiction.
12 Author interview with Carlos Frederico Marés, 17 December 2000.
13 Strictly speaking, it is for an officer of the court to go and inform occupants that they must leave or be evicted. Author interview with Roberto Requião, 5 April 2000.
14 Author interview with Roberto Requião, 5 April 2000.
15 Author interview with Carlos Frederico Marés, 17 December 2000.
16 Author interview with Roberto Requião, 5 April 2000.
17 Author interview with Horácio Martins de Carvalho, 27 November 1999.
18 Ibid.
19 Author interview with Belisário Santos Júnior, 6 December 1999. Belisário, it will be recalled, was a well-known human rights lawyer and Covas' Secretary of State for Justice. Belisário and the rest of the Covas administration were aware of the difficulties that had occurred in Paraná as a result of open advocacy of their new policy. That said, even if the formal position of the Paulista government was to evict, this still left open the question of precisely when, where and how. Matters were not quite as straightforward as Belisário suggests. The devil always lies in the detail. Furthermore, he acknowledges that his own government's policy was only tenable because it had a plan for resettling landless workers.
20 Author interview with Horácio Martins de Carvalho, 27 November 1999.
21 Ibid.
22 Ibid.
23 Ibid.
24 A similar sort of approach was later tried in the Pontal do Paranapanema. Major legal obstacles were overcome in such a way that the federal government was able to funnel substantial funds through the state land agency.
25 Author interview with Roberto Requião, 5 April 2000.
26 Ibid.
27 Ibid.
28 Ibid.
29 Author interview with João Pedro Stédile, 18 March 2000.
30 Author interview with Roberto Requião, 5 April 2000.
31 Author interview with Roberto Baggio, 11 August 2000.
32 Author interview with Roberto Requião, 5 April 2000.
33 Ibid.
34 Ibid.
35 Author interview with Horácio Martins de Carvalho, 27 November 1999.
36 Author interview with Maria de Oliveira, 20 October 1999.
37 Ibid.
38 José Gomes da Silva: *Caindo por terra: crise da reforma agrária na nova república*, São Paulo: Editora Busca Vida, 1987, p. 49.
39 Ibid., pp. 185–7.
40 The scale of the fraud is truly breathtaking and only came to light in a 300-page dossier on Agrarian Debt Bonds. According to the report's compiler, Petrus Emile

Abi-Abib, 'Veritable fortunes were paid for lousy land and where the demand for settlement was not particularly high. It was a lot of land for very few people. Today many of the expropriated areas that have already been paid for don't even have a single family on them. This money could have been used in expropriation of other areas and attended to the needs of the landless in other parts of the country'. He goes on: 'if overpayments for land had not occurred and all the financial resources had been properly applied, the country would be living with the social movements of landless workers rather than confronting them'. (Report accessed January 2010 at www2.correioweb.com.br/cw/2001-09-30/mat_14737.htm It is no longer available online.) See also Ministério de Política Fundiária e do Desenvolvimento Agrário and Instituto Nacional de Colonização e Reforma Agrária – INCRA, *O livro branco das superindenizações*, Brasília: Ministério da Política Fundiária e do Desenvolvimento Agrário, 1999.

41 See www.secretariageral.gov.br/secgeral

42 One newspaper report of the time suggested that 'the 1,200 people encamped in the area correspond to 15 per cent of the 8,000 landless workers who live in the 87 MST encampments in the state'. 'Região é novo Pontal do MST', *Jornal do Brasil*, 10 February 1998.

43 Author interview with Maria de Oliveira, 20 October 1999.

44 See for example the comments of the mayor of Bovis in 'Região é novo Pontal do MST' in *Jornal do Brasil*, 10 February 1998.

45 While the identification of crops by satellite is possible, satellite tracking of animals is not viable. This is one reason why emphasis is placed upon tax returns and vaccination certificates.

46 José Arbex Jr, 'Terror no Paraná', *Caros Amigos*, no. 27, June 1999, pp. 10–15.

47 Ibid., p. 12.

48 'Sem-terra é assassinado no Noroeste', *Folha do Paraná*, 8 February 1998.

49 A landowner, Marco Antônio Cutino, cited in 'Fazendeiros vão combater as invasões com milícias', *O Popular*, 28 June 1998.

50 'Juíza alerta para risco de violência', *Folha de Londrina*, 22 May 1997.

51 'Advogado da UDR diz que Lerner "implorou"', *O Estado do Paraná*, 20 February 1998.

52 'Justiça Cega', *Folha de São Paulo*, 14 May 1999, cited in José Arbex Jr, 'Terror no Paraná', *Caros Amigos*, no. 27, June 1999, p. 12.

53 I was witness to one of these bogus cases when Darci Frigo, a lawyer for the CPT, was charged with breaking the leg of a policeman during an eviction of landless workers from the Centro Cívico in Curitiba on 27 November 1999. It transpired that nothing of the sort had happened. Inadvertently, I caught the real events on film.

54 'Balanço da nossa jornada de lutas', *MST Informa*, no. 182, 23 April 2010, available at www.mst.org.br/node/9719

55 Cited in 'Juíza alerta para risco de violência', *Folha de Londrina*, 22 May 1997.

56 Ibid.

57 Mimeo letter from president of the Sociedade Paranaense de Medicina Veterinária, to the Secretary of Public Security, 7 July 1999.

58 Mimeo CPT-MST, *Despejo no Centro Cívico: violência, arbitrariedade e terror*, Curitiba, 27 November 1999.

59 'De quem é a culpa pelos conflitos?', *Jornal do Estado*, 10 February 1998.
60 Source: 'INCRA monta unidade avançada em Paranavaí', *Folha de Londrina*, 29 July 1997.
61 Author interview with Maria de Oliveira, 20 October 1999.
62 Ibid.
63 Author interview with Raul Jungmann, 5 April 2000.
64 Ibid.
65 Author interview with Carlos Frederico Marés, 17 December 2000.

Chapter 5

Pushing and Redefining Legal Boundaries through Social Movement Pressure

> Today the social movement is taking a road towards the invasion of productive land. ... A struggle of this kind re-ignites a much more ideological struggle or purely ideological struggle in the countryside, rather than one that is truly about land.
> Belisário Santos Júnior, Secretary of State for Justice, São Paulo[1]

> In the case of some specific regions there aren't large unproductive ranches ... So the workers are obliged to choose areas which, although they are productive, can lead on to the debate over their social function.
> João Pedro Stédile, Leader of the MST[2]

One feature that emerges from previous chapters is just how unfavourable the socio-legal terrain upon which the MST operates is. That landscape is characterised not so much juridically, by questions and constraints that pertain to the written law, as by legal practise that is heavily imbued with ideologies that favour absolutist notions of property, that value formal over and above substantive legal equality, and that harbour a distain – even fear – of social movements. As for aspects of legality that are more favourable to interests of social movements, whether constitutionally or in the fine detail of enforcing land audits, these have been shown to be ineffective to the extent that they are mediated by forces exercising veto powers over change.

The one-sided nature of the terrain does not mean, however, that it is unilaterally constructed. On the contrary, it is contested – sometimes fiercely so – both internally and externally. Although such contestation is important, because it opens up some possibilities for progressive action, its significance can more readily be gauged in a practical context rather than extrapolated theoretically.

To this end the first case discussed in this chapter concerns progressive sectors within São Paulo's Public Ministry which have tried to bolster the legal case for land reform itself. Some prosecutors there have taken the bold and unusual stand of emphasising landed property's socially contingent nature and the corresponding legitimacy of occupations of some productive lands (a line forcefully rejected by Belisário Santos Júnior in the introductory quote above). The chapter examines their actions in the context of an occupation of productive land carried out by the MST near the town of Matão, in the centre of the state of São Paulo (see Figure 6) in February 2000.

Since 2000 investment in rural land has mushroomed, has increasingly crowded out alternative land-use strategies, and further highlighted the significance of productive land. As well as underlying the difficult political and legal choices this poses for the movement, the events of Matão reveal the MST's sophisticated and changing relationship with law, a relationship that has taken an increasingly offensive (i.e., agenda setting) form rather than a more defensive one. Although some will argue that developments of this kind represent an ideological distortion of a hitherto legitimate struggle for land, others (including this author) see it as a necessary, legitimate and legal response to chronic land shortages and legal failures.

The other case dealt with in this chapter concerns resistance by São Paulo's Public Ministry to pressure by the federal Minister of Justice, Nelson Jobim (1995–97) to prosecute the MST more aggressively. What is important about the case is not simply the substantive outcomes (Jobim's efforts were rebuffed by the Public Ministry, thereby leaving increased room for manoeuvre for it and the MST), but also the deep tension it reveals within the legal field over the issue of land reform. Crucially, the passage of time has done little to diminish the significance of these institutional conflicts. Jobim was later elected to head the Supreme Court in 2004. While the personnel and institutional

Figure 6 Map of São Paulo including Matão

settings have changed, to all intents and purposes many of the underlying fault lines have not. Thus, for instance, President Lula da Silva's appointment of a radically inclined politician, Tarso Genro, as Minister of Justice (2007–10) saw the latter become the object of numerous attacks by landed classes precisely because of his reluctance to take a punitive stance towards the MST.[3] Ironically, as if to hint at some of the political accords that lie beneath ministerial selection, both Presidents Lula da Silva and Dilma Rouseff also counted upon the services of Nelson Jobim, albeit as Defence Minister (2007–11) rather than Minister of Justice.[4]

The Case Against Occupying Productive Land

At the heart of the controversy surrounding the Matão occupation lies Article 185 of the 1988 constitution. It puts forward the notion of 'productive property' and asserts that it 'shall not be subject to expropriation for agrarian reform purposes'.[5] It is the apparently categorical nature of this legal injunction that would become the subject of such heated legal and political controversy.

The factors that originally led to the introduction of productive property and associated guarantees into the constitution are not the concern of this book. The key point is that although they were introduced against strong opposition from pro-land reform groups, the text nevertheless became the cornerstone of all subsequent discussion. The MST might dislike this aspect of the constitution but it clearly worked within its confines – so much so, it may be argued, that the dominant feature of the movement's occupation strategy throughout the 1980s and 1990s was the occupation of unproductive land. Among other things it was an easier target. As one movement document put it, 'unproductive lands must be appropriated. In not being appropriated by virtue of the inertia of the public power, the occupations are legitimate and necessary'.[6] Whether by force of circumstances, or design, unproductive land was elevated from a mere legal category into a source of political legitimation and mobilisation.

The MST's nascent targeting of productive properties was therefore bound to prove controversial. The comments of two key players, both politicians, give a sense of why the move was seen as a step too far. The first comes Belisário Santos Júnior, São Paulo state's Secretary of State for Justice. Although he was not a supporter of the MST, in fact he was a member of Fernando Henrique Cardoso's Brazilian Social Democratic Party (PSDB), he could be counted as broadly sympathetic to many of the movement's aims. In this context it is worth recalling Mançano's earlier assertion that Belisário's appointment had signalled the undermining of the alliance between state and powerful land grabbers.[7] Belisário is forthright about the perceived dangers:

> Today the social movement is taking a road towards the invasion of productive land. For us this is, shall we say, incoherent with the whole

struggle we have had and where a common limit existed. We want agrarian reform. We want the use of unproductive land. We want the use of public land for the ends to which the law has said it must be assigned. For this reason productive land must not be used in this kind of struggle. But the younger leaders, I don't know to what extent they will influence things. At the moment that is my concern. That a struggle of this kind re-ignites a much more ideological struggle or purely ideological struggle in the countryside, rather than one that is truly about land.[8]

At the time of this interview, Belisário was speaking in an official capacity and therefore within politically circumscribed constraints. Nonetheless, his concerns should not be dismissed lightly. It was, after all, under the ideologically polarised conditions of 1964 that the mere whiff of land reform was transformed into a pretext for the military overthrow of President João Goulart's government.[9] Surely, though, the Secretary of State for Justice did not have the spectre of a military putsch in mind when he made these comments. Conditions had changed beyond recognition. Underlying his observation, therefore, was the view that the MST might be expanding its range of activities too far and too fast and with too much ideological aggression, thereby losing its allies and diverting it from the real prize: land reform.

The Minister of Agrarian Reform, Raul Jungmann, offers a similar, but more extended analysis.

Many people have criticised the constitution of 1988. The great criticism of the '88 constitution is that it made a division between productive and unproductive lands. I believed this to be the case, but later I came to the view, partly from an extrapolation of the juridical terrain, that this represented an enormous political conquest. Look, if it brought problems for us, which it undoubtedly did, it also divided rural owners. This is because the productive owner feels protected by the constitution so he will not become a source of leverage. In this way a division that is immensely important for us is accomplished. Firstly, because there is an abundance of unproductive areas, in other words no shortage of land. Thus for land reform to occur in Brazil it does not require productive areas – the latter notion is nonsense, although there is greater difficulty in the south and south east of the country ... But what I perceive is that this makes the landowners feel more secure – 'It's OK. I am productive. I am inside the system, so it doesn't affect me.' And in a certain way this has led to a situation of political isolation of large landowners. Initially I was faced with a situation in which people fell into line behind the traditional landowners. But today, being in the midst of major negotiations, the changes and the laws, I really ask myself, and end up concluding, that this has indeed been beneficial.[10]

Right-wing interests had first introduced the concept of productive property into the constitution as a means of forestalling land reform. As noted earlier, Article 185 stated that expropriation of such properties was 'not permitted'. And yet 12 years on from those events the Minister of Agrarian Reform felt that the productivity clause had, in fact, been an 'enormous political conquest' and his initial assessment wrong because at last large landowners were 'politically isolated'. Juridically speaking, Article 185 might be the highest form of law, but the minister was, in effect, suggesting that it ultimately took the form of a law of unintended consequences that had confounded the expectations of drafters and opponents alike. Not only had a juridical fracture running the length and breadth of the country been introduced in 1988, but Jungmann seemed to argue that it took eminently practical forms that were overwhelmingly positive – an inversion of the left's (and his earlier) political wisdom. Now, apparently, vast swathes of unproductive land could be split off at considerably diminished political cost, thus obviating the necessity of targeting productive areas.

The devil in the detail: gaps in the argument

On the face of it Raul Jungmann's argument deserves to be taken seriously. There is, for instance, some merit to the suggestion that the legal recognition of the case for expropriating unproductive properties diminished the relative costs/obstacles associated with occupying them, a fact readily exploited by the MST (even if the costs remained horrendously high and the outcomes uncertain). But there are limits to his argument. Although the minister acknowledges that things may not be quite so simple in the south and southeast of the country, the evidence presented in this book shows that the devil almost invariably lies in such details. The case study of Bagé, for example, demonstrated the highly contested nature of productivity as a concept and how, when it failed to suit the interests of landowners, they succeeded in moving the goal posts in accordance with their interests to such an extent that legality itself became a moot point. A striking feature in that instance was how the great divide between groups of landowners, specifically productive versus unproductive groups, never materialised. Not only did the translation of productivity clauses into practise prove extremely messy, but, productive owners increasingly questioned whether they might be caught up in a more rigorous definition of productivity and therefore should rally to their colleagues' cause. Indeed, one fear, voiced by the minister himself, was that events in Bagé might provoke a chain reaction throughout Brazil, as various factions coalesced in opposition to productivity indices and existing accords fell apart.[11] Clearly this raises questions about the real extent of political divisions between productive and unproductive landowners. One may go further. Even now, following the completion of Lula da Silva's two presidential terms productivity indices have been left untouched. To all intents and purposes, the division between productive and unproductive landowners has never lived up to the great expectations.

To be sure, there are divisions among landowners, but any political divisions between the productive and unproductive must be put into some kind of perspective. As Rolf Hackbart noted in relation to productivity indices,

> At its core I think that the question of the productivity indices illustrates well the current dispute over both the right agricultural model for Brazil and the use and ownership of land. ... The debate crystallises the dispute over models. The large commercial capitalist landowning sector says no, we must avoid anything that could signal a risk. I would argue the opposite, that the absence of land regularisation generates greater risks.[12]

So although their material interests differ from unproductive landowners, there is a degree of risk aversion among even the most advanced landowning interests that propells them towards the maintenance of the status quo.

A similar point applies in relation to arguments about there being 'no shortage of land'. To assert the existence of huge tracts of unproductive land as proof positive of the misguided nature of productive occupations is a politically loaded form of abstraction. It obscures the fact that the issue is not whether huge tracts of unproductive land exist in Brazil, which everyone accepts they do, but the precise modalities governing their availability. Therein lies the rub. As chapters on the Pontal do Paranapanema have demonstrated, although land there belonged to the state and should by law have been given over to agrarian reform projects, it remained in the hands of private individuals and therefore a mere abstraction for decades. Transforming that situation proved a herculean task – not only for landless workers themselves, but also for the local state and its allies in the federal government. Even then, with all that effort, only a relatively small proportion was regained by the state. To talk, therefore, in terms of millions of hectares available is, to say the very least, problematic. The issue in Brazil has never been about the quantity of notional land in existence, but the modalities governing access to it. If, as so frequently happens, provision comes by way of a drip feed mechanism, then it becomes of academic interest whether there are one million or, as the minister suggests, hundreds of millions of hectares available.

Belisário's comments are best assessed in the light of these modalities or practicalities. His suggestion that targeting productive land 're-ignites a much more ideological struggle' is true to the extent that it carries a much weightier ideological charge. However his statement is also problematic on several counts. Methodologically and socially speaking it represents a somewhat top-down view of the problems. When the issues are examined from below, i.e., from the actual experiences of landless rural workers, a quite different picture and set of priorities emerge. When the social setting of occupation is detailed, when the reasons why individual workers gravitated to this occupation are clearly spelt out, and when the basis for the selection of target properties explored, it becomes infinitely more difficult to reduce events merely to a matter of ideological struggle, and its supposed dangers, let alone to a matter of 'purely ideological struggle', or the destabilising impact of young hotheads within the movement. Rather than an abstract clash of ideologies one finds that much of the struggle arises out of necessity. Only on the back of those real needs does ideology enter the picture let alone maintain its force.

By way of clarification consider the following comments from MST leader, João Pedro Stédile.

> You see it isn't a central movement organism that decides the area to be occupied. There is no point in coming up with a general or national 'line'. It is the rank and file that must decide upon the area to be occupied. So the general policy of the movement in the base is 'which area here, in the municipality produces badly, or is everyone angry about, and, as a consequence, will lead local society to support us?' That is the general line. There is a second aspect. In the case of some specific regions there aren't large unproductive ranches (about which, evidently, everyone is unhappy). So the workers are obliged to choose areas which, although they are productive, can lead on to the debate over their social function. What is the real social function of property? So here in São Paulo, and some regions in the north of Paraná, productive areas have been occupied.[13]

What is evident from the comments of Stédile (and, to some extent, Jungmann's own acknowledgement of the 'greater difficulty in the south and south east of the country') is how the peculiar characteristics of states like São Paulo and Paraná, i.e., the lack of available unproductive land, have necessitated this shift in movement tactics. These are populous regions of the country so it is not as if the social demand is absent. Occupation of land in the Amazon by poor multitudes from the south is not an option, and in any case, one which when tried under the military government in the late 1960s and early 1970s failed miserably.[14] An essential part of the MST's outlook from its inception has been the necessity of people's struggles within their locality rather than the displacement of contradictions for fear of their ideological or other implications. Does this mean that any form of struggle is valid? Certainly not – it simply means that the movement's integration of social demands within its struggle has compelled it to re-evaluate hitherto marginalised political and legal options. The occupation of the Fazenda Ximbó near Matão, and emergence of the debate on the social function of property should be seen as part of that organic process.

Origins of the Occupation at the Fazenda Ximbó

A notable feature of the Matão occupation, which took even its organisers by surprise, was the speed at which it grew. The encampment began its formal existence on 18 December 1999, when 600 families moved into a corner of the Ximbó ranch. Within 10 days that group had mushroomed to over 1,000 families. Finally, on 20 January 2000, when the population reached 1,200 families, or 6,000 individuals, the gates to the encampment were closed to newcomers as consolidation became the order of the day.

Organisational and socio-economic factors were key to these spectacular rates of growth. The occupation had been meticulously planned. Its preparatory stages had begun almost a year earlier, as families throughout the area were invited to assemble in nearby regional centres such as Ribeirão Preto, Araraquara (see Figure 6, page 152) and Franca. The catchment area went beyond this, to include a small group from the port city of Santos, some 500 kilometres distant, and some families from the inner-city Brás neighbourhood of the state capital, São Paulo. According to one occupation leader, the latter group formed 'part of a project to rehabilitate people living in the streets'. They were 'invited to come and recover their dignity working on the land.'[15]

A related aspect of organisation was the choice of the Fazenda Ximbó itself. If the MST was going to pick a fight on the difficult issue of productive land's social function then it could not have chosen a better location in which to test these arguments. As will become clear later, the movement's choice was likely to enjoy substantial support from the local community and beyond, thereby enhancing its capacity to attract new adherents. Indeed, to many outside observers, including politicians, judges, journalists and members of INCRA itself, the occupation appeared eminently reasonable.

The second explanation for the occupation's sustained growth was the region's socio-economic character. The movement was tapping into a vast reservoir of unmet need, just as it did with varying degrees of success throughout the country. The difference in this instance was that those needs had been identified in an area of exceptionally high agricultural productivity, an area that, on the basis of a quick reading of the Brazilian constitution, was widely held to be legally off limits and, for many observers (including Raul Jungmann and Belisário Santos Júnior), should remain politically off limits too. For the MST, though, that still left open the obvious but as yet unanswered question of how those needs should be addressed. Should they simply be ignored because they were politically or juridically inconvenient? To a large degree this question lies at the heart of the Fazenda Ximbó occupation. It was designed to highlight the issue of property's social function and the plight of landless workers – even in regions of high productivity.

Brazil's California and the social function of property

There should be no doubt as to the uphill nature of the MST's struggle over the Fazenda Ximbó. After the passage of the 1988 constitution, a widespread perception had developed that productive land was legally impregnable and politically sacrosanct, an impression to some extent reinforced by the MST's own concentration upon unproductive properties. A brief comparison between the situation in the Pontal do Paranapanema, which helped legitimise the movement, and that faced by landless workers in Matão, gives insight into the magnitude of the new challenge. It will be recalled that not only did the former region possess lands with historically low levels of productivity, but also that the lands had been privatised illegally, a fact recognised by a 1958 court judgment of which the MST would subsequently make full use. By contrast there was no such judgment hanging over the Matão region where ownership claims were undisputed. As for productivity, land here was fertile and agricultural activity some of the most productive and lucrative anywhere in Brazil.

At one level, therefore, the MST was engaged in the difficult task of questioning the very parameters and ideology of the productive model itself. That ideology was powerfully symbolised by eulogising media references to the region as 'Brazil's California', not a reference to levels of debt or cheap agricultural labour, but to the idea that it constituted a technologically advanced agricultural area. Leaving aside the hyperbole, the reference did draw attention to the region's pre-eminent role in agricultural production, most notably sugar cane (in which it remains one of the leading global players), but also areas like orange, soya and peanut production. On top of these activities came the processing industries, like vast sugar mills and fruit processing plants. These gave further stimulus to manufacturers of fixed and mobile agricultural capital equipment. The net result was the development of a powerful agro-industrial complex.[16]

Just like the so-called 'economic miracle' of the early 1970s, however, 'Brazil's California' had a darker side. For those actually labouring in the cane fields and orange groves, low wages, poor working conditions and unstable employment were the norm. Liberation from this cycle often took the form of unemployment as workers – most notably in the sugar cane industry – were replaced by mechanical harvesters. Although there was more diversity and 'complexity' in this situation (industrial and service sectors do absorb labour too), for numerous landless labourers the situation was brutally simple and unjust. Taking this as a point of departure, it becomes easier to understand not only why the MST moved into the region, but why it could serve as such a powerful pole of attraction.

Clearly, if the intention behind the occupation of the Fazenda Ximbó had been to subvert an entire system of production, it would have been doomed from the outset. Instead, the objective was more modest: to call aspects of the system to account by exposing the social and environmental costs of production and highlight the contradictions between that model and constitutional provisions on the social function of property. Given these objectives the Fazenda Ximbó was an obvious candidate for occupation.

The plantation was owned by a company, Agropecuaria Riopedrense, which had debts of R$95 million (US$51 million) owed to the federal government's

National Institute of Social Security (Instituto Nacional de Segurança Social –
INSS). This was important because, according to Gilmar Mauro, an MST
leader closely associated with the occupation, in meetings with the MST
'President Fernando Henrique Cardoso agreed with us that there are many
INSS debtors who could see their lands taken over for the purpose of land set-
tlements and as a means of paying the debt.' Despite this agreement, however,
there was an absence of substantive results. As a consequence, Mauro noted,
'We occupied in order to press for that process to be accelerated.'[17]

With the value of Fazenda Ximbó estimated at around R$10 million (US$5.4
million), this also seemed an effective way of killing two birds with one stone.
One potential flaw in this argument arose from the fact that Riopedrense had
leased these lands to a third party, the Grupo Corona. The latter, the fourth
largest sugar group in the country, was a formidable operator. It owned two
sugar cane factories (the Usina Bonfim, near the town of Guariba (see Figure 6,
page 152), and the Usina Nova Tamoio, near the town of Araraquara), as well as
administering 75,000 hectares stretching across the Ribeirão Preto region. The
MST's charge, though, was that Corona was anything but an innocent third
party. As Mauro explained, 'The Fazenda Ximbó is very well known in Matão,
where many workers were dismissed without receiving any kind of rights,' a
reference to the closure of a third sugar cane plant near Matão a few years earlier.
'Many are encamped there today. It is a kind of retribution and a way of receiving rights that they did not get from this company.'[18] Indeed, some of these
former employees had worked there for 10 years before being dismissed without
compensation. As another MST leader put it, for them the occupation possessed
'great symbolic value, because in addition to the recovery of this land, it
represents the recovery of 10 years of sweat and struggle'.[19]

In addition to these labour relations issues there was the matter of Corona's
environmental record. In 1999 the company was the subject of forestry police
investigation due to its failure to preserve vegetation adjacent to riverbeds.[20]
Practises of this kind were common to the region and had resulted in silting
rivers.

As a microcosm of large-scale agro-industrial production, the Fazenda
Ximbó offered powerful insights into common problems, in particular the
routine practise of socialising human costs and externalising environmental
costs while privatising the gains. Even if the MST could not hope to change
this entrenched model, it could question its long-term impacts and sustainability. Thus the movement noted the cane industry's abusive use of pesticides,
the negative impact of these chemicals upon soil toxicity and river systems;
processes of accelerated soil erosion and desertification (again impacting upon
river systems) and changes in the micro-climate itself. The MST was not alone
in expressing these concerns. These had long been articulated by the environmental movement. However, setting 'green' issues within a 'red' framework of
social and political action represented a powerful combination. Beyond the
positive social impact that a redistribution of land would have, there was a

feeling among Ximbó occupants that, as one of their number put it, 'if we plant rice, corn, beans, food and grains here, we believe that we can even influence the region's future environmental condition.'[21] It may sound utopian, but the perception of proximity between environmental concerns and the interests of landless workers was very real.

One leader describes the movement's shifting strategy in the following terms:

> What we want to discuss is what is meant by the concept of productive land. That's the question. We want to discuss what the constitution refers to as its 'social function'. You see it is very easy to say what is and what is not productive land. It is much more difficult to explain what its social function is. Can one say that a vast area of land occupied by sugar cane is fulfilling its social function? Let's take a closer look. What labour guarantees do those people working there enjoy? To what extent is the environment there properly protected? To what extent do workers on a property live under slave-like conditions? To what extent do those areas productively generate employment? You see, productivity is not simply a question of producing sugar cane, alcohol or sugar. It is also a matter of generating employment and a diversity of foodstuffs. That's the question we want to discuss and we are saying yes, monoculture is unproductive and it does not fulfil its social function.[22]

Offensive Legality

The above formulation strikingly crystallises the movement's new direction, a tendency increasingly aligned to a positive rather than defensive conception of the legal issues. It is clear that a more offensive stance had been developing over a long period of time. In the MST's early days in Rio Grande do Sul legal activity was largely confined to cobbling networks of lawyers together in a last minute effort to extract landless workers from jail. The last minute nature of legal action was not simply due to the precariousness of radical legal networks. It was also partly due to the movement's own deep scepticism regarding the role of law and legal practitioners.[23] Over time, however, these precarious networks became larger, more stable, skilled and increasingly proactive. One of the most notable developments in this direction was the National Network of Popular Lawyers (Rede Nacional de Advogados e Advogadas Populares – RENAP). Its supporters, mostly composed of sympathetic lawyers drawn from trade unions and non-governmental organisations, provided much needed legal support to the MST. In fact for many years real numerical strength centred in Paraná state, where the MST and outside lawyers were sympathetic to the possibilities of more systematised forms of collaboration. Other notable groups that emerged in the 1980s included the National Association of Popular Lawyers (Associação Nacional de Advogados

Populares – ANAP) centred in Goiânia, and largely composed of lawyers working for the Catholic Church's Pastoral Land Commission (Commissão Pastoral da Terra), and the Institute of Popular Legal Support (Instituto de Apoio Juridico Popular – IAJUP), an organisation based in Rio de Janeiro which was an important intellectual source of legal support.[24]

By the late 1990s the MST was highly conversant with a range of legal issues. It had become what some refer to as a repeat player. Leverage from its engagement with legal issues in the Pontal do Paranapanema is just one illustration of the possibilities that were available. Matão represented the extension and intensification of that process.

Central to both events was the capacity of the movement to create facts on the ground through social struggle. While references to the legal situation undoubtedly played a significant part in the Pontal, in the case of Matão they were at the forefront of action since this was an explicit attempt to begin to reframe culturally accepted legal parameters. In a striking formulation, one of the MST's highest ranking leaders even suggested that occupying the Fazenda Ximbó formed part of a wider strategy aimed at 'creating jurisprudence'[25] favourable to the organisation. That sets it apart.

The MST's legal case

Crucially, the MST was not alone in its belief that the law demanded new interpretations. A growing body of legal opinion was challenging prevailing views about property on the grounds that it could not be considered a free-standing (in effect unexpropriable) category. In 2003, for instance, Brazil's attorney general was caught up in controversy over his comments that, in declaring the legitimacy of orderly and peaceful occupations of unproductive land, he appeared to provide some support for the MST's line.[26] In the same year 30 leading legal figures, ranging from judges to prosecutors and law academics, signed a Manifesto of Brazilian Jurists for Agrarian Reform (Manifesto de Juristas Brasileiros Pela Reforma Agrária). That document refers to the importance of Article 186 of the constitution as well as to high court decisions ascribing a degree of legitimacy to the MST's actions and criticism of the state's failure to act.[27]

In short, there was increasing recognition that rural property simultaneously had to conform to Articles 184 and 186 of the constitution. It will be recalled from the introductory chapter that Article 184 states:

> It is within the power of the Union to expropriate on account of social interest, for purposes of agrarian reform, the rural property that is not performing its social function...

While Article 186 says:

The social function is met when the rural property complies simultaneously with, according to the criteria and standards prescribed by law, the following requirements:

I - rational and adequate use;

II - adequate use of available natural resources and preservation of the environment;

III - compliance with the provisions that regulate labour relations;

IV - exploitation that favours the well-being of the owners and labourers.[28]

It is hardly surprising that the MST should have latched on to these areas. The issue of compliance was like a wedge waiting for a hammer blow. From a legal perspective what is significant is that not only was the MST capable of delivering that blow, but it was in the almost unique position of being capable of delivering the numerous other blows (occupations) that would inevitably be required if things were to change, much as it had done in the Pontal do Paranapanema.

This relationship between the immanent aspects of law and movement action underlies the Fazenda Ximbó occupation and subsequent occupations, as well as references to 'creating jurisprudence'.[29] Articles 184 and 186 opened the way to some basic and highly pertinent questions, like precisely what status should be accorded to labour and environmental rights when set alongside the competing demands of productive property, and whether the former should simply be negated in favour of the latter. Those challenging the judicial consensus charged that that was exactly what had been happening. To all intents and purposes, Articles 184 and 186 had been devalued and deprived of all meaning by judicial interpretations of Article 185 that elevated productive landed property to an untouchable status. One critic, Domingos Dresch da Silveira, who became the the National Ombudsman for Human Rights in 2011, noted the absurd consequences of this:

> If [Article 185 is] interpreted in isolation, this leads us to the curious situation in which it becomes impossible to expropriate a rural property that has become productive as a function of the indiscriminate felling of significant parts of the Atlantic Forest (an ecological offence) and with the use of child slave labour (a social offence).[30]

It was not just lawyers like da Silveira who were receptive to the MST's arguments. So too were leading members of the State of São Paulo Land Agency, ITESP and INCRA. In other words, the movement commanded a much wider constituency of support on the question than one might expect. Speaking in the immediate aftermath of the Matão occupation, Rose Beltrão, the head of INCRA's land acquisition department in São Paulo, welcomed the

MST's newfound emphasis on the social function of property. 'I think it is very good that the Movement raises this banner more often,' she said.[31] In common with the MST, she noted the prevalence of anti-environmental practices, tax evasion and labour exploitation. At the same time, though, there was a marked difference. Beltrão argued that changes to the Agrarian Law (No. 8629/93) were essential. According to her, 'INCRA is totally in favour of expropriation on account of the failure to fulfil the social function, but we don't have the legal authority to carry this out.'[32] Ultimately, therefore, 'the concept of productivity should be changed'.[33]

For the head of ITESP, Tânia Andrade, the time had also come to 're-examine the mechanisms that limit property'.[34] Speaking on the occasion of the First Brazilian Meeting on Human Rights, little more than two weeks before the Matão occupation began, she argued the need for 'a global concept of property'. Such a notion, she suggested, would incorporate agricultural productivity, but it would also 'demand a certain level of environmental and labour relations productivity before an area could be declared not subject to expropriation.'[35] Most significantly, and in contrast to her INCRA colleague, Andrade made no reference to Law 8.629/93. Instead, as someone with a background in law as well as agronomy, she emphasised the possibilities already available within the existing legislative framework.

In an article published in cooperation with the Brazilian Land Reform Association (Associação Brasileira de Reforma Agrária – ABRA), Andrade readily admitted the legal difficulties.[36] For this reason, she argued, it was 'to be hoped that, as a matter of urgency, the duly constituted powers revise the lacunae that exist and intervene so as to correct them.'[37] Nevertheless, she suggested, 'The constitution itself opens doors to this [correction] by establishing social function parameters, including agricultural productivity, as well as environmental and labour questions.'[38] Indeed, she went on, there was the additional matter of Article 5.[39] In effect, she argued, Article 5's specific reference to the notion that 'property shall observe its social function', precluded the possibility that property *of any kind* could somehow free itself of this fundamental obligation. On a range of grounds, therefore, it was time for the judges to revise 'the restrictive interpretation that had hitherto been applied.'[40]

It should be evident, from the above, that a head of steam was building up around the question of the social function of property. However much the Minister of Agrarian Reform might regard the MST's line of argument as politically inconvenient, unnecessary and even irresponsible, the fact remained that an increasing number of individuals, including intellectuals and practitioners, took the opposite view. In early 2000, for example, the MST received strong support from eminent legal scholars, including Fábio Konder Comparato and Luiz Edson Fachin.[41] Not only did they discuss the social function of property in terms similar to the MST, but they also referred to the necessity of – and above all scope for – a new framework of judicial interpretation.

The real question, though, is how such complex technical arguments would translate into reality. On which side of the argument would the judges come down when faced with an eviction request by the owners and administrators of Fazenda Ximbó? Past evidence suggested the outlook was far from promising. To help them decide, though, the Public Ministry would weigh into the debate in a positive and unexpected manner.

The Public Ministry and the 'Carta de Ribeirão Preto'

On 13 December 1999, just under a week before the Ximbó occupation began, members of the federal and state Public Ministries met in the town of Ribeirão Preto for a seminar on the environment and land reform. Inasmuch as prosecutors rarely grant the issue of land reform a platform, the mere fact that such a meeting was taking place at all indicated that something unusual might be afoot. Just how unusual, though, only became apparent at the end of the seminar when prosecutors adopted a letter of intent, the so-called 'Carta de Ribeirão Preto' (Open Letter of Ribeirão Preto, hereafter known as the CRP). One MST leader would later describe this text as 'far more advanced than some of our own documents'.[42] A close reading of the text bears this observation out.

The broad concerns of the CRP, which covered 32 specific points, may be divided into three broad areas: (1) the constitutional concept of rural property's social function; (2) the relationship between that concept and the action of the Public Ministry; and (3), the meaning of social function in the context of collective struggles over rural land. For present purposes attention will be devoted to the first and third areas and discussion of the Public Ministry reserved to a later section.

One of the key assertions made by the text was that the social function was an inalienable or constitutive element of property from which it followed that: 'Property that fails to fulfil its social function cannot be the object of legal protection. There is no legal basis for attributing the right to property, to the titleholder of a property that is not fulfilling its social function.'[43]

This was remarkably radical, but the CRP went further, asserting that property could 'not be considered productive, from a juridical constitutional point of view'[44] if it was predicated upon environmental destruction or upon the negation of labour relations legislation. Even if 'from a strictly economic point of view' a given property was deemed productive, it '*could* be expropriated for the purposes of agrarian reform if it failed to comply with either one of the requisite characteristics of the social function (the social or environmental element).'[45]

Moving on to the third area (social function and collective land struggles), the CRP noted that in practical terms only certain kinds of ownership merited legal protection, i.e., ones based upon Civil Code notions of 'justice' and 'good faith', and constitutional notions of social function.[46] The use of laws of legitimate possession was deemed 'illegal' if put to the service of lands that did not fulfil their constitutional obligations.[47] In what amounted to a dramatic reversal of existing practise, the CRP argued that 'The onus of proof, that a possession in need of court protection relates to land that fulfils its social function, lies with the author.'[48] On a technical note, the letter added, the court's failure to correctly cite respondents to litigation (a common practise in relation to MST militants) rendered such orders invalid (under Article 282 of the Civil Penal Code).[49] Those evictions that did take place, the CRP went on, should be conducted in accordance with Article 620 of the Civil Penal Code, i.e., in the least humiliating or onerous manner.[50] And finally, in conformity with the constitution and more recent legislative changes, it befell the Public Ministry to intervene directly in cases involving collective struggle over land.[51]

As well as being dense and meticulously crafted, these arguments are, without doubt, truly radical. Their source gave them considerable credibility. Although the CRP was not a legal document in the narrow sense of the term, the fact that it had first been drafted and then approved collectively by Public Ministry 'insiders' with an intimate knowledge of the law gave it real weight. The CRP was clearly designed for use, offering adherents protection as well as an effective basis for countering conservative legal tradition using instruments so beloved of that tradition – the constitution and the Civil Penal Code. When, therefore, Judge Silvia Estela Gigena de Siqueira received the Ximbó owners' request for an eviction order, on 21 December 1999, members of the Public Ministry quickly intervened by drawing her attention to the provisions of the CRP.

In addition to the 'insiders' and lawyers, of course, there was the matter of some 6,000 'outsiders' encamped on the Ximbó estate itself. The stakes were extremely high, with an immensely powerful industry seeking rapid eviction on one side, and landless families a favourable precedent on the other. A great deal therefore now depended upon the verdict.

An unprecedented decision

The result, when it finally came on 23 December 1999, was a shock for most of the parties concerned. In a move described by the land agency as 'unprecedented' in Brazil, Judge de Siqueira not only refused the owners' eviction request, but did so in forceful terms. The MST would celebrate the news as a great, even if totally unexpected, victory, while the head of the Corona sugar company, Eduardo Pontes, acknowledged, 'this decision opens an important precedent'.[52]

An unusual aspect of the decision was the methodology underlying it. Rather than simply relying upon the testimony of those seeking eviction, as is so often the case, Judge Siqueira heard other arguments put forward by the Public Ministry, and ordered that an independent assessment of the area under occupation be provided for her. This made common as well as legal sense, factors often absent in decisions of this kind. Only 20 days earlier, for instance, in a nearby judicial district, another judge had upheld an eviction order against 98 landless families from the MST who had occupied the Fazenda Santa Rita near the town of São José dos Campos. As the assistant head of INCRA in São Paulo, Moyzés Schenker, made clear at the time: 'This is an absurd decision because the expropriation of the ranch is in its final stages.'[53]

As part of her deliberations Judge Siqueira sought to assess the scale of occupation, and real extent of the damage allegedly being inflicted upon the environment by the MST. The judge concluded that although thousands of men, women and children were on the Fazenda Ximbó, they were occupying a miniscule proportion of the property, less than 1 per cent. As for the nature of the encampment, far from destroying the environment, it was carefully managed. This, after all, was what one militant had described as the movement's 'calling card'. Rather than hiding its land management practises the movement wanted as many people as possible to see what was going on. That was precisely why it had chosen to site the encampment near the busy Washington Luís highway (see Figure 6, page 152).

Given serious doubts about whether the property was fulfilling its social function, the absence of an alternative site for the landless families and an infinitesimal risk to the property in question, Judge Siqueira decided to refuse the application for an eviction order.

Implications of the judgment

Rarely, if ever, do judicial decrees lead to seismic shifts, especially if those decrees are made in a first instance court. That said, Judge Siqueira's actions undoubtedly intensified the political pressure. From the MST's perspective it made all the difference between an inevitable defeat and unexpected victory. A crack, albeit a small one, had appeared in the edifice of productive rural property, room enough for the MST to stay. Obviously many more such cracks brought about by similar struggles would have to appear before more fundamental change could come about. But whatever the higher court might do on appeal, it could not expunge this result from the record, let alone popular consciousness, especially as events were beginning to acquire a momentum of their own.

This was not simply for the obvious reason that the encampment received extensive coverage in the media, or because it was located alongside one of the great highways of Brazil, and therefore impossible to ignore. From the very outset, the occupation had depended upon links with the local community. Although some of these links were nurtured and fostered, as the movement sought to engage politically with the community (for example, by debating the issues publicly, holding meetings and demonstrations), in other instances it was more a case of activating existing ties. It should be recalled that a large proportion of the landless workers came from neighbouring towns and cities. The overlap between the two was very real. When, for example, the mayor of Jabuticabal was invited to explain her support for the encampment, one of the chief reasons she cited was the presence of 35 families from her town. She felt she owed them a duty of care.[54] Similarly, some priests offered their solidarity. This had been much in evidence during the preparatory stages of the occupation, when parishes opened their doors to MST meetings, and it continued afterwards, as collections were held, and supporters – and even the plain curious – were bussed in.

The MST was keen to reach out for support. It found it in another prominent local figure, the mayor of Matão, Adauto Scardoelli, a member of the PT. As well as offering rhetorical legitimation, through speeches, he provided valuable logistics, like sanitation, water and refuse collection. Popular legitimation also came through the support of Dom Joviano de Lima Júnior, the bishop of São Carlos. On 28 December, during a delayed Christmas Mass celebrated inside the encampment, he cut a symbolic piece of wire fencing while making it clear that 'God doesn't want large estates, he wants the land to be shared.'[55] His declaration (not unusual for such a senior figure in the Catholic hierarchy[56]) reflected and reinforced the widespread grassroots support for the landless workers' action.

Eventually, though, the focus of events moved back to the High Court where predictably Judge Siqueira's decision was overruled. The MST was given its marching orders. What happened next, though, was far from predictable. In a meeting to discuss the arrangements under which the MST would leave, attended by the head of the army, Judge Siqueira, and the mayor of Matão, the latter announced his intention (ostensibly on behalf of the municipality) to commence an entirely new set of legal proceedings. He outlined two approaches. The first would entail expropriating and then permanently donating to the landless workers the few acres of land then under occupation. Indeed, he had already set events in train by officially publishing his motion. The second approach would entail requisitioning the area for a temporary period under powers granted to municipalities when faced with the possibility of major public disturbance. The effect of this would be to maintain the status quo. Although Judge Siqueira forcefully contested the merit of these arguments, the fact was that the mere superimposition of a new wave of litigation, and a corresponding timetable, could well delay matters. Despite her reservations, she acknowledged that the case was entering into completely uncharted territory.[57]

There is little doubt that the mayor was helping his friends in the MST. He was also raising an issue of genuine importance, namely did the power to engage with the land question extend to local authorities (and if so, in what form), or did it lie almost exclusively with INCRA? At first glance the answer seemed to be with the latter. The difficulty here was that if the earlier comments from INCRA's own head of land acquisition were anything to go by, on the issue of the Ximbó at least, the organisation was characterised by powerlessness. Nor, as we have seen, was powerlessness confined to this episode.

As has been shown in other chapters, it is often as a consequence of the power vacuum generated by these gaps and contradictions that the question of local state intervention arises. To this extent there was nothing new or unique about the problem. Furthermore, the proposal for a so-called 'municipal option', i.e., the search for creative local alternatives, had been made many years earlier (in 1985) by intellectuals frustrated at the absence of progress under centralised control.[58] Similar problems had surfaced in 1997 during land conflicts in the Pontal do Paranapanema, when 22 mayors from the region met Belisário and expressed their concern at being marginalised from the agrarian reform process, while ultimately feeling responsible for addressing many of the consequences of its failure.[59] Thus, the mayor of Matão had again placed an issue on the agenda that in substantive terms had never been far from the surface.

In the event, the path chosen by Mayor Scardoelli proved too tortuous. The case was dropped and the issues were never tested in open court. On tactical and legal grounds it was decided that this was neither the best case to fight nor the time to do so. A real danger existed that opponents would entangle the municipality in a wave of legal actions over which it had little or no control, and this might result in the destabilising of the administration itself.[60]

Although unsuccessful, the Scardoelli episode nonetheless highlights the increasing degree of legal and political sophistication with which the movement and its supporters were operating. It also demonstrates the capacity of the movement to reach out and develop creative partnerships in the political fields and capacity to respond to the dynamics of the situation. Having embarked upon a flawed course of action (albeit one that contributed to the movement's short-term objectives), both parties judged it better to withdraw for reasons that related to the longer term interests of the Workers' Party administration rather than the MST. In the meantime, of course, the action had helped to sustain the pressure, which in turn created the wider conditions under which the movement was able to stay in the ranch for more than 100 days. While its immediate objective, the expropriation of a productive property, had not come to fruition, its short-term objective, the opening and development of a serious debate on the social function of property, proved highly successful.

A radical Public Ministry and prosecutorial autonomy

There is little doubt that prosecutors within the Public Ministry played a crucial role in amplifying the debate within the legal realm. They gave greater credibility to the arguments advanced by the MST. Ribeirão Preto's prosecutors emphasised that their own approach was 'nothing more than what the

1988 Constitution itself foresaw for the Public Ministry.'[61] They simply sought a rebalancing of the institutional centre of gravity, away from traditional administrative frameworks of action towards extra-institutional ones, i.e., by developing active relationships with progressive social movements and non-governmental organisations to form 'an alliance ... that would challenge the powerful'.[62] Certainly a key issue facing the Public Ministry was its own lack of social legitimation. For the vast majority of the population it was an alien and inaccessible institution, a problem compounded by its inability to give efficacy to numerous legally enshrined social rights. It was essential to give greater emphasis to the social aspects of the constitution, and that might entail the formation of social pacts and alliances with sectors of civil society, including the MST.

Prosecutorial autonomy

The approach adopted in Ribeirão Preto was the exception and not the rule. Prosecutors were working against a background of institutional adversity of which they were highly critical. They envisaged 'rethinking the Public Ministry' and 'the paradigms that structure the culture and the activities of public prosecutors'.[63] Despite the constitution's assertion of prosecutorial autonomy, they also noted its fragility. Autonomy from pressure by senior prosecutors might be real, but autonomy could be undermined from within, i.e., by the career ambitions of prosecutors themselves and or pragmatic survival strategies in the face of controversy or adversity.

In February 1997, however, that autonomy was tested from outside the institution at a meeting between the federal Minister of Justice, Nelson Jobim, and the head of the Public Ministry in São Paulo, Luiz Antônio Marrey. The meeting was set up at the behest of Minister Jobim himself and formed part of his grand tour of five states (Pará, Rondônia, São Paulo, Paraná and Rio Grande do Sul) where land conflicts had become particularly acute. His declared aim – to enlist the support of various legal organs in helping to pacify the land conflict – seemed harmless enough, but by the time he arrived in São Paulo the agenda had acquired more ominous connotations. As Marrey noted, 'the media reported that the Minister ... was going to demand a firmer hand in repressing the Landless Workers Movement'.[64]

Such reports were to be taken very seriously. Over the previous weeks government-inspired anti-MST rhetoric had reached a peak. President Cardoso himself had criticised the failure of state governments and Public Ministries to act to contain conflict. When launching the Jobim initiative the president even made a point of suggesting that if conventional legal means failed then troops could be sent in.[65] Empty or not, these threats set the stage to the February encounter.

The encounter itself took place in a highly ritualised atmosphere amid the plush surroundings of the Public Ministry's head office and bristling skyscrapers of São Paulo city. In this sense the meeting was a world away from the brutalities of rural conflict. And yet even here the tensions were never far below the surface. They were reflected in the ritual itself.

Referring to the preparatory stages of the meeting, the host, Marrey explains that:

> [E]very single detail was carefully considered. We even thought about the defining role of spaces in that meeting. It was held around a long table at which I was placed at the head, because in my institution, in my house, the presiding official always was – and will be – the Attorney General.'[66]

This was not a question of pomposity or personal pride. The ritual was clearly designed to symbolise relations of power. At that moment Marrey was on home ground and representing an institution that under his stewardship was determined to make a reality of its formal autonomy. Neither he nor it were about to be lectured. 'We live in a federation. The minister could ponder like any other person, and with a degree of authority that merited respect, but he could not determine anything.'[67] This was important, in Marrey's view, because 'at other times in the life of the institution the minister would have been received with great apprehension,'[68] a clear reference to the military dictatorship.

On the substantive issue of land conflict and the future role of the Public Ministry, an exchange of views did take place. As Marrey explains:

> The minister came. He manifested the preoccupation of the federal government. I explained to him what we were doing and saying. ... I noted that even the president of the Republic had said the other day in the papers that he was against the imprisonment of members of the MST. So now, where did we stand? 'Ah', the minister said, 'but they articulate invasions'. 'But', I said, 'you know that according to Brazilian penal law, the planning phase is not punishable.' And it went on like that. The conversation was cordial, but differentiated. ... It was cordial, but one in which the Public Ministry of São Paulo made it clear that it would not accept any kind of pressure or be diverted.[69]

What conclusions should be drawn from this episode? Firstly, it highlights the political nature of legal institutions and the prosecution process. It underlines the fact that merely maintaining the status quo, let alone developing the more radicalised version envisaged by Ribeirão Preto's prosecutors, required a degree of contestation. Under different leadership events could have gone in a different direction, with negative consequences for the MST. Indeed, one is tempted to ask how the minister was received on his tour of other states like Pará and Rondônia.

Secondly, it underlines the extent of ideological differences within the legal sphere. Jobim was expressing the views of many Brazilian prosecutors and judges (of whom he became the most senior judge in 2004), when he suggested that the MST was a conspiratorial organisation, which 'articulated invasions', and which therefore needed to be taught a lesson. His favoured method entailed criminalising the MST's membership and enmeshing the organisation in myriad court cases. For Marrey, on the other hand, criminalisation was not the answer. The days of 'treating a social problem simply as a matter for the police', were over.[70] He also took the view that 'all forms of social struggle against social exclusion are valid, and in this sense the MST fulfils a very important role'.[71]

Thirdly, the episode underlines the importance of ideological aspects of law that are often difficult to pin down but of vital significance. This epsiode was not about the structure or letter of the law, but about its spirit and future direction.

Fourthly, and finally, there is the related question of the nature and distribution of power within the Public Ministry. In view of the fact that there was nothing the minister could do to make the Public Ministry comply with his wishes, it seems odd that he came to São Paulo at all, or that the Public Ministry felt it had to prepare so carefully for the meeting. The explanation for this seems to be that the minister was hoping to shift the political and ideological climate inside the Public Ministry, either by putting it on the defensive or in the expectation that this would lead to the propagation of new, more aggressive strains of action, in other words convictions of MST militants. One way of fostering the requisite shift in orientation was to secure the support of São Paulo's attorney general, in the expectation that his influence would cascade down the ranks. Although the attorney general could not compel junior colleagues to adopt a particular line, his support and patronage of colleagues could act as a stimulus for those prosecutors wanting to adopt a more aggressive stance. Officially, there is considerable scope for patronage within the Public Ministry. The attorney general has the right to nominate 60 advisors with extra-benefits amounting to 30 per cent of an already substantial salary, which stands in excess of R$200,000 per annum even for local prosecutors with less than five years' service. The attorney general also has a direct influence over the council that deliberates upon the designation of prosecutors' functions and specialisms. During the 1996 elections, Marrey would refer to this network of influence as a 'machine'. Indeed, he attributed his own electoral defeat to the power of that machine and the 'generous distribution of rewards'.[72]

Crucially, support for the Jobim line was not forthcoming. However this was not the end of the story. By upping the rhetorical stakes, the Minister had generated his own sphere of influence, appealing directly to prosecutors of a more conservative disposition, many of whom were still smarting from Governor Covas' appointment of Marrey despite his defeat at the polls a year earlier.[73] A substantial part of Marrey's response, therefore, entailed maintaining his own (initially precarious) influence within the Public Ministry.

That meant emphasising not so much the substantive ideological differences over land reform (which would command more limited appeal among prosecutors), as emphasising the heavy-handed nature of the minister's intervention (a proposition that would command widespread support among prosecutors). As Marrey notes, 'We told him [Jobim] that the Public Ministry was very familiar with the Penal Code – in other words, that neither the Public Ministry, nor anyone, was omissive, and that nobody needed to come lecture us on this issue.'[74]

It should be clear, by now, that the impact caused by the minister's intervention, and the responses to his actions, were part of a very complex series of dynamics. Jobim's call for a tough line needs to be seen in another context too. As noted in Chapter 2, only a few months earlier one São Paulo prosecutor had adopted precisely the sort of high profile punitive stance now being advocated. The net result of his efforts had been a crushing defeat in the courts, a stunning legal victory for the MST, and substantial damage to the reputation of the Public Ministry. In part it was precisely this bitter experience that had paved the way towards the adoption of the more flexible approach to the land question, of which the minister now complained.

All these machinations not only highlight the charged atmosphere in which decisions are often taken, but give the lie to the notion that the institution could somehow rise above land and associated ideological conflicts. Prosecutors in Ribeirão Preto took the view that the chronic/structurally embedded nature of injustice meant that intervention should take a proactive form 'committed towards the workers',[75] rather than a supposedly neutral one that effectively preserved the status quo. Their proximity to a current of thought known as 'alternative law', which gained ground in the 1980s, meant that they actively questioned the neutrality of law and juridical positivism, regarded law as rooted in class structures of domination and subordination, and most controversially of all, sought to transform the practice of law from a deeply conservative force into a socially progressive one.[76] Their approach would necessarily involve ideological choices, but so too, as we have seen, did the approaches of Marrey and Jobim.

Conclusion

The events of Matão point towards the possibility of a progressive and interventionist model of legal action that addresses broader aspects of land reform. Quite apart from the decision itself, Judge Siqueira's approach marked a novel way of doing things. Getting to this point was in no small part attributable to the actions of prosecutors within the Public Ministry in Ribeirão Preto. Their radical model of action was philosophically attuned to the goal of land reform and capable of reaching beyond the confines of institutionalism. In this sense Matão represents a kind of high water mark. It suggests that the legal balance can be struck in a different way, one that lawyers like Nelson Jobim would surely disagree with. While the Matão case provides important insights into how things could be – where judges and prosecutors could go, it also underlines where they actually are, since landowners successfuly appealed to the High Court in São Paulo. The institutional centre of gravity still lies against radical decisions, even of the sort proffered by the most senior judges, like Judge Cernicchiaro in the Pontal do Paranapanema.

Seen in this light the contribution of the MST, and movements of its type, becomes all the more significant. For among other things, Matão also represents the ability, no matter how limited, of such groups to drive the legal agenda. The social function of property was and to a large extent remains a constitutional dead letter. The only reason it came to public attention was because of the MST's willingness, some might say obstinacy in putting it before the public eye, just as it had done in relation to occupations of unproductive land some 15 years earlier. Productive property constituted a much more difficult terrain upon which to operate because it ran contrary to the received wisdom of where the law stood. But that was precisely the point. The MST was not about to let this version of the law go unchallenged. This chapter has shown that in so doing it attracted a surprisingly wide constituency to its cause – even helping to galvanise that constituency into action. From a socio-legal perspective Belisário Santos Júnior's concern that the MST's approach was ideologically incendiary, or Raul Jungmann's view that it struck an own goal of sorts by uniting landowners, is to a large extent irrelevant. The key issue is that the movement felt it had reached a point in its own development whereby it could make the sort of case that should have been made back in 1988, when the constitution was first promulgated. One can argue over the political wisdom or necessity of such an act (with which this author happens to be in agreement), but that is not the conclusion being drawn here. Rather it is that Matão was the result of a process of internal maturation which included the development of more stable legal networks (including prosecutors, practitioners, intellectuals) upon whose advice and support the movement could count. Occupying productive land in the heartland of Brazil's agro-industrial economy raised the political and economic stakes, but it simultaneously raised the long marginalised question of what the constitution's reference to the social function of property was and how it could be given real substance. This was offensive legality.

Notes

1 Author interview with Belisário Santos Júnior, 6 December 1999.
2 Author interview with João Pedro Stédile, 18 March 2000.
3 A March 2009 article by the UDR entitled 'Tarso Genro, minister of the MST and of illegality' is unsparing in its vitriol. 'Tarso Genro, ministro do MST e da ilegalidade', www.udr.org.br/invasao46.htm
4 Jobim resigned in August 2011 from the Rouseff administration after reportedly clashing over fighter contracts. Relations had already been strained after he had

called one minister a 'weakling' and complained of being surrounded by 'idiots'. 'Brazilian Defence Minister Resigns', BBC news online, 5 August 2011, available at: www.bbc.co.uk/news/world-latin-america-14414760

5   Article 185, Constitution of the Federative Republic of Brazil, 2nd edition, translated and revised by Istvan Vajda, Patrícia de Queiroz Carvalho Zimbres and Vanira Tavares de Souza, Brasília, 2009. Available at: www2.camara.gov.br/english/brazilian-constitution-2

6   Human Rights Divison, *MST, As ocupações de terras são constitucionais, legítimas e necessárias*, São Paulo, September 1998, p. 10.

7   Bernardo Mançano Fernandes, *MST: Formação e territorialização*, São Paulo: Editoral Hucitec, 1996, p. 190.

8   Author interview with Belisário Santos Júnior, 6 December 1999.

9   Goulart's government had signed a decree opening the way to the compulsory acquisition of land located within 10 kilometres of federal highways and railway lines. By present-day standards, this can be seen as a timid move. In December 1999, for instance, President Cardoso's government passed a decree cancelling fraudulent property registrations corresponding to 93.6 million hectares, or 11 per cent, of national territory. One of the key differences between these two moments was that on the latter occasion landowners were locked into rather than at loggerheads with the networks of government passing those reform measures. For further details on the cancellation policy see: Ministry of Agrarian Policy and Agrarian Development, National Institute of Colonisation and Agrarian Reform – INCRA, *O livro branco da grilhagem de terras no Brasil, Ministério da Política Fundiária e do Desenvolvimento Agrário*, Brasília, 1999.

10   Author interview with Raul Jungmann, 5 April 2000.

11   Ibid. See Chapter 3 for full details.

12   Author interview with Rolf Hackbart, 6 July 2007.

13   Author interview with João Pedro Stédile, 18 March 2000.

14   Poor soil quality was one reason why small farmers found it hard to survive. This demanded ever rising quantities of expensive fertilisers merely in order to stand still.

15   Author interview with Kelly Maford, a São Paulo state MST leader and leader of the Matão occupation, 3 February 2000.

16   The region still boasts a leading international agricultural technology fair, the Agrishow, by far the biggest such event in Latin America. According to the leading equipment manufacturer, John Deere, it is one of the big-three such shows in the world by volume of trade.

17   'Fazendas de monocultura entram na mira do MST', *O Estado de São Paulo*, 22 December 1999.

18   Ibid.

19   Author interview with Kelly Maford, 3 February 2000.

20   'Incra não vai desapropriar Chimbó', *Tribuna Impressa*, 22 December 1999.

21   Author interview with Kelly Maford, 3 February 2000.

22   Author interview with José Rainha, 20 March 2000.

23   Author interview with human rights lawyers Jacques Tavora Alfonsin, 17 June 1997, and Sueli Belato, 12 June 1997.

24   For the development of RENAP see Leandro Franklin Gorsdorf, Advocacia Popular na Construçãode um Novo Senso Comum Jurídico, unpublished Master's

thesis, Federal University of Paraná, Curitiba, 2004. For a useful English-language introduction to IAJUP see Eliane Junqueria, 'Legal policy: models of legal services in Brazil and the U.S.A.', *International Journal of Economic Development*, vol. 2, no. 2, April 2000.

25 Gilmar Mauro of the MST as cited by José Ângelo Santilli, 'Negada reintegração de posse de fazenda invadida', *O Estado de São Paulo*, 24 December 1999.

26 'Fontelles volta a apoiar invasão de terra improdutiva', *O Estado de São Paulo*, 14 August 2003.

27 *Manifesto de Juristas Brasileiros Pela Reforma Agrária*, 21 July 2003, available at www.social.org.br/manifestos/manifesto003.htm

28 Constitution of the Federative Republic of Brazil, 2nd edition, translated and revised by Istvan Vajda, Patrícia de Queiroz Carvalho Zimbres and Vanira Tavares de Souza, Brasília, 2009, Articles 184 and 186 respectively. Available at: www2. camara.gov.br/english/brazilian-constitution-2

29 Gilmar Mauro of the MST, as cited by José Ângelo Santilli, 'Negada reintegração de posse de fazenda invadida', *O Estado de São Paulo*, 24 December 1999.

30 Domingos Sávio Dresch da Silveira, 'A propriedade agrária e suas funções sociais' in Domingos Sávio Dresch da Silveira and Flávio Sant'Anna Xavier, eds, *O direito agrário em debate*, Porto Alegre: Livraria do Advogado Editora, 1998, p. 21.

31 Rose Beltrão, cited in 'Incra não vai desapropriar Chimbó', *Tribuna Impressa*, 22 December 1999.

32 Ibid.

33 Author interview with Rose Beltrão, 8 February 2000.

34 Tânia Andrade on the occasion of 1 Encontro Brasilieiro de Direitos Humanos, Pontifical Catholic University, São Paulo, 3 December 1999.

35 Ibid.

36 Tânia Andrade, 'Três perguntinhas difíceis', in *Reforma Agrária: Revista da Associação Brasileira de Reforma Agrária – ABRA*, vol. 28, nos 1, 2 and 3, January – December 1998; vol. 29, no. 1, January – August 1999.

37 Ibid.

38 Ibid.

39 Headed 'Individual and collective rights and duties', Article 5 enjoys prominent status because it comes under that section of the Constitution dealing with 'fundamental rights and guarantees'.

40 Tânia Andrade, 'Três perguntinhas difíceis', in *Reforma Agrária: Revista da Associação Brasileira de Reforma Agrária – ABRA*, vol. 28, nos 1, 2 and 3, January – December 1998; vol. 29, no. 1, January – August 1999.

41 See, for example, Fábio Konder Comparato, 'Direitos e deveres fundamentais em matéria de propriedade' and Luiz Edson Fachin, 'A justiça dos conflitos no Brasil' in Juvekino José Strozake, ed., *A questão agrária e a justiça*, São Paulo: Editora Revista dos Tribunais, 2000. Both authors discuss at length the social function of property.

42 Author interview with Gilmar Mauro, 10 August 2000.

43 Carta de Ribeirão Preto, 13 December 1999, section 4.

44 Ibid., section 8.

45 Ibid., section 11. My emphasis.

46 Ibid., section 22.

47 Ibid., section 23.
48 Ibid., section 24.
49 Ibid., section 24.
50 Ibid., section 27.
51 Ibid. This is a clear reference to changes in the Civil Penal Code brought about by Law No. 9.415 of December 1996.
52 'Decisão de juíza de Matão è inèdita', *Tribuna Impressa*, 24 December 1999.
53 Cited in 'Juiz quer expulsar MST de área', *Valeparaibano*, 3 December 1999.
54 'Bispo elogia MST durante missa em área invadida', *O Estado de São Paulo*, 29 December 1999.
55 Ibid.
56 Although the bishop's comments appear to hark back to the radicalism associated with the Brazilian episcopacy of the 1970s and 1980s, in fact his views on property were very much in keeping with decades of Catholic social teaching. As noted in the introductory chapter Pope John VI had declared that: 'it is the right of public authority to prevent anyone from abusing his private property to the detriment of the common good. By its very nature private property has a social quality which is based on the law of the common destination of earthly goods.' He had also noted that 'insufficiently cultivated estates should be distributed to those who can make these lands fruitful'. Second Vatican Council, *Pastoral Constitution on the Church in the Modern World: Gaudium et Spes*, Promulgated by Pope Paul VI, 7 December 1965, Rome, section 71, available at: www.vatican.va/archive/hist_councils/ii_vatican_council/documents/vat-ii_cons_19651207_gaudium-et-spes_en.html
57 Based on author interview with Kelly Maford, 3 February 2000.
58 See, for example, Sônia Helena Novaes Guimarães Moraes, 'A opção municipalista', *Revista Arquivos*, no. 166, October 1985, pp. 88–92. At the time of writing, Moraes was a director of the Brazilian Land Reform Association (ABRA) and Professor of Agrarian Law at the Catholic University of Campinas. Her article demonstrated a keen sense of both the legal constraints upon and possibilities for action.
59 These points were made at a meeting, on 13 February 1997, attended by Belisário Santos Júnior, São Paulo's Secretary of State for Justice. Source: Mimeo, Special Working Group on Land Issues in Western São Paulo, *Relatorio de Atividades e Conclusões*, São Paulo: Ministerio Publico Procuradoria Geral de Justica, 20 February 1997.
60 Author interview with Gilmar Mauro, 10 August 2000.
61 Author interview with Marcelo Pedroso Goulart, 10 September 1999.
62 Ibid.
63 Antônio Alberto Machado and Marcelo Pedroso Goulart, *Ministério Público e direito alternativo: O MP e a defesa do regime democrático e da ordem jurídica*, São Paulo: Editora Académica, 1992, p. 15.
64 Author interview with Luiz Antônio Marrey, 17 March 2000.
65 'FHC culpa estados por invasão de terra', *Folha de São Paulo*, 5 February 1997.
66 Author interview with Luiz Antônio Marrey, 17 March 2000.
67 Ibid.
68 Ibid.

69 Ibid.
70 Ibid.
71 Marrey was careful to exclude violence as a legitimate form of struggle. Ibid.
72 See 'Marrey vai apurar gratificações de promotores', *O Estado de São Paulo*, 23 February 1996.
73 Even though it was entirely within the rules, Mario Covas' selection of Marrey, in February 1996, created tremendous bitterness among the grassroots. Another candidate, José Emmanuel Burle Filho, had won 859, or 60 per cent of the vote, as opposed to Marrey's 640 votes. It meant that the new incumbent came to power with a distinct lack of authority. According to one of Marrey's colleagues, from the Movement for a Democratic Public Ministry (Movimento do Ministério Público Democrático – MMPD), this was his 'original sin'. Eventually, though, this sin was expiated. Marrey was 're-elected' in 1998. He then supported the successful candidacy of his former chief of staff, in 2000, and finally stood once again, successfully, in 2002.
74 Author interview with Luiz Antônio Marrey, 17 March 2000.
75 Author interview with Marcelo Pedroso Goulart, 10 September 1999.
76 For a good introduction to this field see Lédio Rosa de Andrade, *Direito Alternativo Brasileiro*, Porto Alegre: Livrario do Advogado Editora, 1996.

Conclusion

This book has offered a socio-legal account of the Landless Workers' Movement (MST) as well as Brazil's land reform laws and institutions. While the strategic role of law with regard to the prospects of land reform was documented and acknowledged, greater emphasis was placed upon other less visible and often overlooked social, economic and political connections between law and society. Far from being the extraneous factors they are too frequently portrayed as, they not only shape the production of law (constitutional law being a prime example), but subsequently mediate it in ways that give it much of its substance, structure and even meaning. To a large extent this book has been about what happens after the legislative ink has dried. In Brazil's particular case it is the presence and specific correlation of these extra-legal factors, most notably personified by powerful landed interests, which goes a long way towards explaining not only why the record on land reform has proved so limited, but why, in the absence of changes in power relations, that record is unlikely to improve dramatically over the next few years, notwithstanding reforming governments.

Given this apparently sobering conclusion it may seem surprising that the focus of this book was not upon the desirability of severing these connections altogether. That is largely because it concludes that the reality of landed power cannot be overcome simply by reference to the need for greater legal autonomy (whatever that might mean in practise given the problem of judicial conservatism), or to the need for new laws, of which there has long been a surfeit. There is no doubt that as tendencies or desiderata they have some value, but as the evidence presented herein repeatedly attests, they also suffer major internal – and in many senses unavoidable – external limitations. Rather than being resigned to the inevitable impact of these external forces, however, the emphasis of this work is upon the impact which other progressive social and political forces, like the MST, can have. This is not simply as drivers of political change, as one might expect, but as drivers of legal change; in other words, giving Brazilian land law greater substance and meaning.

That may sound a little far fetched, but nowhere is this assertion more clearly and practically demonstrated than in Chapter 1 ('Shocking the

System: Social Movement Pressure as the Catalyst of Political and Legal Change'). Like all the case studies in the present volume, it deals with a particular aspect of the land/law problem, in this instance the failure over decades to enforce the state's claims to its own lands (known as *terras devolutas*) against powerful private interests that had illegally occupied them. To all intents and purposes the law on this issue, as in so many other areas dealt with in this book, was a dead letter. That is a striking fact because the events discussed occurred in São Paulo state, Brazil's political and economic powerhouse and widely regarded as the state with the best equipped legal apparatus in the country (one reason why it was chosen as a case study). Landowners enjoyed a status of near untouchability which neither the state nor the legal authorities seemed able to markedly alter.

. The chapter noted the more favourable political background (especially at a state level in São Paulo) against which the MST occupied land and how this constituted an important variable and opportunity. Unfortunately, political leverage of this kind cannot be counted on in most other Brazilian states. While fully acknowledging the São Paulo state government's distinctive contribution, this study ultimately concludes that it was the pressure of these conflicts that gave new found urgency to the government's, the state land agency's and courts' search for creative legal solutions in the civil sphere. The MST provided land reform agencies and legal practitioners with an historic opportunity and the kind of leverage necessary in order to overcome some of law's limitations. Practitioners and administrators not only had to be shocked into action through social mobilisation, but sustained in it. By altering the political correlations of force that are so central to the effectiveness of legal enforcement (an issue present throughout this volume) the MST enabled the state to reacquire devolved lands and put these towards a land resettlement programme. This is what is meant by giving new substance and meaning to land reform law.

For the most part the efforts of the MST discussed in Chapter 1 are presented as a success story. By giving the political and legal status quo a much-needed jolt, rates of land expropriation accelerated markedly. As a consequence, these events were reportedly described by José Gomes da Silva, a champion of land reform (and architect of the ill-fated first National Plan for Agrarian Reform), as the closest thing he had seen to land reform in Brazil. At the same time, however, the chapter tempered these achievements with an acknowledgement of their inherent limitations. Some of these relate to the colossal investment of organisational resources involved, i.e., personnel and political capital, to say nothing of the personal risks involved (an issue discussed in Chapter 2). The fact was that mass struggle, the occupation of land, was an exhausting and risky process that could only be sustained under determinate conditions and for limited periods of time. It could not be rolled out exponentially. Chapter 1 also notes that while the issue of land ownership and redistribution was moved forward, it was not resolved. What emerged instead was a compromise that attended to some of the MST's immediate and longer term demands, but which also allowed landowners to retain a stake on the land. The solution recognised the de facto strength of both sides, including landowners who still wielded enormous economic and political power, were dug in, and intended to stay that way. Thus, the law here was only partially vindicated.

Given the close association between MST activism and progress on the enforcement and substantiation of land reform laws, it is ironic that Chapter 2 ('To Criminalise or Not to Criminalise: Conflicting Legal Responses to Social Movement Pressure') charted the extremely negative response of sectors of the legal establishment to the movement. There is little doubt that the attempted prosecution and imprisonment of militants had major ramifications for the movement, challenging its basic methodology and viability, and in the process further stimulating the development of sophisticated legal strategies. At the same time, however, the movement was used to this type of struggle. Its activists had long been the target of arrests and imprisonments and had adopted new strategies and tactics accordingly. The choice of devolved land as the terrain upon which to struggle for reform was partly a reflection of that process. For the legal system, which was largely taken by surprise, the implications were also far reaching. When, for instance, authorities announced the imperative of upholding the rule of law against landless workers, after years of legal inertia in a region characterised for decades by lawlessness, those authorities suddenly found themselves on public trial for double standards. Judges and prosecutors might argue that land reform and property rights were two entirely separate issues to be treated on their individual merits, but this line lacked credibility given their poor track record.

Land occupations also exposed legal authorities as being deeply divided on ideological and jurisprudential lines. Conservative sectors within the police, prosecution service and judiciary were keen to indict the MST, even developing expedited procedures for bringing militants to 'justice'. By contrast, however, the Supreme Court (STJ) rejected absolutist notions of private property which underpinned these approaches in an historic judgment which backed key aspects of the MST struggle. This result, quite literally a reflection upon the profound nature of the social divisions, not only underlines the interplay or dialectic *between* law and society, but is another example of what was earlier referred to as MST attempts to give new substance and meaning to land law. It would not have happened without the movement's sustained intervention.

Significant though this decision was in qualitative terms, its precise impact is difficult to gauge and in some respects limited. The peculiarities of Brazil's system of non-binding precedents, for instance, means that lower courts are not obliged to follow the Supreme Court's decision and therefore its broader impact is constrained despite its symbolic importance. Even when social movement pressure encounters a degree of understanding within the highest echelons of the legal establishment, substantive legal change remains an extremely slow process.

When seen in the light of why São Paulo state was initially chosen as a case study, the implications of the first two chapters are disturbing. São Paulo's relatively robust legal infrastructure is routinely contrasted with the precarious and conservative structures of northern Brazilian states where, if anything, the influence of landowners is even greater. That it took decades to begin to address – and even then only partially – such a relatively straightforward issue as devolved lands, and that significant sectors of São Paulo's judiciary and prosecution service felt it was more important to make an example of the MST instead, demonstrates what an uphill task land reform proponents face throughout Brazil. The chapters also underline how legal institutions constitute a significant part of the problem.

In marked contrast to this, Chapter 3 ('Why Law Fails: the Administration of Land Law in the Context of Power Relations') deals with instances where the legal system did indeed seem to offer a way forward. Put simply, judges and prosecutors in the state of Rio Grande do Sul were determined to enforce a key aspect of land reform law, i.e., that which relates to the auditing of land (a necessary prelude to its possible expropriation for the purposes of land reform). Once again, the MST was a significant contributory factor in agitating for audits, but not in the same way it had been in São Paulo, where both a high degree of legal inertia had prevailed on the issue of devolved land as well as open hostility towards the movement itself. The case of Rio Grande do Sul was different. Key elements within the legal establishment, as well as the land reform agency itself, were behind land audits. To this extent the MST was pushing against an open door. Again, though, the findings of this chapter are somewhat disturbing, for despite this fortuitous coincidence of factors, the eventual result was abject failure.

The reasons for this are multiple and complex. The key point to note, though, is that although judges and prosecutors showed a remarkable degree of intellectual independence from landed interests, and a genuine willingness to make this critical aspect of land reform work, perhaps a reflection of more progressive attitudes in this state, they were nonetheless frustrated in their efforts by a negative series of power relations. Too often, especially in development discourses promoted by international organisations like the World Bank, the failure of legal personnel and systems is attributed to amorphous variables like 'corruption' (usually defined in terms of the abuse of public power for private gain). Certainly there is plenty of anecdotal evidence to suggest that corruption exists, but as an analytical category it is extremely problematic (reflected in the fact that international indices are based on fluid perceptions of corruption). More problematically, corruption discourses tend to deflect attention from other factors related to class, political and economic power.

In the case of Chapter 3, an anti-corruption discourse would find little if any traction and offers little by way of explanation. The failure of the land agency to carry out land audits had nothing to do with corruption. Instead it had everything to do with extensive networks of power that sought to frustrate the possibility of change at virtually every turn and level. Thus when landowners failed in their attempts to undermine the scientific validity of productivity indices through specially commissioned academic reports, they turned to obstructive actions in the courts as a source of leverage. When they failed to find succour in the courts they turned to various forms of civil disobedience, for example refusing to countersign audit forms and blockading access to properties. Finally, when the courts still refused to countenance their actions, and when the land agency continued to pursue its strategy of land audits with resolution, they put pressure upon the federal government (aided by allies within the government) to get the land agency to withdraw its plans. The head of the land agency in Rio Grande do Sul, Paulo Emílio Barbosa (who happened to be a federal prosecutor seconded to the organisation), was sacked for his efforts to enforce the law. As for the man who sacked him, Raul Jungmann, the Minister for Agrarian Reform, he felt he had no alternative. This was not because of corruption, but because of the relation of forces at that time. For him it was not 'all a question of the law – that I have to carry out the law. Look, the law emerges from a complex of relations. Sure, you have to carry out the law, that's right, but it is folly to go into combat on the terrain of the adversary because he wins – and there, with the relation of forces, they [landowners] always win.'[1]

One can argue over whether the Minister's specific diagnosis of the problem at the time was correct, especially given the diametrically opposing analyses of other participants in these events. What all of them seem to agree upon, though, is the bounded or contextually defined nature of law. Pro-reform prosecutors did not take the land agency to court for its failure to act because they felt they would gain insufficient traction in the courts. Land law's lack of substance arose precisely from these mediations operating at state and federal levels, within and outside the legal apparatus. The Minister of Land Reform even suggested that on one occasion the MST itself stepped back from pushing the land audit issue because of its alliance with the Workers' Party government of Olivio Dutra in Rio Grande do Sul (the latter had been negotiating with landowners over another issue, Expointer, one of the largest agricultural trade fairs in the world, and did not want to risk losing it by pushing hard on audits). It is a plausible scenario which highlights the sense of multiple forces leading to (or in this instance holding back) from legal change.

Although the specific events discussed in Chapter 3 happened some years ago, the issue of land audits and productivity indices remains as topical as ever and still goes to the heart of enforcing land reform in Brazil. The story of land audits in Rio Grande do Sul has a depressingly familiar ring to it. It echoes earlier failures at a national level, notably the watering down of the first National Plan for Agrarian Reform (1985), and gives an insight into why two subsequent governments, led by President Luis Inácio Lula da Silva, would prove incapable of updating land productivity indices, despite his repeated promises to update them. Like the Minister for Agrarian Reform, Lula was either unwilling or unable to take on sectors of the landed establishment that formed part of his own congressional alliance. Which of the two does not really matter for present purposes. More important is the fact that it substantiates Raul Jungmann's assertion that law emerges from a complex of relations. It also correlates with the suggestion of Lula's own appointee as president of INCRA (the federal land agency) that 'The lack of laws isn't the issue.'[2] No matter how robust or relatively progressive a legal system may be, legal determination on its own is not enough to bring about change, certainly not when the political and economic stakes are so high and weigh so heavily as they do in relation to land.

Chapter 4 ('The Limits of Progressive State Action') discussed yet another example of a southern state, Paraná, with a comparatively robust administrative and legal apparatus but where relations of power rather than formal legality come to play a preponderant role. Such progress as there was had to be hard fought for. The chapter began by acknowledging that the development of a favourable political conjuncture under the governorship of Roberto Requião was critical to the opening of important legal spaces. Against the will of conservative sectors of the judiciary he responded positively to pent-up social demands expressed by groups like the MST, by refusing to expedite the eviction of landless workers on the one hand, and pressing for a negotiated settlement on the other. However, the chapter concluded that his brokering of conflict, through various conciliatory mechanisms that gave real weight to the interests of landless workers, could neither accelerate the process of land reform significantly, nor overcome structural constraints that were largely the responsibility of the federal administration. Such limitations, and the consequent build-up of social tension, would ultimately lead to an implosion of Requião's model and a violent parting of the waves between his government and the MST.

Prior to that rupture, the movement engaged intensively with Requião's government, seeing it as an important local ally in a much broader struggle. Leveraging the local state, by helping it to shift its cultural – including legal – practises, may explain why the MST's leading national spokesperson, João Pedro Stédile, accepted an invitation to give a lecture to state police officers on the subject of the land question and limitations of repressive police tactics. Under the Jaime Lerner governorships, however, any such room for manoeuvre evaporated. Legal avenues were closed, land struggles were criminalised, and a cycle of violence ensued. State security policy was handed to groups opposed to the MST. As for attempts by the federal land agency to instigate land audits, this too ran into sustained local opposition from landowners who successfully resisted the policy and, to all intents and purposes, forced the removal of the head of INCRA in Paraná.

Chapter 5 ('Pushing and Redefining Legal Boundaries through Social Movement Pressure') returned to the theme of the MST as a driver of legal change. However, rather than the vindication of rights to devolved or unproductive lands (theoretically speaking obvious candidates for inclusion in a land reform programme), it discussed an occupation which targeted a much more difficult object: productive land, regarded by many as categorically excluded from expropriation by the 1988 constitution. As the chapter makes clear, the MST's occupation was neither an adventure in opportunism nor illegality, but a carefully calculated attempt to reinvigorate other constitutional clauses, notably those dealing with the social function of rural property. This may have been premature in political terms; the movement itself recognised that outright victory at this stage was unlikely. At the same time, though, there is little doubt that the MST's occupation, like numerous other more conventional occupations of the past, was part of a process of public education. Despite the unfavourable odds, significant sectors within the Public Ministry and the land reform agency came out in open support of the movement. They too felt that discussion of this vital issue had been marginalised and needed an airing. To everyone's surprise the movement would score a notable victory in the first instance court, as the presiding judge ruled in its favour.

What are some of the broader conclusions that should be drawn from the foregoing chapters? One concerns the significant and positive role law can play in relation to land reform, offering a much needed source of ideological leverage (legitimation), and practical leverage (enforcement). That may appear surprising given the weight of negative evidence presented in many of the foregoing chapters. That this conclusion is partly based on the view that some of these developments can be traced to within the legal establishment itself rather than to external movement pressure may appear more surprising still.

A cursory look at the evidence, however, shows that major contradictions – and with them opportunities – are imbricated within the fabric of law. Far from resolving political conflicts definitively, constitutions frequently postpone and ossify them at the same time. Brazil offers a prime example of this. Its constitution has been described by leading politicians of the left and right (Florestan Fernandes and former President José Sarney (1985–1990) respectively) as a patchwork quilt and a Frankenstein's monster, references to its stitching of contradictions into an uneasy compromise, rather than their synthesis. Crucially, though, those compromises leave open all sorts of political and interpretive possibilities, not just for those outside the legal establishment seeking change, but for those within it too.

When one travels across Brazil there is no shortage of evidence of counter currents to judicial conservatism. Commentators frequently refer to the more radical outlook of Rio Grande do Sul state's judiciary, for example, and the more innovative nature of its findings. Its impact should not be exaggerated but its presence needs to be recognised. Likewise, law schools are slowly, but increasingly, adopting more contextual and socially oriented approaches to the study of law, which among other things means addressing issues of substantive and not just formal legality. In fact the historic failure of Brazil's judiciary to address questions of substantive legality in the context of land has even been acknowledged by some of its most senior figures.

Of course none of this means that lower ranking judges have either taken a cue or automatically followed suit (a peculiarity of Brazil's system of non-binding precedents); but for those willing to follow the lead the opportunity is there more than ever before. There have also been significant institutional changes, like the creation of the national agrarian ombudsman (ouvidor agrário nacional) led by a senior judge. This office is not without its problems. To a large extent it is dependent upon and driven by personality and its role is confined to troubleshooting. Nonetheless, troubleshooting, which in this instance means creating more flexible spaces of institutional negotiation, has its place even if it is clearly not the answer. Among other things it offers a platform of authority under which other judges may be educated and even encouraged to act without their customary authoritarian zeal.

Vital spaces of action, most notably within the Public Ministry, or prosecution service, have also been documented. With the promulgation of the 1988 constitution, real possibilities for radical legal action in relation to land reform were opened up. Some of these opportunities were proactively embraced by prosecutors. One should acknowledge, however, that these efforts have remained somewhat episodic and marginalised, pursued by talented, creative, but relatively isolated individuals, rather than becoming institutionally rooted or part of a genuinely collective consciousness.

Within the Public Ministry leverage has assumed other less radical, but nonetheless significant, forms too, notably the protection afforded by sectors of the Public Ministry against the incursions of landed interests within the legal establishment. The heartfelt defence by Brazil's federal attorney general of the right to struggle for (occupy) land, and the refusal of São Paulo's attorney general to succumb to the pressure for a socially conservative approach to land disputes (i.e., more prosecutions of landless workers) are examples of this. And there are nuances in between, such as the instigation of clusters of prosecutors specialising in land disputes, the formation of investigative committees on the land question involving senior prosecutors, and the more favourable tone of senior prosecutors in both the media and the Public Ministry itself. All these mark a gradual but significant shift of perspective and are part of a process of institutional evolution. These shifts in the justice system and legal culture have been encouraged by Lula's governments, and doubtless will be by that of President Rouseff.

In its early years the MST's engagement with law was somewhat limited and defensive. The stereotypes discussed in the Introduction to this work contain significant grains of truth. At best law was viewed as an occupational hazard, while at its worst it was considered a mere expression of ruling class interests, which in numerous instances it was and unfortunately still remains. Over time, however, that has evolved into a deeper understanding of its potentialities.

Just as landowners used the legal framework as a means of prosecuting their narrow interests (putting landless workers in the dock), so too the MST came to understand that a more sophisticated understanding of law could open up a range of possibilities and offer valuable leverage. That sense of the possibility immanent in law, no matter how limited, is demonstrated throughout this study.

Notwithstanding the significance of legal opportunities available, the documented willingness on the part of an increasing number of practitioners to take them up, and the positive impact this is having upon legal culture in general, this book ultimately puts more store upon the significance of social movement pressure as a source of legal change than it does upon the internal capacity of the legal establishment to drive matters forward. To a large extent this is as it should be because in many respects legal practice is reactive to and, especially in relation to landed interests, reflective of its surroundings, rather than the independent agent of change some hold or would like it to be. By contrast, social struggles can and must take the lead. A prevalent feature of land struggles is the challenge that they pose not only to the political status quo, but also to the legal status quo, i.e., to its cultures, practices and understanding of itself.

Since its earliest days the MST has pushed generally accepted legal boundaries, more latterly with increasing insight and confidence. It is important to stress, however, that what drove it in these new and innovative directions was political necessity and pent-up social demand. Above all else land occupations are a response to a social rather than legal problem. The Minister of Agrarian Reform's acknowledgement that in regions like the south and south east of Brazil there is a shortage of unproductive lands,[3] and João Pedro Stédile's observation that 'in the case of some specific regions there aren't large unproductive ranches ... [s]o the workers are obliged to choose areas which, although they are productive, can lead on to the debate over their social function',[4] reinforce that sense of causality.

Tensions arising from the MST's stance have increasingly been played out against two forces. One is the relative diminution of absolute levels of rural poverty that have occurred in the light of policies conducted under the Lula administrations. This has seen some diminution in rates of social mobilisation as economic alternatives to land occupations presented themselves to workers. Another force is the transformation of the Brazilian land question under the impact of national and transnational capital. Put simply, the crowding out of alternative land use strategies, criticised by international food agencies like Oxfam,[5] has accentuated the significance of productive land and with it the difficult political and legal choices facing the movement. It has had to decide whether to withdraw in the face of these interests and accept the political, economic and legal constraints thereby imposed, or whether to challenge them. To accept these constraints would see the movement's margin of action diminishing in key states of the federation. This makes President Lula da Silva's and

Dilma Rouseff's embracing of agro-industrial interests all the harder to swallow and explains why the truce that has persisted between their governments and the MST has been so uneasy. The result is contradictory in the extreme. Occupations on productive land occur episodically rather than systematically.

It is in this extremely difficult political context that law has, if anything, acquired added significance. As thorny political problems like productivity indices have been pushed aside under pressure from landed interests, law's tactical significance as a potential source of leverage is accentuated. Political expediency and other pressures have led to the shelving of campaign promises and closure of opportunities, but constitutional and other legal guarantees on land reform remain conspicuous by their presence. Whether their actual significance i.e. material impact will increase is a matter which, on the basis of past evidence, this book argues must remain an open question but one in which social mobilisation will continue to play a crucial mediating role. In *Drowning in Laws: Labor Law and Brazilian Political Culture* (2004), John D. French argued that 'In the end, the labour laws became "real" in Brazilian workplaces only to the extent that workers struggled to make the law as imaginary ideal into a practical future reality.'[6] Precisely the same can be said of the Brazilian constitution's potentialities in relation to land reform. If there is a single lesson to be drawn from this book, it is that in the end land laws and the politics of reform will only become real to the extent that rural workers struggle to make them so.

Notes

1   Author interview with Raul Jungmann, 5 April 2000.
2   Author interview with Rolf Hackbart, 6 July 2007.
3   Author interview with Raul Jungmann, 5 April 2000.
4   Author interview with João Pedro Stédile, 18 March 2000.
5   See Robert Bailey, *Growing a Better Future: food justice in a resource-constrained world*, Oxford: Oxfam International, June 2011, available at: http://policy-practice. oxfam.org.uk/publications/growing-a-better-future-food-justice-in-a-resource-constrained-world-132373
6   John D. French, *Drowning in Laws: Labor Law and Brazilian Political Culture*, Chapel Hill: University of North Carolina Press, 2004.

Index

Page numbers in italic refer to figures and tables.

Abrão, José 111, 112
Administrative Decree 97, 170
agrarian courts 70
agrarian reform *see* land reform
agricultural estates *13*
agricultural exports 13, 105
Agricultural Federation of Rio Grande do
    Sul (FARSUL) 96, 97, 99, 102, 103, 108,
    109, 113
agricultural productivity *see* productivity
agricultural superpower status 13
Agriculture Commission of the Chamber of
    Deputies 97
agro-industrial complexes/interests 13–14,
    188
Agropecuaria Riopedrense 159–60
Água da Prata plantation 143
Alckmin, Geraldo 50
Almeida, Marcio Portes de 112
alternative law 173
Amazon 13, 157
Amazonia 26
Amazonas 62, 115
Amnesty International 73
Andrade, Tânia 42, 46, 48, 49, 83, 164
anti-audit movement 121
anti-land reform government 16
Araraquara 158, 160
Araújo, José Carlos de 144
armed evictions 41, 63–4
Arns, Dom Paulo Evaristo 68
arrest: of landowners 143; mass, Paraná 136;
    of MST militants 57, 67, 71
Arruda Sampaio, Plínio de 80
assassinations: rural workers Eldorado dos
    Carajás 73, 82, 127, 143, 146
Association of the Public Ministry (AMP) 80

Atlantic rainforest (Mata Atlântica)
    28, 163
attitudes: judicial 3–4, 5
attorney general: deputy 79, *see also* Marrey,
    Luiz Antonio
autonomy: judicial 70; legal 4, 179;
    prosecutorial 74–5, 84, 170–3
Azambuja, mayor 99

Bagé region: bringing land reform to 91–5;
    conflict over productivity indices *see*
    productivity indices; farmers union 97
Baggio, Roberto 135
bail regime 75
Bandeirantes ranch 141
Barbosa, Laércio 67, 71
Barbosa, Paulo Emílio 106, 107–8,
    109–11, 112, 114, 116, 117–18, 120,
    122, 183
Barreto, Márcio 67, 68, 71
Barros, Adhemar de 32
Barros Filho, Antônio Emídio de 32
Beckhausen, Marcelo 121
Beltrão, Rose 163–4
Benedelli, Olivo 135
Beraldo, Darci Lopes 67, 70, 71
Bicudo, Helio 74
biodiversity destruction 13
Bogo, Vincente 97, 103, 118
Boller, Juvenal 37, 39, 44, 46, 51, 52
Bolsa Família 16
Brasília 41, 75, 96, 97
Brazil: agricultural exports 13; agricultural
    and livestock estates *13*; agricultural
    superpower status 13; economic boom/
    miracle 20, 92, 159; geographical
    proportions 7–8

Brazilian Constitution (1988) 4, 185;
    Article 5 164; Article 184 162, 163;
    Article 185 153, 155, 163; Article 186
    162–3; Article 188 5, 6, 15
Brazilian Land Reform Association
    (ABRA) 164
Brazilian Popular Party (PPB) 105
Brazilian Social Democratic Party (PSDB)
    12, 153
Brazil's California 158–61
BRICS economies 13
Britto, Antônio 96–7, 105, 110
Brizola, Leonel 39

Carandiru prison 67, 68
Cardoso, Fernando Henrique 8, 9, 19, 81,
    85, 104–5, 115, 130, 146, 170
Caros Amigos 141
Carta de Ribeirão Preto (CRP) 165–6
Carvalho, Horácio Martins de 128,
    132–3, 136
Carvalho Rocha, João Carlos de 100
case selection: federalism and 6–12
Catholic Church: deception of priests in
    relation to devolved lands 31; Pastoral
    Land Commission 39, 127, 133, 143,
    162; reservations about occupations 58–9;
    social teaching 6, 110
cattle ranchers: conflict over productivity
    indices see productivity indices; Paraná
    141, 142, 143, see also landowners
cattle ranches: purchase of 113
cattle ranching: Bagé region 92;
    Paraná 141
Cernicchiaro, Luiz Vicente 76, 77, 78, 79,
    82, 85, 174
Cerrado 13
Chaves, Valdemir Rodrigues 36–7, 52
Chomsky, Noam 1
civil disobedience 22, 84, 96, 100, 121
Civil Legal Code 41, 48, 49, 111
Civil Penal Code 67, 166
class 3, 5, 14, 30, 45, 62, 74, 77, 79, 85,
    90, 105, 173, 182, 186
collective interests: defence of 111
collective rights 58, 73, 102, 111
collective struggle 165, 166
Comparato, Fábio Konder 164
compensation 50, 63, 93
compromise(s) 145–6, 181, 185
conflicts: see land conflicts; legal conflicts;
    social conflict

conservatism: judicial 4–5, 38, 44, 75,
    184, 185
Constituent Congress 42, 94, 116, 118
containment 5, 16, 138, 143
convictions: landowners 143
corporate interests: judiciary 131, 138
corruption 15, 31, 33, 47, 51, 90, 128,
    134, 182, 183
Costa, Fernando 32
counter-hegemonic movement: MST as 19
Covas, Mário 6, 12, 39, 40, 41, 42, 43, 44,
    45, 47, 69, 71, 80, 146
Cox, Maximiliano 12
criminal conspiracy 70–1
criminalisation 85, 143
crisis management 41
Curitiba 131, 137

DATALUTA 11
Decree 42.041 (1997) 39, 45, 46–7
Decree 91.766 (1985) 139
Decree 643 (1991) 130, 132
Decree 900 (1969) 30
defence: of collective interests 111
delict: general theory of 76
Demarchi, Paul Expedito 141
Democratic Labour Party (PDT) 96
developmental discourse 182
devolved lands 6, 14; 1850 Land Law 14,
    29–30; area occupied by 15; dominion
    over 15; establishing provenance 38;
    failure of law in regard to 180; illegal
    transfer into private hands 27, 30–1; land
    market 31–2; legal moves for
    reacquisition of 44; legal procedure for
    reasserting control over 38; list targeting
    reacquisition of 46; occupation of see land
    occupations; Pontal do Paranapanema 52;
    'public land for land' policy 44;
    underlying legal principle 37–9
Diário Oficial 98, 109
direct action 1, 2, 4, 5, 33, 35, 51, 58
discretion: prosecutorial 84
Discriminatory Actions 37, 38, 46, 70
Dois Córregos ranch 142, 143
Drowning in Laws: Labor Law and Brazilian
    Political Culture 188
Dutra, Olívio 11, 105, 106, 107, 109, 183

economic boom/miracle 20, 92, 159
Eldorado dos Carajás: massacre at 73, 82
employment 14, 30, 60, 141, 159, 161

environmental: concerns; and landless
workers' interests 161; costs 159, 160;
destruction 13, 28, 165; record: Grupo
Corona 160
eviction orders 35, 82; Bagé region 107;
injunction requiring them to be passed
up the chain of command 130; judicial
enforcement of 11–12; Paraná 141, 142;
refusal of 166–7
evictions: armed 63–4; corporate interests
and 138; court sanctioning of 57; judicial
attitudes 5; legal and illegal, in Pontal 41;
local state intervention 128–9
executive: relations between judiciary and
130–1
exploitative labour relations 12, 160
Expointer Agricultural Fair 108, 111, 183
expropriated lands: prices paid for 93
expropriation: in the event of no alternatives
to purchase 113; legal defence against 6,
92; legal framework for 103–4
External Commission of the Chamber of
Deputies 41
Extraordinary Land Reform Secretariat 105

Fachin, Luis Edson 129, 164
falsification: of title deeds 31, 32
families: numbers in land occupation
(1988-2011) 18; numbers settled in land
settlements (1985-2011) 17; tenacity in
face of violence 59–60
fascist legislation 62
fazendas: Anoni 61; Arco-Iris 63; Canaã 71;
Capivara 107, 108, 109, 110, 112, 116;
Flor Roxa 63; Haroldina 63; Nova do
Pontal 34, 59; Rancho 4 63; Rodeio
Colorado 103; Santa Cruz 63; Santa Rita
71, 167; São Bento 34, 35, 60, 61, 62–3,
63–4; state attempts to reacquire control
48–9; Washington Luiz 63; Ximbó
157–61, 167
Federal Public Ministry 11, 41, 79; analysis
of INCRA 101; functions 101–2;
involvement in Bagé region 98–100,
111, 119–20; jurisdiction over land
reform 8, 74
Federal Regional Court (TRF) 103
federalism: and case selection 6–12
Fernandes, Bernardo Mançano 40,
62, 153
Fernandes, Florestan 185
Filipe, Márcio Sotano 48

Fleury, Luiz Antônio 46, 51
Fogolin, Marco Antônio 72
Folha de São Paulo 69, 103–4, 114, 142
Fome Zero 16
forced possession 76, 78, 79, 82
forestry clearance 28
forestry police: investigation of Grupo
Corona 160
French, John D. 188
funds: related to land reform projects 16

Genro, Tarso 139, 153
Gini index: for land 12–13
Gonçalves, Wagner 41
Görgen, Frei Sérgio 105–6
Goulart, João 154
Goulart, Manoel Pereira 31
Gouvêa, Antônio José de 31
Grande Reserva do Pontal 32
green revolution 13, 94
Greenhalgh, Luiz Eduardo 67, 70,
72–3, 78
Griffith, John A.G. 3
grilagem 31, 32
grileiros 33, 42, 45, 135
Grupo Corona 160, 166
Guabiju ranch 106

habeas corpus 67, 70, 75, 78, 79, 82, 85
Hackbart, Rolf 91, 156
High Court of Justice (STJ) 5, 57, 67, 70,
71, 73, 84, 168
Hoffmann, José Hermeto 113
Houtzager, Peter 19
Hulha Negra 95, 96, 97, 107
Human Rights Secretariat 80

ideological aspects: of law 172
ideological divisions 36, 41, 65, 80, 85, 102,
171, 181
ideological leverage 185
ideology: of productive model 159
imprisonment 5; media coverage of workers'
41; MST militants 57, 64, 67, 71, 72,
181; political 68; as public relations
disaster 68–9, see also preventive
imprisonment; re-imprisonments
INCRA see also National Institute of
Colonisation and Agrarian Reform
indigenous inhabitants: slaughter and
liquidation of 28–9
inequality 12, 15

injunctions: land audits 96, 99, 103, *see also* eviction orders; interim control 41, 48–50, 64, 71
Institute of Popular Legal Support (IAJUP) 162
Instituto de Terras, Cartografía e Florestas *see* Land, Forest and Cartography Institute
Instituto de Terras do Estado de São Paulo *see* State of São Paulo Land Institute
Instituto Nacional de Colonização e Reforma Agrária *see* National Institute for Colonisation and Agrarian Reform
interim control (tutela antecipada) 41, 48–50, 64, 71
interventionist model: legal action 173
invasion 64–5

Jobim, Nelson 84, 139, 152, 170, 171–2, 173–4
judiciary: attitudes 3–4, 5; autonomy 70; conservatism 4–5, 38, 44, 75, 184, 185; corporate interests 131, 138; cultures 10; decision-making 4, 77–8; need for a new framework of interpretation 164; neutrality 3, 4; relations between executive and 130–1; response to occupations 65, 66, *see also* High Court of Justice; Supreme Court, Brasília
Jungmann, Raul 8, 9, 97, 103–4, 108–9, 113, 114–15, 116, 117, 119, 120, 137, 145, 147, 154, 155, 174, 184
jurisprudential divide 65, 181
justice: recourse to legal 35; social 2, 4, 58, 84, *see also* High Court of Justice; injustice(s)
justice system: inadequacies of 73

Kaingang 28
Kaiuás 28
Khater, Elizabeth 141, 142–3

La Via Campesina 2
labour laws 188
labour relations: 6, 12, 160, 163, 165
land: investment in rural 152; population growth and demand for 32; prices for expropriated 93; productivity indices *see* productivity indices; purchase by consent 97, 102, 112, 113; redistribution 16–19, 136, 160, 180; speculative value 45; unequal access to 15; unequal distribution of 12–13, *see also* devolved lands; productive land; unproductive land

land audits 41, 92–3; armed enforcement of 103; decision to go for mass surveys 93–4; INCRA announces intentions to start, Bagé region 112; INCRA defeat over 96–8, 182–3; resistance to 95–6; significance of MST in agitation for 182; suspension of 97, 98, 106, 109, 112, 113–14
land conflicts: as challenge to political and legal status quo 187; mediations 10, 100–3, 133, 138; MST involvement *see* Landless Workers' Movement; Paraná 135; and productivity indices *see* productivity indices; righting of injustice 27
Land, Forest and Cartography Institute (ITCF) 10, 128, 133
Land Institute (ITESP) 9–10, 33, 38, 42, 46, 48, 144, 163
Land Law (1850) 14; administration in context of power relations 90–122, 182; 30; legacy of 29–33; reality of 188; underwriting the efficacy of 43–6
land market: devolved lands 31–2
land occupations: Church's reservations about 59–60; containment of 16; high price of 57; ideology of private property invoked against 31; legal responses 63–83, 181; MST's reassertion of tactic 20; number of families in (1988-2011) 18; organisation of militia to deal with 95; Paraná 11, 127, 135–6, 140, 144; perceived as organised vandalism 65; Rio Grande do Sul 11, 61, 107, 108, 109, 110, 112, 116; São Paulo *see* Matão; Pontal do Paranapanema; state response to 40–3; statistics 11; total number by 2009 1
land ownership: 12, 14, 30–1, 81, 165
land reform: Bagé region 91–5; overview 12–19; and conflict *see* land conflicts; failure, Querência do Norte 140–6; funds related to 16; implementation *see* National Institute for Colonisation and Agrarian Reform; jurisdiction over issues of 8, 74; justifications 12; landed interests 179; limits of progressive state action 127–47; and the MST *see* Landless Workers' Movement; need for explanation of failure of 4; precondition for implementation 44
land scarcity 14, 156

land settlements: accord between state and MST (1995) 71; Covas's self-imposed target of 47; INCRA targets 112; low rate, 1990s 16; number of families in (1985–2011) 17; total by 2009 1

landed estates 13, 29, *see also* cattle ranches

landed interests 5, 103, 114, 118, 139, 182; Bagé region 92; illegal transfer of devolved land 27, 30–1; limited land reform 179; opposition against 58; organised violence and intransigence 1; power 9, 29, 120, 138, 140, 146, 147, 179; *see also* Rural Democratic Union

landless workers 14; assassinations 143; environmental concerns and interests of 161; execution of 141–2; massacre at Eldorado dos Carajás 73, 82; media coverage of imprisonment 41

Landless Workers' Movement (MST) 1–2; accord between state and (1995) 71; arrest, imprisonment and trial of militants 57, 64, 67; Barbosa's views of 110; criminalised membership 85; criticism of other rural movements 35; difficulties facing 20, 34, 172; direct action tactics 1, 5, 33, 51, 60–1, 64; 77–8; embracing legal discourse 52; engagement with law 186–7; engagement in Matão region 159; ideological discourse 36; impact of 52; INCRA interest in Paraná as a response to pressure from 141; as leading contender in the Pontal do Paranapanema 33–7, 40; legal activity, Rio Grande do Sul 161; legitimacy of actions 162; leverage 40, 61, 139, 162, 187; multiplier effects 61–3; offensive legality 161–73; power 1–2, 9; professionalisation of in-house legal advice 58; reaction of legal establishment to civil disobedience of 84; relations with government 71; relations with the law 2, 35, 152; Requião's agreement with 135; resistance of Public Ministry to aggressive prosecution of 152; significance in agitation for land audits 182; state's response to 40–3; support from eminent legal scholars 164; targeting of productive properties 153–4; views on intensive agro-industrial complexes 13–14; in the wider spectrum of rural struggle 19–21

Landless Workers' Movement of the West of the State of São Paulo (MASTER) 34

landowners: arrests 143; divide between productive and unproductive 155–6; law 51, 91; organisations 62, 143; state monopoly of devolved lands 14, *see also* cattle ranchers; registered landowners

latifudios see landed estates

Law 4.925 (1985) 37, 39

Law 8.629 (1993) 39, 99, 164

Law 9.415 (1996) 81, 82

law: conflicting responses to land occupations 63–83, 181; engendering respect for 70; failure in regard to devolved lands 180; ideological aspects 172; and land reform 185; of legitimate possession 165–6; MST's relations with 2, 35, 152, 186–7; and politics 2–3, 44, 116–17; significance in pursuit of MST's objectives 52; social movements and change in 27–52, 181, 183, 184–5; and society 179, *see also* force of law; Land Law; rule of law

law schools 185–6

lawyer: networks/associations 58, 78, 85, 161–2, 174

Leal, Vincente 75–6

legal action: interventionist model 173; radical 186

legal: autonomy 4, 179; boundaries: social movements and redefining of 151–74; conflicts 15; fetishism 70; imperatives: marrying political and 46–8; institutions: autonomy and efficiency 4; landowners' collision with 98–100; networks: radical 161–2; positivism 3; profession: deception in relation to devolved lands 31; protection: ownership and 165; rectitude 66; scholars: MST support from 164; sufficiency: Public Ministry, São Paulo 11; system: Bagé region 90; capacity to deal with mass litigation 115–16; class injustices 77; Paraná 143; power of the individual 75; vitiation of prospects of land reform 93

legal-political divide 69–70

legitimate possession: laws of 165–6

legitimation 153, 168, 170, 185

Lei de Terras see Land Law

Lerner, Jaime 134, 137, 138, 142, 146, 184

Lima Júnior, Dom Joviano de 168

livestock estates: number and area 13, *see also* cattle ranches

local states: accord between MST and (1995) 71; control of devolved lands 15, 36; dialectic of social movement action and 37–40; intervention, evictions 128–9; limits of progressive action 127–47, 184; response to land occupations 40–3, *see also* Paraná; Rio Grande do Sul; São Paulo
Luchesi, Fábio 139

Macedo, Marcos Vinicius Aguiar 99–100
Maciel, Adhemar 76
Macielo, Benedito 45
Manifesto of Brazilian Jurists for Agrarian Reform 162
Marcondes, Fernando Florido 72
Marés, Carlos Frederico 129–31
market oriented approach: to land conflict 102
Marrey, Luiz Antonio 80, 82, 83, 84, 162, 170, 171, 172–3
mass arrests 136
mass mobilisations/occupations 1–2, 20, 21, 33, 39, 40, 41, 50, 61, 63, 83, 93, 96, 180
massacre: at Eldorado dos Carajás 73, 82
Mata Atlântica 28, 163
Matão 152; Carta de Ribeirão 166; legal judgement 166–9; MST's legal case 162–5; occupation at the Fazenda Ximbó 157–61
Mato Grosso do Sul 7, 28, 127
Mauro, Gilmar 61, 160
Medeiros, Leonilde Sérvolo de 20, 35
media coverage: occupations 41, 63, 67, 68, 69
media: landed interest 139
mediation of land conflicts 10, 22, 82, 100–3, 127, 133, 138, 140, 146
Médici, Emílio 92, 105
Mello, Dirceu de 67
Mello, Fernando Collor de 16, 105, 128, 135, 146
Mercosul 95
militants 34; arrest/imprisonment 57, 64, 67, 71, 181; massacre of 73, 82
militarisation: of conflict 141; social policy 138
military dictatorship 20, 35, 39, 68, 74, 92, 105, 154, 157, 171
military police 73, 82, 97, 130, 133, 134, 136, 143

militia 95
minimum wage 16
Minister for Agrarian Reform *see* Jungmann, Raul
Ministério Público *see* Public Ministries
Ministry of Agrarian Reform 97, 102, 106, 111, 113, 117
Ministry of Agriculture 19, 103, 113, 117
Mirante do Paranapanema 48, 59; Association of Rural Property Owners 63; devolved lands 52, 64; land occupations 63, 66, 67, 71
mobilisation *see* demobilisation; mass mobilisations; political mobilisation; social mobilisation
Montoro, Franco 33, 37, 38, 39, 43, 44
Moraes, José Roberto de 48
Moraes, Marcus Vinícius Pratini de 105, 109, 113–14, 115, 117, 145
Morro do Diabo reserve 32, 33
Movement of the Democratic Public Ministry (MMPD) 80
Movimento dos Sem-Terra do Oeste do Estado de São Paulo *see* Landless Workers' Movement of the West of the State of São Paulo (MASTER)
Movimento dos Trabalhadores Rurais Sem-Terra *see* Landless Workers' Movement (MST)
municipal option 169
Mussolini, Benito 62

Napoleonic Code 78
National Agrarian Ombudsman 10, 108, 186
National Association of Popular Lawyers (ANAP) 161–2
National Confederation of Agricultural Workers (CONTAG) 19, 20, 35, 36
National Confederation of Agriculture (CNA) 98
National Day of Struggles for Agrarian Reform (2011) 1–2
National Indian Foundation (FUNAI) 130
National Institute for Colonisation and Agrarian Reform (INCRA); challenges to INCRA power 22, 93, 95, 96, 98, 99; devolved land estimates, 15; enforcement land audits, *vistorias* 22, 41, 90–122; Fazenda São Bento, 61; federal powers 8, 9; financial compensation 93, 112;

importance of state support 8, 10;
internal divisions 100–3; José Gomes da
Silva, 139; land use estimates, 14; legal
powers 92–3, 99, 114, 115, 119; Maria de
Oliveira 144–5; Paulo Emílio Barbosa
109; productivity indices 92, 94–6;
Public Ministry 101, 110, 111, 112,
121; relations with ITESP 42; relations
with MST 62, 107, 210–11; record in
Paraná 141, 144; social function of
property, 164
National Institute of Social Security
(INSS) 160
National Network of Popular Lawyers
(RENAP) 161
National Ombudsman for Human
Rights 163
National Plan of Agrarian Reform (PNRA):
first 114, 139, 183; second 14
nature reserves 32–3
Navarro, Zander 40
nepotism 32
Neto, Sandoval 62
neutrality of law 3, 4, 121, 138, 173
non-binding precedents 181
non-confrontation 34–5, 60–1

offensive legality 23, 152, 161–74
Oliveira, Ariovaldo Umbelino de 15
Oliveira, Cândido Martins de 143
Oliveira, Maria de 128, 137, 141, 144,
145, 147
ownership *see* land ownership
Oxfam 187

Pantanal 13
Pará 7, 73, 170, 171
Paraná 6, 7, 8, 10, 28, 64, 127; correlations
of power 137–40; failure of reform in
Querência do Norte 140–6; land
occupations 11, 127, 135–6, 140, 144;
lawyers 161; Lerner administration 137;
limitations of Requião's approach 133–7;
limits of progressive state action 127–47;
map of *140*; positive political climate 12;
Requião administration (1991–94)
128–33
Paranavaí 144
Parnaiba, Visconde de 31
Party of the Brazilian Democratic Movement
(PMDB) 12, 110
Party of the Liberal Front (PFL) 105

Passos, Oliveira 82
Pastoral Land Commission (CPT) 39, 127,
133, 143, 162
Patterson, William 75, 76
Paula, Paulo Afonso Garrido de 81, 82
Paulista Association of Magistrates
69, 85
Peasant Leagues 68
Pereira, Gedeão 97, 99
Pereira Leite, Sérgio 13, 14
Pernambuco 10, 127
Picarelli, Judge 96, 99, 101, 103
Picolli, Antônio Prates 108
Pirapó 31
Pirapozinho 64, 68
police: response to occupations 65, *see also*
forestry police; military police
political cases as defined by Griffiths 3–4
political: expediency 188; imperatives:
marrying legal and 46–8; imprisonment
68; leverage 61, 180; mobilisation 19,
153; process: underwriting the efficacy of
Land Law 43–6; radicalism 20
political-legal divide 69
politics: law and 2–3, 44, 116–17; of
selection 80
The Politics of the Judiciary 3
Ponta Grossa 145
Pontal do Paranapanema: history of 28–9;
development of property relations 30;
dialectic of state and social movement
action 37–40; illegal transfer of devolved
land into private property 27, 30–1;
instability 69–70; interim control 48–50;
land market for devolved lands 31–2; land
occupations 34, 35, 36, 37, 48, 58–63,
71; legal responses to land occupations
63–83, 181; nature reserves 32–3; power
relations 51; role of MST in 33–7, 40;
state response to land conflict 40–3; visits
of senior delegates to 41, *see also* Mirante
do Paranapanema
Pontes, Eduardo 166
Pope John VI 6
population growth: demand for land 32
Porangabinha ranch 141
Porto Alegre 91, 107
poverty: rural 12, 15, 141, 187
power: of attorney general 80, 82;
correlations of 137–40; of landed interests
9, 29, 120, 138, 140, 146, 147, 179;
of MST 1–2, 9, *see also* state power

power relations: administration of land law
in context of 90–122, 182; Pontal do
Paranapanema 51
predatory speculation 29
Presidente Prudente 28, 41, 62, 79
Presidente Venceslau 32
Pressburger, Miguel 14, 30, 39, 43, 45
preventive imprisonment 67, 69, 70, 75,
76, 99, 141
prices: expropriated lands 93
private property: ideology invoked against
land occupations 31, 65; illegal transfer of
devolved lands into 27, 30–1; rejection
of absolutist notions of 181; social quality
of 6, 110
pro-reform government 16, 147
proactive justice 65
Prochet, Marcos 143
Procopio, Felinto 71
productive land: accentuated significance of
187; assessment of see productivity indices;
the case against occupying 153–7;
perception of legal impregnability 158–9
productive property: legal defence against
expropriation 6, 92; origins 119
productivity: cattle ranching, Bagé region
92; in Constitution 92; problem of 94
productivity indices 16–19, 155–6;
announcement of a new 117; appointment
of Barbosa and significance of law 109–11;
commission to re-examine 97, 102;
conflict over 94; scientific validity of 183;
farmers' document contesting 95;
INCRA's defeat 96–8; landowners'
collision with legal institutions 98–100;
landowners' refusal to countersign audit
notifications 96, 112; landowners'
resistance to AU measure 95–6,
97–8; landowners' wrong-footing of
INCRA 98; Lula da Silva's failure to
update 16, 19, 90, 183–4; politics of
mediation and prosecution 100–3; ruralist
block 97; sustainability of 117–18
property: need for a global concept of 164;
social function of 164, see also private
property; productive property; rural
property
prosecution: of landowners 143; of militants
57, 181; politics of 64–6, 73, 100–3
prosecutorial autonomy 74–5, 84, 170–3
public education 185
public land see devolved lands

'public land for land' policy 44
Public Ministries 6–7; influence of state 8;
Rio Grande do Sul 101, see also Federal
Public Ministry; São Paulo Public
Ministry
public order 70, 75, 76, 77, 82
Public Prosecution Service see Public
Ministry

Quadros, Jânio 32
Quércia Orestes 59
Querência do Norte: failure of reform
140–6

radical legal networks 161–2
Rainha, José 34, 36, 60, 67, 68, 71, 72, 77
Recadastramento (RECAD) 100, 101
Reclaiming Actions 47–8
reforming governments 11, 37, 91, 179
registered landowners: as legitimate
interlocuters 42–3; compensation 50, 63;
overturning injunctions 71; legal and
illegal evictions 41; Mirante do
Paranapanema as Achilles' heel of 62;
political and economic crisis 45
repression: of Indians 130; of occupations 59;
of rural movements 128; of social demand
5, 21, 138
repressive policies: anti-land reform
government 16
Requião, Roberto 12, 128–37, 146, 184
resistance: right to 76; to land audits 95–6
Ribeirão Preto 158, 160, 165, 170, 173
Ricci, Rudá 20, 35
rice sector: Rio Grande do Sul 92, 94
right-wing interests/forces 2, 105,
138, 155
Rio Grande do Sul 6, 7, 79; agricultural
economic crisis 95; judicial culture 10;
land occupations 11, 61, 107, 108, 109,
110, 112, 116; MST legal activity 161;
Public Ministry 101; rice sector 92, 94,
see also Bagé region
Rio Novo ranch 141
risk perception: land market formation and
31–2
Rondônia 7, 170, 171
Rosetto, Neuri 59
Rossi, Clovis 69
Rouseff, Dilma 20, 117, 139, 153, 188
rule of law 5, 66, 85, 90, 100, 116, 119–20,
142, 181

Rural Democratic Union (UDR) 62, 93, 96, 137, 138, 142, 144, 145
rural poverty 12, 15, 141, 187
rural property: social function 5–6, 82, 159, 163, 165
rural trade union movement 19–20
ruralist block 97

Sandovalina 64, 66, 67
Santana do Livramento 95
Santos, Alcides Gomes dos 59
Santos, Esmeralda Gomes dos 59–60
Sántos Júnior, Belisário dos 40, 42, 43, 44, 45, 46, 47, 49, 66, 71, 152, 153–4, 156, 174
São José dos Campos 167
São Paulo 6, 7, 9; Forestry Institute 28; Land Institute 9–10, 33, 38, 42, 46, 48, 144, 163; land occupation statistics 11; map of 152; Public Ministry see São Paulo Public Ministry; transformation of state policy 42, see also Matão; Pontal do Paranapanema; Ribeirão Preto
São Paulo Public Ministry: arrest and imprisonment of MST militants 57; and the Carta de Ribeirão Preto 165–6; case for prosecution and its politics 66–73; changes in 79–81; prosecutorial autonomy 170–3; resistance to aggressive prosecution of MST 152; response to land conflict 41, 58; response to occupations 64–6; Second State Congress (1997) 82
Sarney, José 139, 146, 185
Sauer, Sérgio 13, 14
Scardoelli, Mayor Adauto 168, 169
Schenker, Moyzés 167
Secretariat General of the Presidency 139–40
Secretariat of State for Public Security (SESP) 130, 134
Seligmann, Milton 97, 103, 104
separation of powers doctrine 2–3, 69, 132
Serra, José 50, 51
Shiki, Shigeo 93
Silva, Diniz Bento da (Teixeirinha) 136, 138
Silva Estimo, Catarina Ruybal da 48, 49, 51–2, 71
Silva Filho, Gercino José da 10
Silva, José Gomes da 139, 180
Silva, Luis Inácio Lula da 1, 15–16, 68, 117, 139, 147, 153, 155, 183–4, 187–8

Silva, Marechal Costa e 105
Silva, Paulo Sérgio Ribeiro da 64–6, 67, 68, 71, 72, 74, 81
Silva, Zelitro Luz da 34
Silveira, Domingos Dresch da 163
Siqueira, Silvia Estela Gigena de 166–9, 173
social assistance programmes 15–16
social demands 5, 15, 41, 157, 184, 187
social function: of property 5–6, 82, 159, 163, 164, 165
social justice 2, 4, 58, 84
social mobilisation 98, 120, 180, 187, 188
social movement action: conflicting legal responses to 57–85, 181; and legal change 27–52, 181, 184–5; redefining of legal boundaries 151–74, see also Landless Workers' Movement
social policy: militarisation of 138
social struggle(s) 5, 37, 77, 162, 172, 187
social teaching (Catholic) 6, 110
society: law and 4, 179, 181
Sousa Santos, Boaventura de 19
Souza, Diolinda Alves de 67, 68, 71, 72
Souza Martins, José de 14, 51
Special Working Group on Land Issues in Western São Paulo (GETAF) 41, 81–3
speculative value: land 32, 45
Sperotto, Carlos 97, 99, 103, 105, 112
state see federal state; local states
State Forestry Institute: São Paulo 28
State Housing Corporation of Rio Grande do Sul (COHAB) 110
state power 3, 8, 33, 127, 133, 138, 139
Stédile, João Pedro 33–4, 107, 109, 134, 157, 184, 187
sugar cane industry 159, 160, 161
Superior Tribunal de Justiça see High Court of Justice
Suplicy, Eduardo 41
Supreme Court, Brasília: implications of decision 77–9; judicial response 75–7, 85, 181

Teixeirinha see Silva, Diniz Bento da
Teodoro Sampaio 41, 64
terra por terra see 'public land for land' policy
terras devolutas see devolved lands
title deeds: falsification of 31, 32
torture 136
trade union movement: rural 19–20

Transval ranch 141
Turra, Francisco 103, 105, 112
tutela antecipada see interim control

unproductive land: hectare estimation 14;
    modalities governing availability of 156
Usina Bonfim 160
Usina Nova Tamoio 160
usucapion rights: exclusion of 49

Vargas regime (1931) 62
veto powers 19, 139, 151
violence: 59–60; organised 1; of police 134;
    rural in Paraná 127
vistorias see land audits

Workers' Party (PT) 12, 20, 45, 68, 95, 105,
    168, 169
World Bank 182